Language Education in a Changing World

NEW PERSPECTIVES ON LANGUAGE AND EDUCATION
Founding Editor: Viv Edwards, *University of Reading, UK*
Series Editors: Phan Le Ha, *University of Hawaii at Manoa, USA* and Joel Windle, *Monash University, Australia*

Two decades of research and development in language and literacy education have yielded a broad, multidisciplinary focus. Yet education systems face constant economic and technological change, with attendant issues of identity and power, community and culture. This series will feature critical and interpretive, disciplinary and multidisciplinary perspectives on teaching and learning, language and literacy in new times.

All books in this series are externally peer-reviewed.

Full details of all the books in this series and of all our other publications can be found on http://www.multilingual-matters.com, or by writing to Multilingual Matters, St Nicholas House, 31-34 High Street, Bristol BS1 2AW, UK.

NEW PERSPECTIVES ON LANGUAGE AND EDUCATION: 79

Language Education in a Changing World

Challenges and Opportunities

Rod Bolitho and Richard Rossner

MULTILINGUAL MATTERS
Bristol • Blue Ridge Summit

DOI https://doi.org/10.21832/BOLITH7857
Library of Congress Cataloging in Publication Data
A catalog record for this book is available from the Library of Congress.
Names: Bolitho, Rod, editor. | Rossner, Richard, editor.
Title: Language Education in a Changing World: Challenges and
   Opportunities/Edited by Rod Bolitho and Richard Rossner.
Description: Bristol; Blue Ridge Summit: Multilingual Matters, [2020] |
   Series: New Perspectives on Language and Education: 79 | Includes
   bibliographical references and index. | Summary: 'This book considers
   the role of language education in a rapidly changing world. Drawing on
   their extensive experience in language education, the authors consider
   how students might be supported in developing the language awareness and
   competences they need in order to participate fully and confidently in
   our increasingly diverse societies' – Provided by publisher.
Identifiers: LCCN 2019047013 (print) | LCCN 2019047014 (ebook) | ISBN
   9781788927857 (hardback) | ISBN 9781788927840 (paperback) | ISBN
   9781788927864 (pdf) | ISBN 9781788927871 (epub) | ISBN 9781788927888
   (kindle edition) Subjects: LCSH: Language and languages – Study and teaching. |
   Language and education. | Language teachers – Training of.
Classification: LCC P51.L3446 2020 (print) | LCC P51 (ebook) | DDC
   418.0071 – dc23
LC record available at https://lccn.loc.gov/2019047013
LC ebook record available at https://lccn.loc.gov/2019047014

British Library Cataloguing in Publication Data
A catalogue entry for this book is available from the British Library.

ISBN-13: 978-1-78892-785-7 (hbk)
ISBN-13: 978-1-78892-784-0 (pbk)

Multilingual Matters
UK: St Nicholas House, 31-34 High Street, Bristol BS1 2AW, UK.
USA: NBN, Blue Ridge Summit, PA, USA.

Website: www.multilingual-matters.com
Twitter: Multi_Ling_Mat
Facebook: https://www.facebook.com/multilingualmatters
Blog: www.channelviewpublications.wordpress.com

Copyright © 2020 Rod Bolitho and Richard Rossner.

All rights reserved. No part of this work may be reproduced in any form or by any means without permission in writing from the publisher.

The policy of Multilingual Matters/Channel View Publications is to use papers that are natural, renewable and recyclable products, made from wood grown in sustainable forests. In the manufacturing process of our books, and to further support our policy, preference is given to printers that have FSC and PEFC Chain of Custody certification. The FSC and/or PEFC logos will appear on those books where full certification has been granted to the printer concerned.

Typeset by Riverside Publishing Solutions.

NEW PERSPECTIVES ON LANGUAGE AND EDUCATION: 79

Language Education in a Changing World

Challenges and Opportunities

Rod Bolitho and Richard Rossner

MULTILINGUAL MATTERS
Bristol • Blue Ridge Summit

DOI https://doi.org/10.21832/BOLITH7857
Library of Congress Cataloging in Publication Data
A catalog record for this book is available from the Library of Congress.
Names: Bolitho, Rod, editor. | Rossner, Richard, editor.
Title: Language Education in a Changing World: Challenges and
  Opportunities/Edited by Rod Bolitho and Richard Rossner.
Description: Bristol; Blue Ridge Summit: Multilingual Matters, [2020] |
  Series: New Perspectives on Language and Education: 79 | Includes
  bibliographical references and index. | Summary: 'This book considers
  the role of language education in a rapidly changing world. Drawing on
  their extensive experience in language education, the authors consider
  how students might be supported in developing the language awareness and
  competences they need in order to participate fully and confidently in
  our increasingly diverse societies' – Provided by publisher.
Identifiers: LCCN 2019047013 (print) | LCCN 2019047014 (ebook) | ISBN
  9781788927857 (hardback) | ISBN 9781788927840 (paperback) | ISBN
  9781788927864 (pdf) | ISBN 9781788927871 (epub) | ISBN 9781788927888
  (kindle edition) Subjects: LCSH: Language and languages – Study and teaching. |
  Language and education. | Language teachers – Training of.
Classification: LCC P51.L3446 2020 (print) | LCC P51 (ebook) | DDC
  418.0071 – dc23
LC record available at https://lccn.loc.gov/2019047013
LC ebook record available at https://lccn.loc.gov/2019047014

British Library Cataloguing in Publication Data
A catalogue entry for this book is available from the British Library.

ISBN-13: 978-1-78892-785-7 (hbk)
ISBN-13: 978-1-78892-784-0 (pbk)

Multilingual Matters
UK: St Nicholas House, 31-34 High Street, Bristol BS1 2AW, UK.
USA: NBN, Blue Ridge Summit, PA, USA.

Website: www.multilingual-matters.com
Twitter: Multi_Ling_Mat
Facebook: https://www.facebook.com/multilingualmatters
Blog: www.channelviewpublications.wordpress.com

Copyright © 2020 Rod Bolitho and Richard Rossner.

All rights reserved. No part of this work may be reproduced in any form or by any means without permission in writing from the publisher.

The policy of Multilingual Matters/Channel View Publications is to use papers that are natural, renewable and recyclable products, made from wood grown in sustainable forests. In the manufacturing process of our books, and to further support our policy, preference is given to printers that have FSC and PEFC Chain of Custody certification. The FSC and/or PEFC logos will appear on those books where full certification has been granted to the printer concerned.

Typeset by Riverside Publishing Solutions.

Contents

Acknowledgements	ix
Introduction	1
Part 1: Language and Languages in Education	3
1 The Crucial Role of Language in Education	5
Language, Thought and Learning	5
Language and Learning Objectives	6
Classroom Language	8
Questioning	9
Scaffolding	10
Multiliteracies	13
Some UK Initiatives around Language and Education	14
Language Repertoire	16
Concluding Remarks	16
2 Changes in Second and Foreign Language Education	19
The End of the Colonial Era and Language Policy	19
Language Issues in Post-War Europe	20
The Common European Framework of Reference for Languages	21
Multilingualism and Plurilingualism	23
Early Language Learning	24
The European Centre for Modern Languages	25
The Bologna Process	26
Developments in East and Central Europe	26
Migration	27
The Growth of Language Teaching as an Industry	28
Information Technology and Corpus Studies, and their Impact on Language Education	30
Concluding Remarks	31

3 The Growing Influence of English in Education — 34

The Special Case of English — 34
Who Does English Belong To? — 36
Intercultural Communicative Competence — 38
The Future Evolution of English — 39
The Impact of English on Education — 40
The Role and Impact of English in Higher Education — 42
The Challenges Implied by the Upsurge of English in Education — 44
English and the Learning of Other Languages — 46
Concluding Remarks — 46

Part 2: Teacher Education and Training — 49

4 Initial Language Teacher Education: Traditions, Trends and Relevance — 51

The 'Philological Route' — 51
Linking Teacher Education to the School Curriculum — 54
Research and Language Teacher Education — 58
Pedagogical Institutes and Colleges of Education — 59
Initial Qualifications — 61
Gatekeeping and Assessment Practices — 62
The Cultural Dimension in Language Teacher Education — 64
Teacher Educator Preparation and Trainer Training — 65
Concluding Remarks — 66

5 Language Teachers' Professional Development — 68

What Does Teachers' Professional Development Include? — 68
Decision-Making about Professional Development — 70
The Role of the Institution — 71
Observation of Teaching as Part of Professional Development — 76
Reflective Practice and the Use of Competence Frameworks — 78
Criteria for Effective CPD for Language Teachers — 79
Autonomous Teacher Development — 79
Concluding Remarks — 81

6 Language in Pre-Service and In-Service Teacher Education for Teachers of all Subjects — 84

Literacy and Oracy — 84
The Place of Language and Communication in Curricula for Teacher Education — 86
Concluding Remarks — 101

Part 3: Stakeholder Interests — 103

7 The Perspectives of Stakeholders in Language Education — 105

- Language Learners — 105
- Parents and their Role — 109
- Employers — 110
- Admission to Higher Education — 112
- Society as a Beneficiary — 113
- The Service Providers — 115
- The Key Role of Consultation with Stakeholders — 116
- Concluding Remarks — 117

8 Policy Making — 119

- Policies Affecting the Teaching of the Main National or Regional Language — 121
- Policies in Post-Colonial Countries — 123
- Policies on the Teaching of Foreign Languages — 124
- Policies on the Status and Teaching of Migrants and Migrant Languages — 127
- Policies in Multilingual Contexts — 129
- Concluding Remarks — 130

9 Commercial Interests in Language Education — 132

- Examination Providers — 132
- Publishers — 135
- The Role of the British Council — 141
- Language Schools — 142
- Quality Assurance Bodies — 143
- Teacher Training Providers — 145
- Concluding Remarks — 148

10 Language in Education and in Teacher Education: Towards New Paradigms — 150

- The Story So Far — 150
- Where Do We Go From Here? — 152
- Ways Forward — 160
- Concluding Remarks — 162

References — 164

Index — 172

Acknowledgements

The authors are very grateful to the following colleagues and various institutions for their ready responses to our somewhat lengthy and sometimes complex questions.

Dr Lukas Bleichenbacher and colleagues at the Pädagogische Hochschule St Gallen for information about the role of language in teacher education in Switzerland, and about the *Profession-Related Language Competence Profile for Foreign Language Teachers*, as well as information about the St Gallen curriculum model discussed in Chapter 4.

Professor Neil Mercer, Emeritus Professor at the University of Cambridge Faculty of Education, for a lengthy and detailed conversation about the importance of oracy in UK education and teacher education.

Dr Yoncan Liu, University of Cambridge Faculty of Education, for detailed discussion on the way scaffolding and other aspects of language are dealt with in UK teacher education, and information about the English as an additional language Assessment Framework.

We wish to acknowledge the invaluable help in the form of information about the content of national or regional teacher education curricula and practices provided by the following colleagues: Carla Carnevale, Gerhard Finster, Jamilya Gulyamova, Viktoriia Ivanischeva, Svetlana Javoronkova, Michael Morawski, Tatiana Neugebauer, Gerda Piribauer, Ruxandra Popovici, Alexander Shalenko and Belinda Steinhuber; and to Clare Harrison for providing important details about Cambridge English teacher training qualifications.

Teachers and academic managers at five EAQUALS member institutions kindly provided detailed responses to a survey concerning continuing professional development for language teachers discussed in Chapter 5: AVO Language and Examination Centre, Sofia; the British School of Trieste; Eurocentres UK; AKCENT International House, Prague; and British Study Centres, London.

We are grateful to the following for permission to reproduce or adapt material used in the book:

- The British Council for permission to reproduce excerpts from the Profile of a Newly Qualified English Teacher in the Ukraine.

- Cambridge University Press for permission to reproduce the diagram on page 77
- John Clark and Angela Scarino for permission to adapt the diagram in Figure 6.1 (p. 92)
- The Council of Europe, Strasbourg, for permission to reproduce sections of the *Reference Framework of Competences for Democratic Culture* on page 89
- Professor Robert Gardner for permission to reproduce the 'Socio-educational Model of language learning' in Figure 7.1 (p. 106)
- The State University of World Languages, Tashkent for permission to reproduce the Reformed National Pre-Service Curriculum for English Teachers in Uzbekistan discussed in Chapter 4.

We are especially grateful to Andrew Littlejohn for his thorough review of the first draft of the book and his useful suggestions.

Introduction

The influence and impact of language and communication on our lives and on society at large is more far-reaching than ever. The 'post-truth' era that we now live in combined with the multiplicity of 24-hour news media leaves us floundering to distinguish fact from fiction, fantasy from reality, realism from pessimism. Moreover, the relentless recourse to social media means that 'hate speech', verbal bullying, humiliation, even death threats are everyday phenomena and are in danger of becoming – have already become – the new normal. Young people around the world working their way through the education system are confronted by all this and by an information and emotional load that has never been greater, as well as with the task of trying to interpret that information and to sift from it what is safe, helpful, empowering or uplifting while trying to ignore what is poisonous and misleading.

During our years of varied and complementary experience in language education at almost all levels from student teacher via teacher educator to senior manager, and in contexts in countries in different parts of the world, the role and power of language and languages in education has always fascinated us. Aware as we are that language teaching and learning have evolved considerably since we started out, and that the relationship between foreign language teaching, the teaching of additional languages and language across the curriculum has become richer and more intricate, we decided to take the opportunity to write this book together and to try to shed some new light on a complex and challenging area of education. We have backed up our discussion with data and case studies from a range of contexts internationally in the belief that, while educational traditions and priorities vary considerably, the issues we raise are relevant to any education system anywhere in the world.

This book is intended for readers who are teacher educators, researchers, postgraduate students, senior teachers, academic managers, and for those involved in the development of policy for language education and for language, literacy and oracy as transversal competences and life skills. Our aim has been to distil from our wide experience, and from informal research within our respective networks in countries around the world, a range of perspectives on the ways in which languages are taught and learnt, and the way language permeates the curriculum and impacts on educational achievement. We also consider in some depth the place of language in teacher education for all teachers before reflecting on and explaining where things in our view could be improved. In other words, for the purposes of the book, 'language education' encompasses a far wider field than the teaching of foreign or additional languages, important though this is. It includes the work that all teachers need to do to develop their learners' language awareness and skills, whether in the primary classroom, in the teaching of the language of schooling (e.g. English in England, French in France), or the teaching of the 'academic' and specific kinds of language involved in other curriculum subjects.

In the book we offer our opinions and make proposals on a range of measures which we believe could, through imaginative concerted effort, lead to a deeper and broader understanding of the central role of language and languages in education systems, and could enable pupils and students to develop the language awareness and linguistic and communicative competences they urgently need in order to participate more fully and confidently in our increasingly diverse societies.

Part 1: Language and Languages in Education

The first part of the book provides an overview of key aspects of both language education and the role of languages in education. Many of these aspects are referred back to in later chapters. The term 'language education' is usually associated with the teaching and learning of foreign or additional languages, and two of the chapters in this part focus on this kind of language education, one of them on the dominant role English now plays. However, in today's world it is harder than it was even 30 years ago to draw a line between this kind of language education and the teaching and learning of the 'language of schooling', generally the language of the community or country in which the school or institution is situated. This is because it is no longer the case – and in many countries it was never the case – that cohorts of students in an educational institution are a monolingual and monocultural group. Even among the majority who share the national or regional language, there is considerable diversity in levels of literacy and ability to use oral language effectively, as well as in the varieties of the language they feel comfortable with. In addition to these considerations, we also discuss the way language is used by teachers in their work and the impact this has on learning.

1 The Crucial Role of Language in Education

We begin this first chapter with a wide-ranging overview of the vital role that language plays in education wherever the learning and teaching takes place, whatever the age of the learners and irrespective of the aims of the educators. Our purpose here is to set out aspects of language and languages in education that we consider to be of prime importance when addressing the challenges and opportunities referred to in our title.

First, we briefly consider the ground-breaking insights of Lev Vygotsky and his followers, and of others who fashioned the shape and principles of contemporary education in Europe and North America. We then look in more detail at how language works to facilitate the development of concepts and the raising of awareness in the interactions between those teaching and those learning. This leads naturally to a reflection on how language used in schools and other educational organisations links up with and prepares the way for coping with the complex multiple functions and uses of language in the real world, for example, to gain and exercise power, to sell goods and services, and in our role as citizens.

Language, Thought and Learning

'Learning, in the proper sense, is not learning things, but the *meanings* of things, and this process involves the use of signs, or language in its generic sense'. This sentence from a chapter entitled 'Language and the training of thought' in John Dewey's classic *How We Think* (Dewey, 1910: 175) is a good example of early 20th century views of education, child psychology and language. The great names in this tradition span the universities of the northern hemisphere from Vermont, where Dewey worked, to Neuchâtel, the home of Jean Piaget, and Moscow, the alma mater of Lev Vygotsky. The ways in which they presented their ideas, and in the case of Piaget and Vygotsky, their research findings, on the question of signs, language, thought and learning, are of their time, but the insights themselves remain important today and are often overlooked by teacher educators and teachers themselves. Broadly, they proposed that thinking and concept development are only possible with the help of language.

Vygotsky's work and ideas have had a controversial history since his untimely death from tuberculosis in 1934. This is partly due to the incompleteness, censoring and amendments of the original Russian versions and the lack of reliable translations, but also to the promotion of simplified versions of his ideas in the West in the 1970s and since. Work is still ongoing on the first ever full version of Vygotsky's complete works. The ideas reproduced here cannot, therefore, be regarded as a full or reliable representation, but they are very relevant to the purpose of this chapter. As Vygotsky put it, '[Word meaning] is a phenomenon of verbal thought, or meaningful speech – a union of word and thought' (Vygotsky, 1986: 212). After close critical analysis of the work of Piaget and many others working in the field up to the 1930s, as well as practical research with children, it was clear to Vygotsky that concept development was dependent on language, and that instruction involving language and other semiotic systems had a crucial role to play in helping children to develop new conceptual frameworks and to enrich their existing understanding. For him it became evident that the learning of new concepts, notably 'scientific' concepts, is mediated by concepts that have already been acquired and by the language and other systems of signs (gestures, diagrams, etc.) in which they are represented.

In most learning from a very early age social interaction involving spoken language is key: even parents showing the world to their babies or encouraging them to eat, sit, walk or play use language of one kind or another as a constant soundtrack. Beyond babyhood, when children's language is often an 'egocentric' accompaniment to their activities, and into adulthood, it is unusual for there to be thoughts and feelings without some kind of inner language, and it is apparent that this inner 'speech', as well as the mediation provided by others, plays its part in our ongoing, never-ending learning.

Language and Learning Objectives

Vygotsky was one of the first to describe the mediating function of language: its use as a tool to bridge the gap between what is familiar, for example known concepts, and what is not yet known or 'other'. This process of 'knowing' was the focus of the *Taxonomy of Educational Objectives* developed by Benjamin Bloom and colleagues in the United States in the 1950s. The resulting model proposed six successive cognitive stages: knowledge > comprehension > application > analysis > synthesis > evaluation (Bloom, 1956). While the underlying assumptions behind the taxonomy have been disputed, the taxonomy has had considerable impact on educational thinking and research, especially in the USA, and has been followed up by revised versions, such as that developed by Lorin Anderson, David Krathwohl and colleagues (2001), and a more radical 'new taxonomy' created by Robert Marzano (Marzano & Kendall, 2007). Whichever of these one considers, and whatever view one has of their validity and usefulness, it is clear how prominently language features at all levels of the taxonomy. This interdependence of language, thought and learning, linking back to Vygotsky, is nicely illustrated by a correlation of action verbs with the categories of the taxonomy as revised by Anderson and Krathwohl (2001). As examples, 'understanding' is quite low in the hierarchy of the *Revised Taxonomy* and is associated with such verbs as 'classify', 'explain', 'interpret', 'rephrase' and so on. On the other hand, 'evaluating' is near the top, one step down from 'creating'. Some verbs that are typically associated with evaluation, according to Anderson and Krathwohl, are 'compare', 'deduct', 'explain' and 'prove'. The interrelationship between learning and using language in various ways is clear from such examples: even when learning autonomously, using words to explore what one is discovering is essential to the process.

As its original title suggests, Bloom's *Taxonomy* was designed as an aid to the formulation of educational objectives for teaching any subject. It specified categories of knowledge as well as a hierarchy of cognitive processes. In Anderson, Krathwohl *et al.*'s revised taxonomy, the knowledge and cognition dimensions are divided into two complementary dimensions in which language remains a key factor. Broadly, as Krathwohl (2002: 213) explains 'statements of objectives typically consist of a noun or noun phrase – the subject matter content – and a verb or verb phrase – the cognitive process(es). Consider, for example, the following objective: The student shall be able to remember the law of supply and demand in economics.' Here he points out that 'the student shall be able to', which is likely to be common to all objectives, can be ignored, leaving the verb 'remember', a cognitive process, and the noun phrase, 'law of supply and demand in economics', an element of knowledge.

The verbs and nouns that can be used to express desired learning outcomes, as exemplified on the *Revised Taxonomy*, reappear in lists of 'teaching and learning language' (see also Figure 1.1). In almost any secondary classroom we could expect to hear teachers giving instructions or invitations such as the following:

'Could you define "botany"'?
'Can you illustrate what is meant by a "deciduous tree", and give an example?'
'Explain why the French revolution happened when it did'.
'Compare the causes of the Mexican revolution and the French revolution', and so on.

Moreover, many of these verbs are also used in instructions in tests and textbooks and are likely to feature in talk between students when they are discussing learning tasks.

Classroom Language

> In order to learn, students must use what they already know so as to give meaning to what the teacher presents to them. Speech makes available to reflection the processes by which they relate new knowledge to old. But this possibility depends on the social relationships, the communication system, which the teacher sets up. (Barnes in National Institute of Education, 1974: 1)

It was clear to both Vygotsky and Barnes that, if language is essential for thought and concept building from an early age, teaching (or 'instruction') involving speech, written texts and the use of other systems of signs must be key to children's development and learning at later ages within the education system. A question that, we believe, is too seldom addressed in teacher education and teachers' reflection on their work is: how can language be used most effectively in the sociocultural space of the classroom – or indeed outside the classroom – to stimulate genuine development and learning?

Since the 1970s and earlier, the role of classroom talk in learning has been the object of research and discussion within a fairly restricted circle of educationalists. In his research into and discussion of what he calls 'learning by talking', described in his book *From Communication to Curriculum* (Barnes, 1976), Barnes successfully demonstrated how exploratory talk within small groups of children in the classroom, for example about a poem, stimulates the 'recoding' and enhancement of their understanding in a way that would have been much harder for them to achieve on their own, or indeed with explanations or 'telling' from a teacher. But in so doing Barnes was addressing a far bigger issue, namely the way in which instruction and the type of language and communication that was – and still is – most often used by teachers to 'transmit' knowledge and concepts reaffirms the power structures in society that militate against autonomy, reflection and equal opportunities, including children's opportunities for learning. By contrast, exploratory talk in the classroom, more recently termed 'dialogic teaching' by Robin Alexander (once a colleague of Barnes's) (e.g. Alexander, 2008), moves away from the traditional transmissive routine that involves initiation by the teacher, response by a student or more than one, and evaluation or feedback by the teacher (IRE or IRF for short), and instead encourages genuine dialogue between the teacher and students, and among students, of a kind that helps them to interpret, reshape and recode concepts and ideas in their own individual ways and on their own terms.

Based on analysis of teacher and learner talk during classroom research projects in the 1990s in five countries (England, France, India, Russia and the United States) and follow-up work in the UK, Alexander proposed the categories listed in Figure 1.1.

Teaching talk	Learning talk
• Drilling, repetition ('rote')	• Narrate
• Recitation (through questioning)	• Explain
• Instruction, exposition	• Instruct
• Discussion (exchange of ideas)	• Ask different kinds of questions
• Dialogue (towards common understanding)	• Receive, act and build upon answers
	• Analyse and solve problems
	• Speculate & imagine
	• Explore & evaluate ideas
	• Discuss
	• Argue, reason & justify
	• Negotiate

Figure 1.1 'Teaching talk' and 'learning talk'
Source: Adapted from Alexander (2008: 38–39)

As Alexander points out,

> Only the last two of these [kinds of teaching talk] are likely to meet the criteria of dialogic teaching ... and while we are not arguing that rote should disappear (for even the most elemental form of teaching has its place) we would certainly suggest that teaching which confines itself to the first three kinds of talk ... is unlikely to offer the kinds of cognitive challenge which children need. (Alexander, 2008: 31)

However, for dialogic teaching to be successful, Alexander and his colleagues believe that teachers also need to work hard on helping children to develop their repertoire of the types of learning talk identified in Figure 1.1, as well as their ability to listen, to 'be receptive to alternative viewpoints, think about what they hear, and to give others time to think' (Alexander, 2008: 40).

Questioning

An area that does not feature prominently in Alexander's list, but which others have written extensively about, is the way in which teachers use questioning. In their book aimed at the teaching profession, Norah Morgan and Juliana Saxton illustrated how different types of teacher questions at primary and secondary school level can relate to the categories proposed in the *Taxonomy of Educational Objectives* discussed earlier. These include, for example, questions that draw on knowledge, questions to test understanding, questions which require application, and questions which promote evaluation or judging (Morgan & Saxton, 1991: 12–15). However, they conclude that questions in teaching need to go beyond the *Taxonomy* because it does not in its original version deal with feelings (this is an issue which is addressed in Marzano's *New Taxonomy* by introducing the so-called 'self-system' (Marzano & Kendall, 2007: 12–13)).

Morgan and Saxton propose a classification of teacher questions into three main groups: 'questions which elicit information'; 'questions which shape understanding'; and 'questions which press for reflection' (Morgan & Saxton, 1991: 41). It is particularly in the second and third of these groups that questions can address the dimensions that have a potentially key role to play in cognitive development.

Our own experience confirms this view of the role of communication and questioning in classrooms. However, the categories of learning talk and questions described above do not feature often enough in discussion of classroom interaction. Moreover, as Barnes and others have pointed out since the 1970s, focusing on the ways in which language and communication are used across the curriculum throws the spotlight on issues which are also important for teacher educators and teachers to reflect on:

- Where does power lie in classrooms and how is it shared?
- Who does most of the talking? The quite large group of students or the teacher?
- How productive is that talk? Is it more often in the form of IRF (which has its place), or does it sometimes involve genuine questions and dialogue?
- Are students from different backgrounds expected to learn in the same way, or is there allowance for different routes to learning?
- How successful is the classroom as a sociocultural space for a learning community where language is used to co-construct ideas and make cognitive progress?

Scaffolding

A concept that is often used when discussing teaching and learning talk, especially in subject teaching, is 'scaffolding'. To fully understand the sense of this term we need to return to Vygotsky and a key concept defined by him: the 'zone of proximal development' (ZPD), which is,

> the distance between the actual developmental level as determined by independent problem solving and the level of potential development as determined through problem solving under adult guidance or in collaboration with more capable peers. (Vygotsky, 1978: 86)

The implication of the ZPD is that a given stage in a child's development opens up the potential for a next step in development, and that this next step needs to be aided in some way, for example, by a teacher (or a parent or another student). The support of scaffolding can, if provided in the right form, aid the child or student to 'bridge the gap' between these phases of development. This does not mean that the helper does the task for the child or student, or tells her or him how to do it, but rather that various means, hints, demonstrations, etc. are used to guide their discovery and learning, gradually reducing the scaffolding along the way as the task is done more successfully. Think of the physical and verbal support given to a child on the verge of learning to ride a bicycle: once the physical scaffolding of stabilising wheels on each side is removed, you may need to run alongside and hold the saddle for a while, or tell the child to steer one way or another, but gradually you need to let go while still shouting encouragement.

An annotated example of oral scaffolding in subject teaching, taken from data collected by Walqui in the USA, is reproduced below:

S(student):	It's like everybody should get the same rights and protection, no matter, like, race, religion.
T(teacher):	Yeah. Everybody. (*The teacher acknowledges the student's response and waits*)
S:	No matter if they are a citizen or illegal, they should get the same protection. (*The teacher evaluates and approves the student's answer*)
T:	I agree with you, but why do you say that with confidence? (*The teacher is asking the student to justify or elaborate her thinking*)
S:	Because it says that.
T:	Because it says that? (*The teacher acknowledges the student's response and continues to wait for justification or elaboration*).
S:	Also because it [the 14th Amendment] says it should not deny any person of the right to life, liberty and property without due process. (*The student draws on evidence for her thinking.*)
T:	Okay, not any citizen? (*The teacher highlights a key aspect of the 14th Amendment.*)
S:	Any person. (*The student consolidates her understanding.*)
T:	Okay, so is the 14th Amendment helpful to you? (*The teacher connects the student's learning to her experience, as an immigrant.*)

(Walqui, 2006: 166)

The key skill on the part of the person providing the scaffolding, such as the teacher, is to provide the right kind and amount of support in the right way at the right time, and then gradually to reduce or remove it. This applies just as much to adults learning to deal with complex academic tasks for the first time as to children developing basic concepts.

The term 'scaffold' in this metaphorical sense was first used in an article by Woods *et al.*, in 1976. The article describes an experiment with 30 children aged 3–5 years old who were asked to build a pyramid using purpose-made wooden blocks. They describe it as:

> a process that enables a child or novice to solve a problem, carry out a task or achieve a goal which would be beyond his unassisted efforts. This scaffolding consists essentially of the adult 'controlling' those elements of the task that are initially beyond the learner's capacity, thus enabling him to concentrate upon and complete those elements that are within his range of competence. [...] it may result, eventually, in development of task competence by the learner that would far outstrip his unassisted efforts. (Woods *et al.*, 1976: 90)

Wood *et al.* (1976) identified six key scaffolding functions:

(a) 'Recruitment', i.e. getting the learner(s) involved in the task
(b) Reduction in freedom i.e. simplifying and focusing attention on the task
(c) 'Direction maintenance' i.e. keeping the learners on the task when attention lapses
(d) Marking or accentuating critical features of the elements in the task
(e) Frustration control, i.e. maintaining motivation: the authors propose that the task should be less stressful with a tutor than without
(f) Demonstrating or modelling solutions that are possibly ideal. (Woods *et al.*, 1976: 98)

Vygotsky, who himself did not use the term 'scaffolding', also believed that this kind of external social support assists children's learning in two distinct ways: they are learning how to cope with the task or the concept, and they are also learning how to organise their learning and reasoning. In a sense, they are acquiring new concepts or awareness while, at the same time, learning how learning works and how to learn.

This dual aspect of learning and education is, in our view, too seldom highlighted: how are children and young people in the education system best helped simultaneously to develop their ability to learn and make sense of the world while also developing their knowledge, understanding and skills in traditional subject areas? And how can language and communication best be used by teachers and students to achieve this?

These questions link up with another important topic: the role of language in the development of the so-called 'transversal competences' that are needed across the school curriculum as well as in life beyond the school or college. Whichever list of such transversal competences one refers to, language, communication and learning how to learn are included as essential elements. The recent re-specification of transversal competences by the European Commission, for example, lists literacy competence, language competence, personal, social and learning competence, and cultural awareness and expression competence as four of eight main transversal competences (European Commission, 2018b: 38). Meanwhile, UNESCO includes reflective thinking, interpersonal skills (including communication skills and collaboration etc.), and media and information literacy, such as the ability to locate and access information as examples of transversal skills (UNESCO Asia-Pacific Policy Brief, 2015: 5).

Multiliteracies

The multiliteracies initiative has its origins in the 1990s, and grew out of a realisation that, given the universal developments taking place in language and communication, 'literacy' as it was defined and exemplified in educational principles and practice was no longer fit for purpose. The underlying rationale for the concept behind the inelegant term 'multiliteracies' is firstly that communication is increasingly multilayered and multifaceted as individuals move from context to context, domain to domain, and from one cultural environment to another. 'These differences are the consequence of any number of factors, including culture, gender, life experience, subject matter, social or subject domain and the like. Every meaning exchange is cross-cultural to a certain degree' (Cope & Kalantzis, 2015: 3). Secondly, an updated concept of literacy is needed because communication itself is multimodal in that spoken words are likely to be accompanied by body language, tone of voice, facial expressions and so on, and the written word may increasingly be mixed in with visual illustrations and symbols of one kind or another, and may be printed in a book, delivered on a screen or handwritten. In other words, diversity of one kind or another and the fast-moving evolution of modes of communication, as well as the intermingling of languages, require teachers to think of literacy more broadly and to ensure that their students learn to cope with and take advantage of its diversity. Thus multiliteracies intersect, on the one hand, with languages and culture since students need to learn to live in multicultural societies and global communities where people with different first languages are communicating with one another, and, on the other hand, with media and literacy in information and communication technology (ICT): the ability to interpret in a considered manner the content and messages distributed via the internet and through printed media, and to take advantage proactively of the opportunities offered by ICT-based communication.

We sense here the growing pressure on teachers and teacher educators: if I am a teacher of, say, history, not only am I to ensure that my students have a clear unbiased view of the history of the nations and societies specified in the curriculum and of the way evidence is used to underpin views of history; I also need to ensure that my work in the classroom enables young people to develop transversal competences such as critical thinking, open-mindedness, teamwork and social responsibility, but also their communication skills, an understanding of how language and communication work in societies, and a multifaceted kind of literacy which will help them with their further learning. These are exciting but demanding challenges, especially given the diversity of cultures, languages and learning aptitudes that I am likely to find in my classroom owing to globalisation and migration flows. But how do I develop the range of skills and awareness that I require to do my job well and to continue doing it well as the needs of the students I work with and the sociocultural environment changes? Moreover, if I am teacher educator, how do I ensure that teachers are equipped with skills and awareness of this kind? These are questions we will suggest answers to later in the book, notably in Chapter 6.

Some UK Initiatives around Language and Education

In the 1970s, well before the advent of the internet and notion of 'transversal competences', the British government instigated an enquiry into language and literacy in education, called *A Language for Life* (Bullock Report, 1975). Notwithstanding the huge social and technological changes since those days, some of the recommendations in the final report, though mostly not or only sporadically implemented since that time, were carried forward in later work and remain as relevant today as they were then, at least in the UK and no doubt in many other national contexts, irrespective of the prevalent language of schooling.

> The following are some examples of recommendations from the Bullock Report (1975):
>
> (4) 'Each school should have an organised policy for language across the curriculum, establishing every teacher's involvement in language and reading development throughout the years of schooling';
>
> (5) 'Every school should have a suitably qualified teacher with responsibility for advising and supporting his colleagues in language and the teaching of reading'
>
> (15) a substantial course on language in education […] should be part of every primary and secondary school teacher's initial training, whatever the teacher's subject or the age of the children with whom he or she will be working.'
>
> (17) 'there should be a national centre for language in education concerned with the teaching of English in all its aspects.'. (Bullock Report, 1975: 514–515)

If we interpret 'reading' here more broadly as what we now call 'literacy', there seems to us to be much food for thought in these recommendations. Like many good recommendations, however, they do imply concerted effort, in the case of the UK across authorities and entities that had and still have considerable independence, as well as investment of funding and time, and efforts and expertise at school level that meet local requirements.

The Bullock Report was followed in the 1980s by two further reports, namely the Kingman Report (1988) on an enquiry into 'the Teaching of the English Language' and the Cox Report (1989) on 'English for Ages 5 to 16'. In different ways, the proposals that the two reports summarise pick up where the Bullock Report left off. For example, the Kingman Report proposed that subject departments concerned with the teaching of language in secondary schools should develop a 'co-ordinated policy for language teaching' (p. 69) and that teacher education courses and teacher training courses should 'contain a substantial component of tuition in language study' (p. 70). Meanwhile, the Cox Report advocated that the curriculum for children between the ages of 5 and 16 should include the 'development of pupils' understanding of the spoken word and the capacity to express themselves effectively in a variety of speaking and listening activities, matching style and response to audience and purpose' (Cox Report, 1989: 11), and laid down a series of 'attainment targets' to be focused on in the curriculum.

These reports gave rise to the Language in the National Curriculum (LINC) project coordinated by Professor Ron Carter. The project developed materials for the professional development of teachers aimed at raising their awareness of and knowledge about key aspects of language, with specific reference to English. The introduction to the project report includes a brief summary of a functional model of language derived from applied linguistics, which underpins the materials themselves:

- The making of meaning is the reason for the invention, existence and development of language.
- All meanings exist within the context of culture. Cultural values and beliefs determine the purposes, audiences, settings and topics of language.
- Texts, spoken and written, are created and interpreted by making appropriate choices from the language system according to specific purposes, audiences, settings and topics. (Carter, 1989: 2)

This brief summary is a very useful as a reminder to teachers – and indeed everyone – of the complex and dynamic nature of language and the need for these dimensions of language to underpin language in education. The materials themselves covered all key aspects of language in the curriculum as recommended by the reports referred to above and a range of media was used, including audio-recordings and television. According to a note below the title, the materials were used with teachers at all schools in England and Wales over a three-year period from 1989 to 1992. Further small-scale rather than national initiatives have followed and continue to the present day.

This series of examples is a clear demonstration of what can be done when concerted and enlightened attention is paid to an educational initiative. Unfortunately, in this case, as in many others, political changes meant that the impetus for continuing this overdue work and integrating language fully into teacher education did not last.

Language Repertoire

Every individual has a 'language repertoire', the capacity to use a range of language and potentially of different languages, for communication. Some areas of the repertoire may be much more developed than others. For example, children up to the age of 6 years may be able to use the language of the home and of interaction with friends fluently, but not yet be able to express themselves confidently in formal language. Some adults may feel quite confident about writing e-mails to work colleagues, but are intimidated when writing a report or formal letter. The internet, (e.g. see http://ilanguages.org/bilingual.php) tells us that at least 60% of the world's population is able to communicate in more than one language and many of them are bi- or trilingual. Many more of us have some knowledge of other languages, however modest, in our repertoires.

The importance of language in education centres on the need for children and older students to gradually develop the breadth and depth of their ability to understand and use the language of schooling effectively, that is, the language in which most subjects are taught. Our ability to progress in our education and to reach our individual potential, whatever the subjects, hinges on our awareness of how language operates and is used in different contexts for different purposes. It also involves gradually becoming familiar with and able to use different types of oral and written language for different academic and other purposes. For example, the language used for explaining or asking about scientific or historical information is different from the language used to complete tasks such as writing about a topic, making oral presentations about concepts or discussing contentious ideas. The gradual broadening of literacy and oracy to encompass a range of varieties and registers of language is an essential aim of education internationally and should be the responsibility of all teachers, whatever their subject specialism.

Concluding Remarks

This chapter has spelt out some key aspects of the role of language in learning and education more generally. Important early explorations of the relationship between language, thinking and learning fed into detailed thinking about how educational objectives should be framed linguistically, and the ways in which language, especially talk, questioning and scaffolding, can most effectively be used in the classroom. As Neil Mercer pointed out in words that neatly summarise points made in this chapter,

> Teachers have a professional responsibility for helping their students to build new understandings upon the foundations of their previous learning, and language is the main tool available to the teaching profession for doing this ... teachers can also help students to learn how language can be used as a tool for making joint, coherent sense of experience. (Mercer, 2000: 52)

But to do this well, teachers need to be well prepared for their work through initial teacher education and then to engage in continuing professional development of their own. The UK examples above show how intensive focus on language in education can lead to potentially far-reaching policy proposals while demonstrating that ongoing concerted and comprehensive programmes of action in schools and in teacher education do not necessarily follow. Language and communication are so central to education that it seems only common sense that 'language across the curriculum' should form a main part of initial teacher education, that there should be a clearly focused language policy in each school, or at least each school authority, which teachers feel they own, and that at least one teacher in each school should have expertise and responsibility in the area of language across the curriculum, and can provide focused mentoring for colleagues when required. Unless some sort of provision along these lines is available, the risk is that the necessary development of teachers' reflection on the role of language and communication in their work, and of their competence in this area, will be haphazard and, given the pressures that teachers are usually under, pushed down the list of day-to-day professional concerns.

It is important to add some caveats at this point. The first is that the sociocultural characteristics of school education vary considerably from country to country and are determined by numerous factors relating to the types of classroom environment and traditions of education that have developed in the national or local context. What is more, the role of the teacher may be seen by students and their parents as very different in one cultural context as compared to another. For example, exploratory talk and dialogic teaching in a classroom in India with 100 students poses different challenges from those faced in a class of 30 in the UK. Secondly, it is hard to prove that students 'learn better' by one means rather than another. In most contexts, much assessment of learning is still geared to the learning of facts and information rather than the cognitive and cultural development of children. This means that the formal evidence available does not provide very reliable information about the quality or even the extent of learning. Thirdly, the kind of exploratory teaching that will 'work well' is itself subject to environmental constraints, such as class size or heterogeneity within the class, and the pedagogic competences that teachers have at their disposal. These constraints may, of course, affect any educational innovation, but this seems often to be forgotten by policy makers. The general idea behind an innovation in approach to classroom teaching such as exploratory talk may be clear to teachers, and, they may even have had some training in procedures for setting it up in the classroom. However, if they are not systematically helped to master the skills needed to set the scene, give instructions clearly, provide scaffolding and maintain order, or if suitable learning resources are not available, their success will be limited and there will be a temptation to revert to relying most of the time on the 'tried and tested' IRF formula referred to earlier in the chapter.

We will return to several of the issues raised in this chapter in our discussion of teacher education and professional development in Part 2. Meanwhile our focus in the second chapter moves from the role of language in learning and teaching across the curriculum to the teaching and learning of second and foreign languages. We will consider how foreign and second language teaching has evolved over recent decades, the place it has in educational curricula, and the links or potential links between the learning of other languages and the development of transversal language and intercultural competences.

Questions for reflection and discussion

(1) In your experience of education (all subjects) how important for your own learning were the ways in which your teachers used language and encouraged students to use it in their classrooms?
(2) In the school environments in your country, how feasible and useful would it be to implement the Bullock Report recommendation that every school should have a suitably qualified teacher with responsibility for advising and supporting all colleagues in language and literacy?
(3) In your opinion, how relevant for teachers is the concept of multiliteracies, and how important is experience and awareness of it for their students' educational careers?

2 Changes in Second and Foreign Language Education

In the period since the end of World War II, the role and status of second and foreign language education has been re-examined and redefined in the light of the profound political, economic and social changes that have taken place across Europe and beyond. In this chapter, we look at the impact of these changes not only on aspects of language teaching and learning, including methodology, curricula, materials and assessment, but also on attitudes, identity, education and cultures. We start with a brief overview of the main milestones during this period.

The End of the Colonial Era and Language Policy

The Spanish and Portuguese colonies in Central and South America had all been liberated in the early 19th century, in each case leaving the legacy of a common language that helped to unify each new nation and to make them governable in spite of the many local and tribal languages that continued to be used by indigenous people. In most cases, liberation was attained through armed struggle.

In the case of the British and French colonies, mainly in Africa and Asia, independence came in the decades immediately after World War II. Here, the linguistic legacy was, and still is, more complex and, in some instances, controversial in nature. In newly independent India, Pakistan (and later Bangladesh) and Malaysia, the sense of nationhood was underpinned by reinforcing the status of Hindi, Urdu, Bengali and Malay respectively as national languages. In each of these countries, this led to a temporary decline in the status of English, which had come to symbolise colonial exploitation and suppression. In most of Britain's former colonies in East and West Africa, English has retained official language status, in most cases because of the need for a lingua franca between speakers of the many local languages. In Malaysia and

Bangladesh in the early years of the new millennium, there was recognition even at government level that they were losing out economically by allowing standards of English to lapse because of the promotion of Malay and Bengali respectively, and policies were put in place to improve the teaching and learning of English across their education systems.

Likewise, French has largely maintained its official status in the African countries that were once colonies, and the same is true of those French territories in the Caribbean, the Pacific and the Indian Ocean which are still seen as a part of France. By contrast, Morocco, Algeria and Tunisia have all reverted to Arabic as the national language. The former Portuguese colonies of Angola, Cape Verde and Mozambique have all retained Portuguese as their national language following independence. Interestingly, in just about all of these former colonies, English, French or Portuguese remain in everyday use among educated people.

Language Issues in Post-War Europe

Scarred by the ravages of two world wars, European nations began to take steps to ensure closer economic and political cooperation by moving in stages to what is now the European Union. The earliest institution to be founded, and for language education perhaps the most significant, was the Council of Europe, which pre-dates the European Union, and was set up in 1949 with the stated aims of upholding human rights, democracy and the rule of law in Europe, and of promoting European culture. In 1954, the Cultural Convention, signed initially by 14 countries, was established with the following stated objectives:

> The purpose of this Convention is to develop mutual understanding among the peoples of Europe and reciprocal appreciation of their cultural diversity, to safeguard European culture, to promote national contributions to Europe's common cultural heritage respecting the same fundamental values and to encourage in particular the study of the languages, history and civilisation of the Parties to the Convention. (Council of Europe, 1954)

From the 1970s onwards, the Council of Europe began putting foreign language teaching and learning centre stage in its actions to promote collaboration and exchange among the peoples of its numerous member states, and over recent decades has made uniquely influential contributions to the field (for an overview of the main 'milestones' in this work, see https://www.coe.int/en/web/language-policy/milestones). The work of international experts on language curricula and language standards resulted in the appearance in 1975 of the *Threshold Level* (van Ek, 1975), a seminal document that was to have a profound effect on the teaching and learning of languages right up to the present day. It was designed as:

> a specification in operational terms first of what a learner should be able to DO when using the language independently for communication in a country in which that language is the vehicle of communication in everyday life, and then of the necessary knowledge and skills. (The European Centre for Modern Languages' website 'help' section; see http://archive.ecml.at/help/detail.asp?i=124, accessed 20th July 2017)

It was this document, and its later extensions at different levels, that was responsible for fundamentally changing traditional thinking among language teaching professionals about how languages should be taught and what should be prioritised in syllabuses and materials. The most significant implication was that language teaching should shift its focus radically from language knowledge to language skills, equipping learners to communicate effectively in a foreign language. Publications by Wilkins (1976) and Littlewood (1981) focused on how to design a syllabus using categories drawn from early European documents such as the *Threshold Level* (van Ek, 1975), and on the methodological implications of teaching language for communication, respectively. Authors of early textbooks designed on communicative lines, such as the *Strategies* series for English (Abbs & Freebairn, 1975–1978), struggled to accommodate grammatical knowledge within an overall communicative approach, at the time resulting in allegations of 'cryptostructuralism'. This also reflected the difficulties which language teachers, especially those in state educational systems, experienced, and in some cases still experience, in trying to change the focus of their teaching from a preoccupation with language knowledge to a prioritisation of developing language skills.

The Common European Framework of Reference for Languages

The *Threshold Level* (van Ek, 1975) and its successors paved the way for Council of Europe-led research and development work on a framework of principles and of levels of attainment in foreign languages based on illustrative 'can-do' descriptors. The year 2001 saw the publication of the *Common European Framework of Reference for Languages* or CEFR for short, now available in 40 languages (Council of Europe, 2001). The CEFR provides sets of skill-based descriptors at six levels, which are intended to offer a basis for designing language learning outcomes and assessment criteria. It has further reinforced the need to see language proficiency and achievement in terms of the ability to communicate rather than knowledge of language systems, although it does acknowledge and document the need for linguistic competence as a foundation.

But the authors wanted the CEFR to be seen as more than just a set of skill-based descriptors:

> The approach adopted here, generally speaking, is an action-oriented one in so far as it views users and learners of a language primarily as 'social agents', i.e. members of society who have tasks (not exclusively language-related) to accomplish in a given set of circumstances, in a specific environment and within a particular field of action. While acts of speech occur within language activities, these activities form part of a wider social context, which alone is able to give them their full meaning. (Council of Europe, 2001: 9)

'The action-oriented approach' is the title of a recent and wide-ranging book (Piccardo & North, 2019), which looks in great detail at the CEFR's contribution to language education and the principles and research underpinning the approach.

In a message to users of the CEFR in their introduction, the authors assert that 'We have *not* set out to tell practitioners what to do, or how to do it. We are raising questions, not answering them' (Council of Europe, 2001: xi). However, the Framework has been seized upon by publishers, syllabus designers, examination authorities and ministries as a means of identifying standards, whether in the blurb on the cover of a textbook, in a syllabus or curriculum document, as a 'badge' for a public examination, or as an aspirational standard for school leavers or graduates to attain by the end of their studies. Some employers use CEFR levels as a way of setting minimum standards required for a specific vacancy which they wish to fill, and, more disturbingly, immigration authorities in several countries now use the attainment of a given level of proficiency in the national language as one of the prerequisites for application for citizenship, residence or even family reunion. For example, a 2013 survey carried out among member states of the Council of Europe found that 15 of the 36 participating countries had language-level requirements for residence permits, of which seven were at CEFR level A2 and three at CEFR level B1. The comparable figures for the previous survey in 2009 were four for A1/A2 or A2, and four for B1, out of a total of 13 countries that had such requirements (Council of Europe, 2014).

The CEFR has been adopted and used for various purposes by ministries publishers and examination authorities in many countries around the world, and its influence continues to grow. Importantly, it also continues to evolve in response to perceived needs as well as gaps and shortcomings in the original document, and a companion volume with new descriptors has recently been published (Council of Europe, 2018b).

One of the purposes of the CEFR was to provide tools for self-assessment. Table 2 of the CEFR (Council of Europe, 2001: 26–27) is a self-assessment grid of descriptors that can be used for this purpose.

A parallel CEFR project (details of which can be found at http://www.coe.int/en/web/portfolio/introduction) developed a model for a replicable language portfolio for self-assessment, the *European Language Portfolio* (ELP), that could be adapted for different purposes in the various sectors of education in European states. The CEFR has been used for different purposes by publishers, examination authorities, ministries, employers and other stakeholders in language education. Not all of these stakeholders demonstrate close understanding of the purpose and detail of the Framework, and in particular of the time it takes language learners to progress from one level to the next in terms of developing language proficiency. This is evidenced by the unrealistic target levels set by some ministries of education for school leavers or for future teachers of English, but also by the claims made by some publishers about the level that users of their books can be expected to reach. The CEFR itself and its later companion publication (Council of Europe, 2018b) are apparently seldom read in their entirety, and this in turn leads to overconcentration on the scales of descriptors or 'can-do' statements at the expense of attention to other important sections on, for example, sociolinguistic and pragmatic competences and (especially in the companion volume) on mediation skills. Also, there is no doubt that front-line stakeholders such as language teachers and teacher educators would benefit from an orientation programme to the CEFR to enable them to use it themselves as a professional tool rather than simply relying on the interpretations offered by ministries, publishers and examination providers. Inevitably, it has come in for criticism for a variety of reasons, and we shall look at its impact more closely in Chapter 9.

Multilingualism and Plurilingualism

The Council of Europe has also been influential, through its Language Policy Programme, in recommending the development of language policies across its 47 member states, many of which were outlined in a *Guide for the Development of Language Education Policies in Europe* (Beacco & Byram, 2007). Embedded in the Council's thinking about policy are the concepts of multilingualism and plurilingualism, and the importance of the distinction between them.

> plurilingualism is the ability to use more than one language – and accordingly sees languages from the standpoint of speakers and learners. Multilingualism, on the other hand, refers to the presence of several languages in a given geographical area, regardless of those who speak them. (Thonhauser, 2012: 3)

Taken to its logical conclusion in policy terms, multilingualism needs to be recognised and accepted where it exists within a nation state.

It represents a move away from the 'one nation, one language' trend of the 19th and 20th centuries, which disadvantaged and threatened the very existence of minority languages such as Basque, Breton, Welsh and Kashubian. In an age of mass migration, a positive attitude towards multilingualism should also mean that the many languages that migrants bring with them are accorded more acknowledgement and support in public services and the education system.

Plurilingualism as a feature of language policy making has led to its widespread adoption as an educational aspiration and a key plank in curriculum design and approaches to teaching and learning, transcending the traditional limits of foreign language classes and extending into the realms of bilingual education and, more recently, content and language integrated learning (CLIL). More on this in Chapter 3.

Early Language Learning

There has been a long-running debate among teachers and academics about the best age for children to start learning a foreign language. However, there is no doubt that proponents of an early start are currently in the ascendancy, as is evidenced by the number of countries which have now made provision for foreign language classes at primary level, and in some cases even in kindergarten. A study commissioned by the European Union to look into the main pedagogical principles of teaching languages to young learners came up with a selection of persuasive reasons for making an early start, some of which are restated here:

- to develop the hidden multilingual potential of every child, which allows a natural acquisition of another language as early as possible and also a better access to other foreign languages once a child starts to understand at least one of them;
- to foster positive attitudes towards language learning;
- to raise awareness of foreign-language learning at a young age and thus motivate children for learning foreign languages;
- to meet demands from parents that their children should learn languages in kindergarten. (adapted from Edelenbos *et al.*, 2006)

Here, too, publishers have been alert to the rise in demand, and materials specially designed to motivate and enthuse young learners are now widely available. This general expansion in provision is probably driven at least as much by parental demand as by hard research evidence. However, there is general agreement, largely based on insights from developmental psychology, that the methods used to teach a foreign language to younger learners need to be different from those used at secondary level, and that teachers need specialised training to be able to work at this level. Herein lie a couple of problems, related to the transition to secondary level, that have yet to be fully addressed and resolved. The provision of foreign language classes at primary level remains uneven, which means that first year secondary classes are often by nature mixed ability. For this reason, but also because some secondary teachers dismiss the worth of play-learning at primary level, they prefer to start again from the beginning, this time with different methods and with textbooks that are specially designed for study at secondary school. Learners who enjoyed their language classes at primary school may lose motivation if their previous learning is explicitly or tacitly ignored as irrelevant. Plainly, there is still work to be done, despite the recommendations as long ago as 2006 (Edelenbos *et al.*, 2006.), which focused, inter alia, on the need for specialised training for teachers of young learners, the need for research into the main models of early language learning and the main learning outcomes associated with them, and also for research into children's motivation and its impact on their progression as language learners.

The European Centre for Modern Languages

The work of the Council of Europe in language education was given added impetus by the founding, in 1998, of the European Centre for Modern Languages (ECML). Its stated vision is of:

> a Europe committed to linguistic and cultural diversity, where the key role of quality language education in achieving intercultural dialogue, democratic citizenship and social cohesion is recognised and supported. (http://www.ecml.at/Aboutus/AboutUs-Overview/tabid/172/language/en-GB/Default.aspx)

The Centre, based in Graz in Austria, currently has 33 member states, and its work focuses on projects aimed at specific areas of language learning and teaching. The project teams are drawn from member states and they work to the following brief:

- to provide training modules, guidelines and toolkits for teacher educators, equipping them to train others within their institutions and networks;
- to provide training and professional development opportunities for multipliers;
- to publish examples of good practice applicable in different contexts. (http://www.ecml.at/ECML-Programme/Programme-Overview/tabid/155/language/en-GB/Default.aspx)

The Centre relies on its publications and on word-of-mouth dissemination by those who participate in its workshops and seminars for its impact, and this inevitably results in different levels of uptake in language classrooms in participating countries. It also goes some way towards explaining why the valuable work done by the ECML is not more widely known, either within the whole of Europe or beyond. Its relative autonomy allows it to respond reasonably flexibly to new trends and areas of activity in the field and to the language education priorities identified by its member states.

The Bologna Process

One further, and very important, development in Europe was the signing of the Bologna Declaration in 1999, initially by 29 European countries, thereby making a commitment to what is commonly known as the Bologna Process, aimed at establishing, over time, a standardised framework of qualifications in higher education and a credit transfer system for modules of study, thus making student mobility easier and more worthwhile. While the Bologna Process continues to move forward, with many more countries now participating, the aim of complete compatibility and standardisation of qualifications remains only partly fulfilled owing to the conservative nature of higher education when it comes to adopting change. Crucially, the Bologna Process has highlighted the need for high levels of language proficiency for those students who wish to pursue their studies in a country other than their own, and this in turn has led to a growth in demand for language qualifications, especially in English.

Developments in East and Central Europe

The collapse of socialism in East and Central Europe and the subsequent deconstruction of the Soviet Union both had important consequences for language policies and language teaching and learning. Almost overnight, in countries such as Czechoslovakia, Hungary and Romania, Russian was rejected as the main foreign language taught in schools and was replaced by English, in most cases by popular demand. Governments had to respond, but this proved to be an immense challenge because of the shortage of qualified English teachers. In some of these countries, English teachers and even fluent English speakers had been regarded with suspicion and sometimes were kept under surveillance by the authorities. Suddenly, everything changed and they were in demand.

In 1989, in response to the beginnings of change across the entire region, the British Government established the 'Know-How' fund, originally to provide technical assistance to Poland, before it was later extended to Hungary and Czechoslovakia, and eventually to Romania, Bulgaria and the Soviet Union. Some of the funding was targeted at educational reform, particularly in English language teaching. Attempts at reforming the teacher training curriculum had a strong initial impact, largely because of the need to meet the demand for English teachers. Fast-track programmes were set up to train English teachers in three years instead of the usual five, with a focus on modern methodology and language improvement rather than on educating philologists. In Hungary, for example, the British Council was able to support these new programmes, and the Eötvös Loránd University in Budapest provided a model that was taken up in several universities across the country. The fast-track programme there turned out classroom-ready graduates with a practical grounding in both language and teaching skills, thereby tackling the nationwide shortage of qualified teachers of English. However, the experiment was relatively short-lived once the immediate demand had been met, and most universities reverted to the five-year programme to be taught strictly and only by those with PhD qualifications. But the fast-track programme left its mark, and the five-year programme now generally embraces a practical approach to methodology, lengthy teaching practice and a school-based mentor scheme.

In many post-Soviet republics, the model for language teacher education has remained largely unchanged, though curriculum reforms have made headway in the field of English teacher preparation in Uzbekistan and Ukraine. In each case, a major area of focus has been the redesign of the methodology programme starting from the premise that it needs to have a strong practical orientation in order to prepare student teachers for their careers, thus supplanting the traditional view of methodology as a knowledge-based, theoretical subject. Reforms like this are difficult to push through in contexts where academic hierarchies prevail and hard-won territory is defended. For more on the reform in Uzbekistan, see Gulyamova and Isamukhamedova (2012). This is covered in more detail in Part 2.

By contrast, the landscape of language teaching and learning has changed quite dramatically in East and Central Europe in the period since 1989. English is now the first foreign language in all the countries in the region, but other languages continue to be taught where there is an existing tradition or a need (e.g. German in the Czech Republic, French in Romania, Russian in Bulgaria). Language policies increasingly address economic realities, such as the employment market and the need to promote international trade and are no longer based solely on political imperatives or the need to bolster national pride and identity.

Migration

A more recent development that has added to the complexity of language policies and language education in many countries in Europe has been the large-scale movement of people from the Middle East and Africa. The massive influx of refugees that started as the Syrian and Iraqi conflicts gained in intensity from 2014 onwards, coupled with an increase in economic migrants from different parts of Africa, has had a significant impact on state education, including language education, in countries across Europe. An Austrian teacher of English reported recently that she has eight different nationalities in a class of just over 20, some of whom speak little German and no English. At the time of writing, it is uncertain whether these migrants will eventually return to their native countries or not. This picture is reflected in countries across Europe, but it is not an entirely new phenomenon. In Germany, for example, the sustaining of the 'Wirtschaftswunder' beyond the 1950s relied heavily on migrant workers invited in from Turkey to fill the vacancies in a range of different industries. In the UK, immigration from Commonwealth countries was encouraged, for similar reasons. Further afield, Australia encouraged immigration for much of the latter part of the 20th century, mainly to overcome skills shortages in the employment market, and from the late 19th century and earlier the USA was regarded as a land of refuge and of opportunity for those fleeing persecution in Europe or seeking a better life. Immigrants came from many different countries with almost as many different mother tongues. In all these four countries, a great majority of these early migrants stayed and have now attained citizenship. All these trends led to a need for a different approach to language teaching and learning, with a focus on adults, and an emphasis on language for survival and for largely functional purposes. At school level, the children of these migrants needed to be assimilated into state education systems, a process which required attention to acculturation as well as the development of language proficiency. Teachers needed to develop new skills in order to cope with these challenges and training courses in second (rather than foreign) language teaching grew in number.

The Growth of Language Teaching as an Industry

Specialist language schools have existed, and in some case flourished, for well over 100 years. Berlitz schools, founded in 1878, were pioneers in this area. But the period since around 1960 has seen an exponential growth in provision, with the opening of small, family-owned schools as well as a number of large corporate groups and franchises. This expansion has been driven by a number of factors, including the poor quality of language teaching in many state schools, the huge increase in demand for English in almost all walks of life (especially among adults), the increase in uptake of internationally recognised examinations (including those required for student mobility, such as TOEFL (Test of English as a Foreign Language) and IELTS (International English Language Testing System for English), and recognition of the benefits of plurilingualism, particularly in Europe.

Side by side with this private sector expansion, there has been an increase in language teaching provision through national cultural-diplomatic organisations: this includes the British Council (founded in 1934, but with a greatly expanded language teaching provision since 1945); the Alliance Française, which has been active in the field of cultural diplomacy since its foundation in 1884, and its sister organisation the Institut Français with special responsibility for language and culture; the Goethe Institut (founded in 1951, as Germany regained its equilibrium after the war); the Instituto Cervantes (founded in 1991); and the Instituto Camões, established a year later. Public funding for adult language learning has also been in place in some countries for many years now. The Volkshochschulen in Germany and Austria, the Escuelas Oficiales de Idiomas in Spain, the Folk High Schools in Sweden and Adult Education Institutes in the UK all offer subsidised classes in foreign languages, in some cases preparing participants for recognised examinations offering certificates of proficiency. Classes at these centres may be larger and less intensive than in the private sector, but they have played an important part in opening up opportunities for language learning to people who could not otherwise afford the fees.

Both state-sponsored institutions and private sector organisations have contributed enormously to innovation in the field of foreign language teaching. Many successful textbook writers learned their trade in private language schools and by becoming published authors made a significant contribution to the field. The very successful *Streamline English* series (Hartley & Viney, 1978–1980), for example, emerged from collaboration between teachers at the Anglo-Continental School in Bournemouth in the 1980s, while the Eckersley School of English in Oxford was founded partly on the success of *Essential English for Foreign Students* (Eckersley, 1938–1942), a textbook written by the school owner's father, which had the market almost to itself in the 1950s. Since its foundation, the Goethe Institut has fostered the development of Deutsch als Fremdsprache or DaF (German as a foreign language) through training and publications and, much earlier, the Alliance Française was partly responsible for the widespread adoption of the audio-visual method for the teaching of French. For decades, method-based teaching prevailed in many language schools and state-sponsored institutes. Some of them, such as the Berlitz schools, stuck to direct method teaching based on their own, in-house textbooks, while others, notably, but not only, in France experimented with audio-lingual and audio-visual methods, usually driven by technology in the form of slide projectors and/or language laboratories. By the 1980s, however, most schools were using materials based or partly based on a 'communicative approach' inspired by the *Threshold Level* (van Ek, 1975) and later the CEFR (Council of Europe, 2001), which were the result of Council of Europe led cooperation between experts from both state and private sector institutions.

From the 1950s onwards, the higher education sector in the UK was involved in providing qualifications in the teaching of English as a foreign language, and later postgraduate qualifications in applied linguistics and English language teaching (ELT) which were needed by people wishing to teach abroad in the private sector, in British Council centres, or in sponsored posts in state sector universities and schools. In Chapter 4, we will return to the topic of initial teacher education for language teachers and the various forms it takes in different sectors and contexts. Some universities developed a reputation for expertise, excellence and influential publications in specific areas of language teaching and learning; Birmingham University for English for Specific Purposes (cf Dudley-Evans & St John, 1998), Lancaster University for testing and assessment (cf Alderson & Clapham, 1995) and for corpus linguistics (cf Garside *et al.*, 1987), Reading University for early breakthroughs in syllabus design and communicative language teaching (cf Wilkins, 1976) and the then Ealing College of Further Education for English as a second language. But these trends extended beyond the UK, for example, with the establishment of CRAPEL (Centre de Recherches et d'Applications Pédagogiques en Langues) at the University of Nancy in France as a centre of excellence in the field of learner autonomy, and the worldwide reputation of Victoria University in Wellington for vocabulary studies, thanks largely to the work of Paul Nation.

Finally in this section, it is worth mentioning that the English language learning industry in general has made an immense contribution to the economies of, for example, the UK, Ireland and Australia, a fact which was illustrated recently in a report commissioned by English UK, the umbrella body for English teaching organisations in the UK. The authors' key findings make interesting reading:

- Around 650,000 students studied English as a foreign language in the United Kingdom at more than 550 accredited institutions in 2014
- Overall, the industry supported around 26,500 jobs in the United Kingdom through its supply chain, employee and student spending, and its direct teaching activity
- The total value of international English language students' spending, including tuition fees, accommodation and other living costs, added £1.2 billion to United Kingdom export revenues in 2014
- The sector added approximately £1.1 billion of value to the economy over the year, or an average of £378 per student for each week they stay. (Chaloner *et al.*, 2016)

Information Technology and Corpus Studies, and their Impact on Language Education

Language education has also been profoundly affected by the dawn of the digital age. Internet resources continue to multiply and diversify, and with them the opportunities afforded to learners to bypass traditional modes of learning and to take more responsibility for their own language learning. Learning materials have in many cases been reconceptualised and both low-tech and high-tech options are being explored and opened up. The 'English in Action' project in Bangladesh, for example, aimed to raise the English language proficiency of 25 million people by delivering language learning resources to mobile phone users (Rahman & Cotter, 2014). The British Council has produced and made freely available a wealth of self-access learning resources for teachers and learners on its website (https://learnenglish.britishcouncil.org/). Teachers in contexts all over the world are setting up contacts with their peers in other countries and involving their language classes in share online projects.

In addition to all this, which has been extensively documented in experience reports in books and journals in many languages, advances in technology have also facilitated research into language on a massive scale. The availability of huge banks of language data, known as corpora, in the form of electronically stored collections of many types of written and spoken text has made it possible for linguists to conduct research into the ways in which language is actually used in the real word outside classrooms. There had already been a move from prescriptive grammar to descriptive grammar in the 1970s and 1980s, but for a while after that most grammars were still based on the written word. Now that corpora of spoken language are widely available, it has been possible to describe elements of spoken grammar that had never previously been recognised (Carter & McCarthy, 1997, 2006, 2011), and several of these insights have now been integrated into teaching materials. Some existing corpora are available (sometimes in reduced form) online; for example, the *British National Corpus* (1991–2007) (http://www.natcorp.ox.ac.uk/) while others are owned by publishers or universities and are accessible mainly to their own authors and researchers. The UK publisher, Collins, holds corpora for French, German and Spanish as well as English (see http://www.collinslanguage.com/language-resources/corpora/). Corpora have also been useful in vocabulary studies, and have, for example, enabled word frequency counts to be made in specific text types, a facility which has been invaluable to materials designers.

Concluding Remarks

Our purpose in offering the overview in this chapter has been to provide a backcloth for a more detailed treatment of many of the key issues in later chapters. We hope it has gone some way towards documenting what has been an unprecedented period of activity in the history of language education, especially but not only in Europe. Whether or not all this activity and change has advanced or held back the development of language teaching and learning is an open question which we shall revisit in different ways in the chapters that follow. What is clear is that the developments that have been discussed have taken place against a background of social, economic and political change on a scale that has sometimes made it difficult for teachers and learners to know what to hold on to and what to discard. A united Europe would have been unthinkable a century ago, and just 50 years ago no-one could have imagined that socialist ideals and systems would collapse so suddenly.

But there are also constants that can be seen collectively as a kind of counterpoint to all the upheaval. Language, in all its varieties and uses, remains a symbol of personal, local, regional and national identity. This affects individual efforts to learn a foreign language as well as national language policies. Hardly anyone speaks the 'Queen's English' or 'Oxford English' these days and those who do are regarded as anachronistic. The BBC now employs newsreaders and reporters with regional accents on the grounds that viewers and listeners identify more readily with them. In Britain, urban varieties are growing in their reach and geographical spread, partly as a result of media coverage. 'Estuary English', a variety that hatched in London around the estuary of the Thames, and which is characterised by features such as the glottal stop, has now taken root in all the home counties. The Liverpool variety of English has spread into large parts of Lancashire, Cheshire and North Wales. These urban varieties are typically seen, especially by young people, as much 'cooler' than rural varieties, which may seem to be slow and laboured by comparison. In the written language, the rush towards ever-faster means of communication has seen the growth of a whole new truncated variety of each language for the purposes of text messaging and using social media. Here, too, there is a shared code among teenagers and even smaller social groups whose messages may be largely indecipherable to an outsider. In all these cases, language choice is heavily influenced by cultural considerations and the identity that goes along with them. A Yorkshire cricket fan, proud of his heritage, is likely to exaggerate elements of his dialect when confronted with a fan from Lancashire or from somewhere 'down south'. Berliners use their dialect to identify themselves and maybe even to achieve ascendancy over Bavarians. Some speakers of 'High German' regard Swiss German as an unfortunate aberration and yet no Swiss German would give up their dialect any more than they would give up their cultural traditions. Significant, too, has been the resurgence of once-suppressed minority languages such as Basque, Welsh, Breton, Kashubian and Sorbian, with positive policies, inspired by the Convention on Regional or Minority Languages (Council of Europe, 1992), which is in place in many countries to ensure their survival. Primary education is now available in many of these languages, sometimes as an option and sometimes as a compulsory additional subject, but this is in most cases not sustained at secondary and tertiary level. Speakers of these languages very often become trilingual as they master a foreign language as well as the compulsory national language.

However, there is every likelihood that the main national languages will continue to hold their ground now that there is a renewed push in many countries for national identity not to be overwhelmed by the tide of 'Europeanness', which some people find difficult to accept, or by the more recent large influx of asylum seekers in some countries. This is a salutary reminder that, ultimately, language change and development is like a force of nature, decided consciously or unconsciously by people rather than policies, by culturally rooted beliefs rather than by proactive social manipulation. Yet in all of this, English has bucked the trend by taking on a role and status that is unique among languages and this will be discussed at greater length in Chapter 3.

Questions for reflection and discussion

(1) Which of the trends and developments described in this chapter has been most influential in your country and/or in other contexts you are familiar with?
(2) As a result of these trends and developments, has a career in language teaching become more or less attractive to young people? Give some reasons for your opinion.
(3) Each of these trends and developments could easily be the subject of a book in its own right. If you had the chance, which one would you most like to investigate in more depth? Give your reasons.

3 The Growing Influence of English in Education

Chapter 2 provided an overview of the recent history of the teaching and learning of foreign languages, especially in Europe. In the context of the growing focus in education on plurilingual approaches and the need for teachers to be able to work with classes that include students with diverse linguistic and cultural backgrounds, the very term 'foreign language' has itself become debatable. In many educational settings, the language of schooling, that is the language in which most subjects are taught, is not the first language of many of the students. A special approach to language teaching and learning may be needed to provide for students who have arrived from other countries and/or who live in a family environment where one or more other languages, including their first language, is used. In such cases the language being learned, the language of schooling, is generally not considered a 'foreign language' but an additional language. Similarly, for adult migrants arriving to settle in another country, the language they need to learn is not generally referred to as a 'foreign language'. These terminological developments reflect the reality of greater mobility in the world as people seek improved economic and educational opportunities or are forced to flee persecution and war. This is especially the case in the European Union because Europe has recently been a primary destination for those from the Middle East and Northern Africa seeking asylum and refuge, but migration from country to country and from one language environment to another is far from being a new phenomenon.

The Special Case of English

The focus of this chapter is on a European language that has become dominant in foreign language curricula across the world. A key development over the last hundred years has been the emergence of English as the preferred foreign language for a majority of people worldwide and our aim here is to explore the impact of English on the wider spectrum of language and languages in education.

The reasons for what some have called 'the hegemony' of English (e.g. Kaplan, 1993), and the resulting surge in demand for English and in the numbers of people able to use it, are largely historical but partly linguistic. As discussed in Chapter 2, the impact of British colonialism, which in different forms spanned the world between the 17th and mid-20th centuries, resulted in the establishment of English as the most widely used language of the USA, Canada, Australia, New Zealand and Ireland, and the adoption of English as a main language in much of Africa, the Caribbean and the whole of South Asia, among other areas. In these parts of the world it has remained a 'second language' ever since colonial times because of its practical, and sometimes political, usefulness, including as a relatively neutral means to enable people with different mother tongues within the same country to communicate.

In the meantime, over the last five centuries, English itself has evolved and lost some of the grammatical complexity related, for example, to verb conjugations and distinctions between more formal and less formal second person pronouns that it had once had. Unlike some other languages, English now makes no distinction between formal and informal or singular and plural 'you', and in the present tense it has only two verb forms – one for third person singular, ending in 's', and another for all other subject-verb combinations. In the past tense, there is only one verb form whatever the preceding subject, except in the case of the verb 'be'. Other changes in English and the ways in which it readily adopts words and expressions from other languages may be considered advantages by some users of it as a foreign language. Thus, while difficulty and puzzlement are caused by the complex relationship between its written forms (spelling) and pronunciation, English is seen by many as a relatively easy language to learn and use. However, as David Crystal has pointed out,

> a language does not become a global language because of its intrinsic structural properties, or because of the size of its vocabulary, or because it has been the vehicle for great literature in the past, or because it was once associated with a great culture or religion ... A language becomes an international language for one chief reason: the political power of its people – especially their military power. (Crystal, 1997: 7)

In other words, the scale and scope of British colonialism over 400 years, backed up by military force and the industrial and economic power this helped Britain to achieve, as well as the far greater economic and military power of the USA that has followed, are the chief factors in the ascendancy of English. Added to this, the huge non-military influence wielded since the early 20th century by the USA in mass media, entertainment, research and innovation, especially since the advent of the internet, has caused a linguistic (and cultural) ripple effect across the world. Commercially, English has increasingly been adopted as the corporate language of multinational organisations, and in the world of academia as the 'working language' of a great many international conferences, partnerships and exchanges, as well as publications. The result is that, according to recent estimates (e.g. Graddol, 2006), English is used by between one and a half and two billion people, but for three quarters of these people English is not their first language.

Who Does English Belong To?

As was described in Chapter 2, there is great diversity in the ways in which spoken English is used in the British Isles, much of it related to geography and socioeconomic as well as ethnic background, and the ways in which it is used in Australasia and North America – the other so-called BANA (Britain, North America and Australasia) countries (e.g. see Holliday, 1994) – are also very varied. The even greater diversity of spoken varieties of English around the world, however, can only be imagined. As Barbara Seidlhofer has put it:

> English is being shaped at least as much by its non-native speakers as by its native speakers. This has led to a somewhat paradoxical situation: on the one hand, for the majority of its users, English is a foreign language, and the vast majority of verbal exchanges in English do not involve any native speakers of the language at all. On the other hand, there is still a tendency for native speakers to be regarded as custodians over what is acceptable usage. (Seidlhofer, 2005: 339)

But, if it was ever the case, English can no longer be considered to 'belong to' those for whom it is a first language, the 'native speakers', and can no longer be associated only or primarily with BANA cultures. English has become the property of the world, and this situation has given rise to considerable analysis and debate in applied linguistics and sociolinguistics over the last 30 years. One strand of the debate concerns the ways in which English is used among the majority of users for whom it is not a first language, but among whom it may be, depending on the purpose and occasion, a lingua franca. The concept of English as a lingua franca, or ELF, for short, and the academic movement that has promoted it, has involved analysing instances and corpora of communication in English among those for whom it is not a first language in order to identify which features do and do not lead to communication difficulties in English. Thus, for example, it has been found in research led by Jennifer Jenkins that certain of the difficult sounds of English (such as the two or more ways of pronouncing 'th' in words) are not crucial in communication and that approximations are effective. Similarly, whether or not a speaker uses the final 's' in the third person singular present tense of verbs does not materially affect communication

(Jenkins, 2000). An argument put forward by promoters of ELF is that time and effort can be saved in the teaching and learning of English if less time is spent on such issues and more on those features that do cause misunderstandings.

It is not clear from the literature what users of English as a second or foreign language think of the idea of simplifying the language in this way. From our experience, many such users still aspire to a kind of 'standard English'. Unlike in the case of French and Spanish, however, no academy was ever set up to safeguard standards in English and make decisions about what is and is not acceptable, and users of English as a foreign, second or additional language may feel frustrated that they can only turn to reference books, which are themselves quite diverse, or to speakers of English as a first language, who cannot necessarily be regarded as reliable arbiters, given the lack of awareness and knowledge that most of us have about English.

In the early days of debate about ELF, the issue was nicely teased out by Seidlhofer who draws a distinction between English as a native language (ENL) and ELF. After a discussion of implied criticism by others of the way in which non-native speakers of English in positions of responsibility use the language, she writes:

> English does not simply transfer intact from one context to another – the E in ENL is bound to be something different from the E in English as a lingua franca [ELF]. However, the difference is still waiting to be recognised, explored and acted upon in much applied linguistics and particularly in mainstream English language teaching. (Seidlhofer, 2001: 138–139)

Her contention, then, was that in a sense, the notion of ELF is independent of ENL, and there is no point in ENL users criticising the ways in which speakers of English as foreign or second language use the language as a lingua franca or otherwise. ELF, as seen by Seidlhofer, now has a life – or several lives – of its own and, up to a point, rules of its own. One argument against such a view is that, in our experience at least, English as used by those for whom it is not their first language is not a single variety of English, but takes quite different forms depending on the situation, communicative purpose and the backgrounds of the speakers. Perhaps what is being argued for by advocates of ELF is simply more tolerance of diverse use, and less puritanical criticism of forms of language and lexis that diverge from ENL. This is a position that we would endorse, but it may not stop users of English as a foreign or second language asking what the 'correct' pronunciation or use of a word is.

Such questions pose a dilemma for native speakers of English and especially for teachers of English: what position should we take on standards and correctness in English? Many weighty grammars and dictionaries of English are now mainly or partly based on 'evidence' found in corpora of written and spoken English and are thus descriptive rather than prescriptive. However, the simplified grammar and usage books commonly used by many teachers and referred to by textbook writers set down rules in many areas that may or may not coincide with the grammar and use found in the corpora, or in everyday interactions. In addition, depending on which country or part of a country native-speaking teachers come from, their views of what is 'correct' may differ considerably, especially where vocabulary and pronunciation are concerned. For example, how should teachers of English, whether native speakers of it or not, respond to potential questions about the recent use of 'I'm like…' as an equivalent for 'I said…' or 'I thought…' or the routine exchange 'How are you?' 'I'm good', both of which are currently common among people in some BANA countries? The English language as taught by teachers of English is quite naturally partly 'inherited' from reference and textbook writers who themselves were influenced by their predecessors, so their version of English may be to some degree 'frozen in time' and in some areas of detail it may be obsolete. On the other hand, adventurous teachers and some textbook writers now include authentic examples of spoken and written English from outside the BANA countries; for example, from India, Africa and elsewhere, in order to enable learners to familiarise themselves with a wider variety of English use.

Intercultural Communicative Competence

A larger problem with the difference between ENL and what we will call international English, as used for international meetings of all kinds from those organised by large international organisations such as ISO, the International Organisation for Standardisation, to those involving business executives from both English speaking and non-English speaking countries, was highlighted in a BBC website article by Lennox Maddison (2016) entitled: 'Native English speakers are the world's worst communicators'. The specialists quoted in the article, Chia Suan Chong and Jennifer Jenkins, referred to the not uncommon problem of the disruption of productive communications in English among non-native speakers of English by native speakers who are unable or unwilling to adapt their interventions to suit the other participants. As Chong was quoted as pointing out:

> A lot of native speakers are happy that English has become the world's global language. They feel they don't have to spend time learning another language. But … often you have a boardroom full of people from different countries communicating in English and all understanding each

other, and then suddenly the American or Brit [British person] walks into the room and nobody can understand them. (Maddison, 2016)

While many native speakers of English do deploy much higher levels of intercultural and communicative competence and sensitivity than exemplified here, we have frequently witnessed this phenomenon in international meetings and have found ourselves in the embarrassing situation of having to 'interpret' unadjusted native speaker English to make it accessible to other participants, or of having to ask the native speaker to adjust his or her delivery by speaking more clearly or slowly and by avoiding slang, specific cultural references, acronyms and other obscure language. The implications are clear: if people for whom English is a first language wish to make themselves properly understood and to have an influential role in such discussions and negotiations, it is essential for them to adjust their language in various ways to ensure that it is easily understood by others, especially at times when they are addressing or in discussion with other native speakers of English. Indeed, this applies to users of any language participating in the increasingly frequent intercultural and multilingual encounters, and teachers of all subjects also need to be mindful of this issue given the increasing cultural and linguistic diversity in their classrooms.

A related and more dangerous issue is the fact that, although they may be less easily understood by those present, native speakers of English feel able – and are able – to dominate proceedings in international meetings run in English, using up an unfair share of talking time and influencing the content and proceedings disproportionately. This is especially likely to be the case when the discussion is about the wording of agreements, standards or other formal documents that are being drafted in English. In such cases, the onus is very clearly on the native speakers of English to ensure that their proposed versions of wording take into account the meanings intended by others, and crucially to 'make space' for others to comment on or seek to amend their native speaker wording.

The Future Evolution of English

Will more and more varieties of English emerge, with different pronunciations, vocabularies and grammatical features? It is a possibility, but several forces work against the ever-increasing diversity of English. One is globalisation itself: the reason why English is used as a lingua franca or international language is so that people can make themselves understood across languages and cultures, and in many cases so that they can work in 'transnational' or multinational environments. This puts an onus on English users, including those for whom it is a first language, to try to ensure that their English is easily understood, even if it is 'non-standard'. Another opposing force is the internet: there is generally far less diversity in the written language than in the spoken language, and in work and leisure massive amounts of communication take place by e-mail and through written social media. Depending on the relationship between the sender and the receiver, this enables users of English to simplify what they write or to use standard conventions such as abbreviations and acronyms, and of course to learn from one another's written language. In addition, even though the hegemony of English on the internet is reducing with the growth of websites in other languages and the use of online translation, vast numbers of internet pages in English are consulted daily. There is relatively little variation in the written English found in these online texts, whatever the source and purpose of the website, except the kinds of variation that reflect different registers and specialisms, such as research reports, promotion and publicity, Wikipedia (encyclopaedia) entries, instructions and guidelines, technical discussion or politicised discourse, as well as the differences of vocabulary and spelling between North American and British English.

Nevertheless, the development of the English language around the world is, like the development of most languages, uncontrollable and unpredictable. As an example, the Oxford English Dictionary publishes updates on new words added to the dictionary every three months. The number of words added is normally at least 500, adding up to no fewer than 2000 new words each year. This is partly due to the readiness with which English allows new words and phrases to be invented or borrowed from other languages.

The Impact of English on Education

This rise in the use of English worldwide may currently be an unstoppable force but its social and educational consequences are not to be underestimated. One of the effects is the drive in non-English speaking countries towards ever more curriculum time being given to English, sometimes at the expense of other languages, from the start of primary school onwards. This change in educational priorities is often due to the pressure of national policy where governments believe that English will support national economic development and international competitiveness. In Japan, for example, successive government policy initiatives to improve the teaching, learning and testing of English over the last decade and more has been driven by international studies which reveal that levels of attainment in English by the end of schooling are lower than in other Asian economies (e.g. see Torikai, 2018). Such policy decisions are reinforced by pressure from parents, whose natural concern is that their children are given as broad a range of opportunities as possible to make their way in life. This may include a desire to enable their children to undertake higher education or job-related training abroad.

A complementary impact is the growth in the promotion of English as one of the languages of schooling through curricula, especially in secondary and higher education, that seek to combine the teaching of certain subjects with the teaching of English, which is very often the language focused on in content and language integrated learning (CLIL) programmes, and in bilingual education at international and specialist schools. CLIL comes in different shapes and sizes for different age groups, but generally it involves teaching one or two subjects at secondary level (or one or two lessons per week at primary level) in English instead of in the language of schooling, and in addition to 'normal' English classes. During CLIL lessons, which may be taught by a teacher of English who is familiar with the subject in question or, in some cases, by a subject teacher with a reasonable command of English, the focus is not only on the subject content but also and explicitly on the way English is used in describing, discussing or writing about the content. In other words, the teaching and learning is intended to have a dual focus.

The declared benefits of CLIL programmes are that, in addition to having more opportunities to learn English as a foreign or second language thanks to the immersion approach used in the additional CLIL lessons, students have the opportunity to learn how to use it in their history or science classes, and to develop their transversal competences. However, there are important issues to consider when introducing and implementing CLIL programmes, especially at secondary level. Following an interesting report on a study carried out over three years in three Basque-medium schools in the north-east of Spain, Aintzane Doiz and David Lasagabaster (2017) discuss two of these issues. The first is whether CLIL should be obligatory for all students, optional according to the wishes of students and their parents or discretionary subject to prior assessment of competence in English. The dangers of making it optional or discretionary are clear: the gap in developing proficiency in English is likely to widen over time. The dangers of making it obligatory may result in students being demotivated by not being able to cope, or, for those coping well, becoming bored if they have to wait while the teacher helps less proficient students. The second issue discussed is whether CLIL lessons should be taught exclusively in English or whether teachers can use the language of schooling or another language in their students' repertoire to assist with more difficult concepts or with class and behaviour management. Here the decisions are likely to be taken by teachers according to the nature of the group and the practical advantages of flexibility on this matter, but a decision either way is likely to have consequences for learning (Doiz & Lasagabaster, 2017: 98–107).

A further option available to certain parents and children in some countries is bilingual education, which presupposes that students already have a competence in English (or depending on the school, in French, German, Japanese, etc.) that is sufficiently well-developed to enable them to study subjects in the way that those for whom it is their first language do. Bilingual education is often chosen because of a desire to obtain a school leaving qualification, such as the International Baccalaureate in

English or in another international language, as well as or instead of national qualifications in the home language, in order to multiply the options available in later education. Such bilingual programmes are generally restricted to designated schools or private international schools, and therefore may not be available to those who are unable to pay the necessary fees or attain the necessary proficiency in both languages. Not all bilingual schools specialise in English: the 'Raising bilingual children' website lists international schools offering bilingual education (see http://www.raising-bilingual-children.com/basics/language-stimulation/bilingual-schools/other-european-countries/other-european-countries-ii). Interestingly, it also lists 'Deutsche Schulen' which offer education in German and the students' first language.

The Role and Impact of English in Higher Education

The gradual transition to a world in which student mobility has become a reality, at least for some, has had a profound effect on higher education institutions. The desire on the part of students, often encouraged by their parents, to be able to pursue higher education in English has led not only to the expansion of universities in the BANA countries, but also to the rapid growth of undergraduate and postgraduate programmes in institutions elsewhere where courses in certain subjects are taught through the medium of English rather than in the national language, or are offered in parallel to those in the national language. Students in many countries are now able to choose university courses in their own countries that are run in English rather than in their home language, or alternatively to join other international students enrolled in English medium courses in another country, including many non-BANA countries. Universities in some countries such as the Netherlands and Malaysia have been quick to understand and act on the benefits of offering undergraduate and postgraduate programmes through the medium of English, and they have seen a corresponding rise in student enrolments from other countries within and beyond Europe. As a further example, most Ukrainian universities offer Ukrainian language courses to enable foreign students to enter their programmes, but an increasing number are offering courses which are wholly or partly taught through the medium of English. The very progressive Medicine Faculty at the University of Uzhgorod, for example, has parallel English- and Ukrainian-medium courses, and recruits large numbers of undergraduates from India who study entirely through English, while most home students opt for study in their mother tongue.

Students enrolling on such courses see this as a way of enhancing their chances of success when applying for posts in multinational organisations or in other countries, or of improving their prospects in their home countries. However, English as a medium of instruction (EMI) means that students on the courses taught in English face the challenges of higher-level study, including lectures, seminars, dissertations, etc. in a foreign language. By contrast to CLIL at school level, which has developed methodologically to allow for dual purpose teaching and learning, there has been almost no corresponding development in EMI in higher education. In many cases, no concessions are made to students with language difficulties. Generally, EMI tutors are unlikely to be willing or to have the time to provide any kind of language support. This means that students have to work autonomously on their academic language skills although, as discussed below, in some cases, preparatory courses and support from the university language centre are available. Foreign students are usually required to show proof of proficiency in English before they are accepted on a degree programme, and in the UK many universities provide a foundation year in which students are expected to improve their English alongside foundation studies in other subjects. Certain universities in English-speaking countries and elsewhere have now established commercial units to enable students to upgrade their language proficiency on specialised English-courses and to obtain the necessary qualifications before entering undergraduate courses. These 'pre-sessional' courses aim to give prospective university students experience in and knowledge of the special type of English used in university level texts, lectures and assignments, and to learn some of the special skills required. Further specialised language support may be provided on a part-time basis by a university language centre where students or their teachers feel more ongoing help is needed; for example, with the written language, or where given departments, such as law or medicine, require their students to have specialised knowledge of the language even where courses are not delivered in English.

In order to help students to prepare for or cope with courses given in English, many university language centres offer preparatory and parallel courses in English. These are frequently described as English for specific purposes (ESP), or in some cases as English for academic purposes (EAP). The courses vary in their degree of specialisation. A general purpose study skills programme, such as the 'pre-sessional' courses mentioned above, may include attention to academic reading and writing skills, practice in note taking from listening inputs, seminar and presentation skills, and an introduction to basic research skills. The approach to this kind of course content is likely to be dictated in part by the prevailing academic culture, norms and requirements in each host institution, and in part by the teaching material that is available. Numerous books on publishers' lists offer practice in all the main study skills.

At the other end of the spectrum are highly specialised courses, for example, in English for oil and gas, English for biochemistry or English for immunology. There are seldom any published materials available in specialisms such as these, and the English teachers (often attached to specialised faculties or departments) have to produce their own, usually text-based, materials for classroom use. These 'home-made' materials are often limited and rather traditional in nature. Where undergraduate and postgraduate courses have a strong vocational dimension, such as international business studies, or tourism and hospitality, English teachers are often expected to look beyond the immediate demands of study, and to prepare their students for the language demands they are likely to face in their future professions.

As the demand for ESP/EAP has gathered momentum, it has become clear that the traditional focus on teaching specialist vocabulary and recycling conventional grammar fails to meet the language needs of students within each discipline. This has led to a much greater focus on recognising the typical genres and analysing the patterns of texts and discourse in different academic disciplines and basing materials on the way specialists construct meaning through the language they use. Most of the seminal work in this area (e.g. Coulthard, 1994; Fairclough, 2003; Swales, 1990, 2004) focused on English, but there is also research going on in other languages.

At the higher levels, postgraduate students and university lecturers and researchers themselves may want specialised coaching in the English needed to understand and write articles for international journals, and participate in international conferences and academic exchanges. The challenges involved for the teacher providing such support are considerable, and specialist materials, such as the *English for Academics* series (British Council, 2014, 2015), have been written for this purpose.

The Challenges Implied by the Upsurge of English in Education

A notable challenge and potential area of risk is that the rising demand for English across educational sectors and beyond has in many cases not been matched by an increase in the supply of competent and well-trained teachers of English nor, in the case of CLIL and EMI programmes, of subject teachers with good competence in and awareness of English. This is particularly the case where English is introduced in the early years of primary education: here teachers with little or no experience of teaching the language, and little or no training in language teaching are often expected to teach some basic English in large classes while meeting all the other curriculum objectives. The result is that, as alluded to in Chapter 2, even if they have already been learning the language for four, five or even six years, students entering secondary school may find themselves 'starting again', either because the English teaching in primary school has been ineffective, or, more likely, because there is no coherence between the secondary and primary curriculum for English. Moreover, in many contexts those secondary school teachers who were trained many years ago and have not benefited from good professional development opportunities may believe that it is essential to take a 'subject' approach to English, which involves transmitting large amounts of grammatical and other linguistic knowledge to students before – or rather than – helping them to communicate effectively in the language.

Where CLIL teachers are concerned, given the demands implied by integrating the teaching and learning of English on the one hand and of a subject on the other, specialised training and ongoing support should be considered a prerequisite. But, apart from the challenge of making adequate training available, success depends on the availability and willingness of subject teachers with a good level of proficiency and teaching skills in English, or a well-trained teacher of English with a good knowledge of the subject in question and an ability to teach it. In many contexts, teachers with such profiles are few and far between.

A similar training and professional development issue exists where English is the medium of instruction in higher education: apart from EAP teachers, few lecturers and tutors at this level have specific awareness of the issues faced by students studying in a language that is not their own, and many would not see it as their concern. Unlike CLIL teachers in primary and secondary schools, whose task involves integrating the teaching of English with subject teaching, EMI teachers in higher education understandably see their job as teaching the subject in question; it is the university's job to ensure that the students admitted to the courses are 'up to the mark', including in this case as regards their language competence. In some contexts, subject specialists may themselves have only an intermediate command of English making it hard for them to adjust to the challenges of teaching the subject in English. In Ukraine, for example, a recent research study concluded that:

> Ukrainian universities have a small and weak base for expanding their EMI programmes, and a large-scale push to upgrade academics' English skills is a priority if universities are to be more international in their research, teaching and rankings. (Bolitho & West, 2017: 94)

Faced with the realisation that teachers of EAP or ESP need specialist training, and that subject specialists need to raise their standards of proficiency in English, a number of countries, including Ukraine and Uzbekistan, have embarked on large-scale projects to address these needs, with the help of funding from the British Council and in some cases also the Ministry of Higher Education. Other countries are watching these developments with interest.

If subject specialists working with international students at universities, especially in BANA countries, have English as their first language, the challenge will be different but equally great, and similar to that confronting native speakers of English who need to negotiate with or work closely with colleagues who are not native-speakers, discussed earlier in the chapter. They need to adjust their communication in English to meet the needs of students with varying levels of proficiency in the language, and to provide mediating support where needed. This requires experience and ideally specialised training. On the other hand, they also need to ensure that the standards achieved by their students match the requirements of the university and are equivalent to those attained by students for whom English is a first language.

English and the Learning of Other Languages

Some see the relentless upsurge of English as a potential threat to their own languages, especially if these are not widely used. Meanwhile, in English-speaking countries such as the UK, there has been a decline in the learning of other languages, presumably based on the misguided assumption that everyone speaks English anyway – or is learning to speak it – and in the equally misguided belief that, because of this, there is no value in learning the languages of the people one may need or wish to communicate with for work or other purposes. In England and Wales, learning a foreign language is optional and less and less common after the age of 14. Some schools have stopped offering Spanish and German alongside French because of funding cuts and low demand, and applications to study modern languages at universities in the UK have dropped year on year for the last decade. It is hard to surmise what the long-term consequences of impoverishing children's education in this way will be. By contrast, around the world more and more people are leaving school with some proficiency in English as well as in the language of schooling (and perhaps other national or home languages), and in the European Union the recommended aim is that people leaving school should be able to use two other European languages in addition to the language of schooling.

It could be argued that, if English now plays such an important role in the wider world and competence of some kind in the language is seen by parents and students, as well as by governments and employers, as a necessity, English should stop being regarded as a foreign language like others in school curricula. If English has now become a 'basic skill', like mathematics or information technology, then it should perhaps be treated accordingly in education systems. This could have the benefit of separating English and its unfair competition with other languages from the foreign languages curriculum and putting it elsewhere, for example alongside computer studies, which, depending how the curriculum is reorganised, might free up more space for other languages.

Concluding Remarks

This chapter has considered how over the last hundred years English has become a language like no other in recent history. This has led to the speedy development of diverse specialised kinds of courses in English (some of them mirrored in other languages) and the increasing use of English across the curriculum in some contexts. This situation poses considerable challenges for national policy, for institutions providing teacher education, for schools with their ever more complex timetables and for teachers themselves.

In an increasingly 'globalised' world, where for many international travel for business, study or leisure is the norm rather than the exception, and where the availability and speed of communication media have evolved exponentially, it is perhaps no surprise that a lingua franca has emerged, and that this has turned out to be an established language rather than Esperanto or another neutral invented language, as many once predicted. The demand from parents and students for more and more time and attention to be paid to English in the education system is a natural consequence. It is also natural that those concerned with the teaching and maintenance of other languages should be nervous about the ways in which demand for English in the various forms in which it is taught is impacting on school and university curricula. The rise of English has been seen by some as a threat to other languages, especially those that are less widely used and learned, and not without reason. However, as also mentioned in Chapter 2, some of these languages, for example Irish in Ireland and Welsh in Wales, like Basque and Catalan in Spain, have been reinvigorated by determined efforts on the part of governments and educators to ensure that they continue to be learned and used. These efforts can serve as examples for other languages that may be under pressure.

Another potentially positive effect of the expansion in the provision of English for language education in general is the large investment of time, effort and finance in language teaching innovations and resources. Carefully examined for their quality and fit with other languages and contexts, the developments in English language teaching in its different forms may provide examples, models and potentially technological solutions useful for all foreign language education. This cross-fertilisation should become a two-way street. Exciting developments are taking place in other languages too, but at present there is little exchange of expertise and ideas among teachers of different languages and creators of language learning resources. Moreover, as illustrated by the discussion of CLIL above, the experience gained from the introduction of new initiatives such as CLIL at school level or EMI at university level bring with them the need to rethink certain important issues concerning language and languages in education. For example, what are the lessons of CLIL with its overt dual focus on a subject and the language related to that subject for all teachers of science, maths, history, geography etc. at school level? If policy makers and teachers take a broader view involving reference to and use of more than one language, what are likely to be the educational advantages and drawbacks, including for children's developing cognition? How much choice and guidance should students be given when options such as CLIL are available, and, in any subject teaching, how can the gap be reduced between those for whom 'academic' and subject-specific language come easily and those who find such language challenging? These are all questions that have a wide relevance well beyond the teaching of English. In this sense, developments in the teaching and learning of English could contribute to research and debate about education in general and the role language plays in it.

Meanwhile, efforts continue in many countries to ensure that young people leave secondary education able to communicate in at least one foreign language, often English, as well as the language of their country of residence, which in many cases for the children of migrants and international workers may not be their mother tongue. In other words, outside the BANA countries, youngsters are leaving school more 'plurilingual' than ever, and more of them are as a result better equipped to communicate and participate in the challenging contemporary world of work and education. It could be argued that the rise of English has in a way contributed to this.

A key challenge for language education and education more widely remains teacher education, and this is the subject of the second part of the book. The demand for more and more proficient teachers of English, including CLIL teachers, has brought with it a need to rethink at policy level the ways in which initial teacher education for language teachers is organised and the methodology and resources that are best suited to meeting learners' need to be able to communicate effectively and, in the case of English, in many cases at a higher or more specialised level of proficiency. As will be discussed in Part 2, beginning in Chapter 4 with a focus on the initial education of language teachers, this incentive to review the long-standing ways in which teachers are prepared, and are encouraged to engage in continuing professional development, is in many contexts an opportunity to make overdue and much needed improvements.

Questions for discussion and reflection

(1) If you are not living in a country where English is the prevalent language of schooling, how important is the role of English in education and employment?
(2) In your context, how widespread are CLIL and bilingual education in primary and secondary schools? How successful are they and/or what difficulties do they entail? If these are rare in your country, how helpful do you think it would be if they were encouraged by national policy?
(3) In EMI and bilingual education, how appropriate and realistic is it to take a dogmatic approach to language 'immersion' and to exclude the use of other languages in the students' and teacher's repertoire?

Part 2: Teacher Education and Training

This part of the book takes a critical look at teacher education for language teachers, both their initial education (Chapter 4) and the provision of opportunities for in-service education and continuing professional development for practising teachers (Chapter 5). Chapter 6 then goes on to explore the ways in which curricula for initial and in-service education of teachers of all subjects and for primary teachers deal with language and communication, which as was discussed in Chapter 1, play such a critical role in all teaching and learning.

Part 2: Teacher Education and Training

4 Initial Language Teacher Education: Traditions, Trends and Relevance

In Chapter 2, we looked at some of the many changes that have taken place in foreign language teaching and learning in the last few decades, and we identified some of the sources of energy and insight that have propelled these changes. In this chapter, we take a critical look at their impact on the pre-service education and training of language teachers.

To establish some background for this discussion, it is worth looking at the contexts in which language teacher education or training has hitherto taken place.

The 'Philological Route'

In most of Europe and in many other countries around the world, universities and other higher education institutions have kept a firm hold on initial teacher education. Future language teachers normally graduate in their major language and go on, often in the same institution, either to top up their degree with a supplementary teaching qualification or, in some countries, simply go straight into teaching on the assumption that their subject knowledge is sufficient as a qualification. This model has been in place for many years and it is underpinned by deeply embedded traditions and practices, which see the teaching of a foreign or second language like the teaching of any other school subject, such as history or chemistry, although in essence learning a language should imply first and foremost acquiring communicative skills in that language rather than just 'language knowledge'. In many European countries and in post-Soviet republics, the programmes are usually taught and administered in the philological faculty of the university and the focus is on declarative knowledge of the language being studied, with courses in grammar, lexicology, phonology, semantics and stylistics. These courses are not always given in the target language, that is, the language student teachers are planning to teach. While some universities insist on language proficiency classes alongside these studies, this is not universally the case, and it is still possible, in some institutions, to graduate in a foreign language without being able to speak it fluently. Where methodology is included in the curriculum, it is often regarded as a theoretical subject and is delivered in the students' first language by lecturers from the pedagogical faculty, who in many cases may never have taught in a school. It is also worth mentioning that the main research areas in these faculties are either linguistics or literature, and that research into teaching and learning is generally seen by academics as outside their field of interest. For this reason, students' final thesis or qualification paper is traditionally on a linguistic or literary topic that is often imposed by their supervisor. Students planning a career in teaching thus often have little in the way of practical orientation before they embark on school practice or their first teaching post, a problem that is exacerbated in some contexts by the fact that this career decision is often taken very late in the cycle of undergraduate studies. Thus, entrants to the profession have little choice other than to teach the way they were taught, which results in the perpetuation of grammar-translation methods such as reading a text aloud and translating it, reciting grammatical rules and learning lists of vocabulary by heart. As a consequence, insufficient attention is given to a view of language as communication rather than just as a school subject. This model of language teacher education is extremely difficult to challenge and reform, as it is integrated into a model of teacher preparation that applies to all subjects across the curriculum, and also because so many academics in philology faculties have a vested interest in the status quo.

In some countries, however, inroads have been made into the philological model and positive developments and reforms have taken place. As was mentioned in Chapter 2, the fast track programmes that were devised to meet the demand for English teachers in the 1990s may have been absorbed into the traditional academic structures of universities in Hungary and Poland, for example, but they have left their mark in a number of ways which seem to be sustainable. In these cases, methodology is now understood as a practical, classroom-relevant area of study rather than as a theoretical subject and it is taught in the target language; teaching practice is carried out in carefully selected 'practice schools' and supervised by mentor teachers as well as by university lecturers; and research papers for qualification purposes are much more often based on classroom investigation rather than on theoretical topics.

Since the turn of the 21st century, this trend has been taken up and refined in several contexts, as the curriculum outline from Uzbekistan discussed next illustrates.

Case study: The Reformed National Pre-Service (PRESETT) curriculum for English teachers in Uzbekistan

Commentary

The curriculum in Table 4.1 is the result of a joint initiative of the British Council, the Ministry of Higher and Secondary Specialised Education and the Uzbek State University of World Languages. It was introduced gradually, year on year, with careful piloting of each module,

Table 4.1 Overview of PRESETT curriculum for trainee teachers of English

Modules/semesters: Hours per week (total in a semester)	1	2	3	4	5	6	7–8
Language courses							
Language skills							
Listening and speaking	2 (40)	2 (40)	2 (40)	2 (40)			
Reading	2 (40)	2 (40)	2 (40)	2 (40)	2 (40)		
Writing	2 (40)	2 (40)	2 (40)	2 (40)	2 (40)	2 (40)	3 (48)
Integrated skills	2 (40)	2 (40)	2 (40)	2 (40)			
Grammar and vocabulary in context							
Grammar in context	4 (80)	4 (80)					
Vocabulary in context	2 (40)	2 (40)	2 (40)	2 (40)			
Discourse analysis			2 (40)	2 (40)			
English as an international language						1 (20)	
Independent study skills	2 (40)						
Total	16	14	12	12	4	3	3
Methodology courses							
Language learning			2 (40)				
Approaches to language teaching				2 (40)			
Teaching and integrating skills					1 (20)	2 (40)	
Teaching language systems for communication				2 (40)	1 (20)		
Assessment and testing					2 (40)		
Classroom language and management						1 (20)	
Materials evaluation and design						2 (40)	
English for specific purposes							1 (16)
Planning for teaching						1 (20)	
Classroom investigation						1 (20)	1 (16)
Developing intercultural awareness							1 (16)
Teaching young learners							2 (32)
Total	0	0	2	4	4	7	5
Overall:	16	14	14	16	8	10	8
Number of weeks	20	20	20	20	20	20	16

Source: British Council, Uzbekistan

and supported by a nationwide programme of training for those university teachers charged with teaching the curriculum. This training has been absolutely central to its successful implementation, as working with it has required a complete paradigm shift in thinking about teacher education, including the way student teachers are assessed. As is evident from a close look at Table 4.1, the curriculum includes a strong language improvement element in the early semesters, deemed necessary because of the relatively poor levels of proficiency reached by school leavers. It also includes a staged introduction to important aspects of methodology from Semester 3 onwards, and provides for an intensive, supervised period of school experience with a strong emphasis on reflective practice. The lighter timetable load in Semesters 5–8 is because students need time to prepare for teaching practice and for writing their 'qualification paper' or thesis. The main areas of subject knowledge remain in place alongside the new curriculum, but there is now a clear realisation that the drive to improve standards of English across the republic, from primary level through secondary and vocational schools, depends to a great extent on improving language standards and building basic teaching skills in students during their initial training, and that time and opportunities lost at this seminal stage cannot easily be compensated for later. The curriculum has been evaluated both internally (in the 17 universities that train English teachers) and externally by an expert consultant, and it has attracted attention from other countries where there is an interest in pursuing similar reforms in language teacher education. While much of the thinking that underpins the curriculum has been stimulated by inputs from international consultants, the ownership of the whole programme remains firmly in the hands of the local university teachers and lecturers who were ultimately responsible for its design and implementation. One of the most striking impacts of the new curriculum has been a marked increase in the number of graduates committing to teaching as a profession as a positive choice rather than as a fallback option after failure to find a post with more lucrative career prospects.

Linking Teacher Education to the School Curriculum

In the UK, and in some other European countries, language teacher education, as with training to teach other subjects and also primary teacher education, is closely aligned to the requirements of the national curriculum for schools. This has led to criticism that the base of teacher education has narrowed and become utilitarian rather than generous and broad in nature. A language class is by definition a window on a wider world beyond the classroom, and teaching a language requires cultural and intercultural awareness and the ability to think critically and reflectively, in addition to subject knowledge and a command of classroom techniques. In short, language teachers need to gain a good working command of most of the transversal skills which are targeted in school curriculum statements. This basic idea has been taken up and elaborated in a number of teacher education curricula.

Case study: The Ukrainian PRESETT methodology curriculum

The new Ukrainian pre-service (PRESETT) methodology curriculum for English teachers, for instance, is built towards an agreed profile of a 21st century language teacher, which is offered here as a case study (Box 4.1).

Box 4.1 The profile of a newly qualified English teacher

A graduate from the PRESETT Bachelor's programme should demonstrate the following knowledge, skills and qualities:

Understanding learners

- Understand how to identify learners' needs as they evolve and adapt teaching procedures and materials accordingly.
- Understand the main theories related to second language learning and acquisition and their implications for practice.
- Reflect on their learners' language learning processes.
- Involve learners in different ways of learning to help them develop their learning strategies.
- Advise learners on how to organise and manage their learning productively.
- Take into account psychological and social factors that influence learner behaviour when planning and teaching.
- Understand the concept of learner autonomy and its implications for teaching and learning.
- Guide learners in finding and using resources in and beyond the classroom that assist their learning.
- Identify individual learning difficulties and cater for different categories of special educational needs in planning and teaching.

Planning lessons and courses

- Plan teaching to meet the needs of learners and to achieve course outcomes according to the curriculum.
- Plan teaching of the language systems in appropriate communicative contexts.
- Evaluate and select materials to engage learners in line with the aims and objectives of a lesson, and the specific teaching/learning context.
- Plan the stages of a lesson in a way that enables language skills to be developed systematically.
- Plan the timing of a lesson in an organised way, allowing time for monitoring and feedback.

- Plan interaction patterns for different activities during the lesson.
- Analyse the language to be presented in the lesson and anticipate the problems that learners may face.
- Set aims, objectives and learning outcomes of lessons and lesson sequences appropriately.
- Plan lessons taking into account insights from previous classes.
- Anticipate non-language problems that may arise during the lesson and plan how to respond to them.

Managing the lesson

- Create conditions and provide facilities for learning in the classroom.
- Organise classroom processes through clear instructions and accurate timing.
- Set up and monitor a range of interactions in the classroom according to learning purposes and learning styles.
- Maintain a proper balance between teacher talk and student talk.
- Identify problems in learner behaviour and deal with them appropriately.
- Provide appropriate feedback to learners.
- Solicit and act on feedback from learners.
- Use classroom resources and technologies to support learning.

Evaluating and assessing learning

- Apply different types of assessment to suit a range of learning contexts.
- Identify and diagnose learners' errors and difficulties and apply the findings in teaching and assessment.
- Use a range of techniques to correct errors in learners' spoken and written language, and provide developmental feedback.
- Help learners to understand their errors and how to deal with them.
- Equip learners with tools for assessing their progress and achievement.
- Use given criteria from an existing assessment scale to grade learners' progress and achievement.
- Refer to the National Curriculum to select texts for teaching and testing.
- Design progress and achievement tests that are based firmly on National Curriculum requirements and CEFR level descriptors.
- Evaluate and select existing tasks/ tests from an online or a printed source for assessing learners' progress and achievement, adapting and/ or supplementing them if needed.
- Administer, mark and give feedback on tests and assessment in a timely and appropriate fashion and maintain accurate assessment records.

Knowing the subject of English

- Have a B2/C1 level in the target language and make justified use of L1 and L2 in class.

- Select language and terminology appropriate to the level of the learners and the type of lesson.
- Give full, accurate answers to queries from students about different aspects of language and usage.
- Anticipate learners' problems while dealing with the language in class.
- Use a range of techniques to guide learners in working out answers to their own language queries and correcting their errors.
- Provide a good model of pronunciation and grammatical accuracy for learners.
- Keep up to date with changes and innovations in spoken and written English.

Knowing the subject of methodology

- Have a sufficient knowledge of theories of language teaching and learning, methodology concepts.
- Provide principled justification for the teaching approaches, range of techniques and materials being used.
- Select and create appropriate tasks and materials for the classroom.
- Develop their range of teaching techniques following up observation of colleagues.

Managing own professional development

- Understand the principles of reflective practice.
- Collaborate with colleagues, regularly share experiences and ideas with other teachers and get support from them.
- Undertake further training.
- Keep up to date with the latest developments in ELT.
- Understand how to observe and learn from other teachers.
- Identify areas for professional development, set goals and plan development to achieve these goals.
- Build learner autonomy in themselves.

Source: The British Council, Ukraine

Commentary

This profile, with its stress on features such as reflection, the development of autonomy and a principled approach to assessment, represents a huge step forward compared with the previous status quo, even if it looks like a rather lengthy checklist of competences. It certainly suggests challenges both for the teaching of the new curriculum and for assessment, but, importantly, it also sets standards which, if fulfilled, will move Ukrainian English teacher education away from the previous 'hit and miss' approach with different interpretations of standards at each of the universities training teachers, and towards a commonly agreed set of outcomes for teacher educators and their students to aspire to. It is hoped that, with time, the model will be adopted for the training of teachers of other foreign languages.

The model favoured in Finland is also resolutely university-based, but it goes a step further by insisting that all aspiring teachers gain a master's degree and that they have to prove themselves capable of carrying out research. Sahlberg describes the model as 'a spiral sequence of theoretical knowledge, practical training and research-oriented enquiry of teaching' (Sahlberg, 2012: 12). This suggests a professional and practical approach to research, in contrast to that in philological faculties, as described above. Significantly, all teacher education programmes in Finland have a strong language and communication component. Here it is also worth noting that teaching is a high-prestige and well-paid profession in Finland, and that there is great competition for places on all teacher education courses (Sahlberg, 2012).

Research and Language Teacher Education

This insistence on teachers as researchers in Finland opens up the wider issue of the relationship between research and practice in the field of education. In an exchange on this matter, Medgyes and Paran (2017) argued from different standpoints, the former claiming that research by applied linguists and other academics is of little use to practising teachers, while Paran advocates a healthy reciprocal relationship between teachers and researchers, with potential for a win–win outcome, and also claims that good teaching is informed by research. For years this latter point was accepted by designers of pre-service teacher education programmes, resulting in a perception that teaching involves the application of insights from research studies. True, language teaching has benefited indirectly from an increased understanding of second language acquisition studies and other aspects of applied linguistics, but there is no single discipline area or body of research that can claim to be the main theoretical basis for language teachers' classroom practice. However, any relevant research may lead to the formulation of theories and some of these theories may have an impact on practice. While action research and other ways of researching classrooms often have low generalisability, they do encourage teachers to reflect on their practice and to formulate their own theories of teaching and learning, which is why it has begun to take a more prominent place in some pre-service teacher education courses.

In their report on the *European Profile for Language Teacher Education*, Michael Kelly and Michael Grenfell (2004) underline the complexity of the relationship between theory and practice in language education:

> Language education should be seen as multidisciplinary and interdisciplinary with a complex range of theories behind different teaching approaches. (Kelly & Grenfell, 2004: 5)

Influences on language teachers are indeed many and varied, and the literature on teaching methodology is characterised by references to disciplines and fields such as psychology, pedagogy, drama, management, sociology and even philosophy as well as to applied linguistics. The approach to the design of programmes such as those in Uzbekistan and Ukraine is based not so much on theory as on an understanding of what a teacher has to do on a daily basis in the classroom, and how these practices can be conceptualised in terms of the knowledge and skills needed to underpin them. In short, modern approaches to the design of language teacher education programmes are increasingly oriented towards the practical challenges of (language) teaching rather being derived from academic theory.

Pedagogical Institutes and Colleges of Education

In some countries, for example Austria, Switzerland, Malaysia and the Russian Federation, an alternative path to teacher education is via specialist pedagogical institutes or colleges of education, where subject knowledge is studied alongside key aspects of education. In some cases, this qualifies teachers only for a post at primary or middle school level, and graduates may need to take a master's level course to teach at a higher level.

In Austria, since 2016 these colleges have been brought under the oversight of parent universities who have taken control of the teacher education curriculum and assessment procedures, thereby depriving the colleges of the autonomy that they had previously enjoyed. The curriculum for prospective teachers at all levels has been revised and there are now fewer credit points for teaching practice, which is generally seen by teacher educators as a retrograde step. However, the curriculum retains a focus on partnership with institutions in target language countries, through which trainee teachers have an opportunity to spend an extended period abroad before qualifying.

In Switzerland, which has three main official languages, researchers at the College of Education in St Gallen have developed a curriculum built around the notion of educating language teachers to be multilingual and able to teach more than one language, to be versed in the dimensions of interculturality, to have a high level of general language awareness and to understand the essence of language as a means of constructing meaning in subjects right across the curriculum. In these respects, the curriculum model derives substantively from recommendations in the *European Profile for Language Teacher Education* (Kelly & Grenfell, 2004). Figure 4.1 on the next page shows how the curriculum is conceptualised to address these objectives.

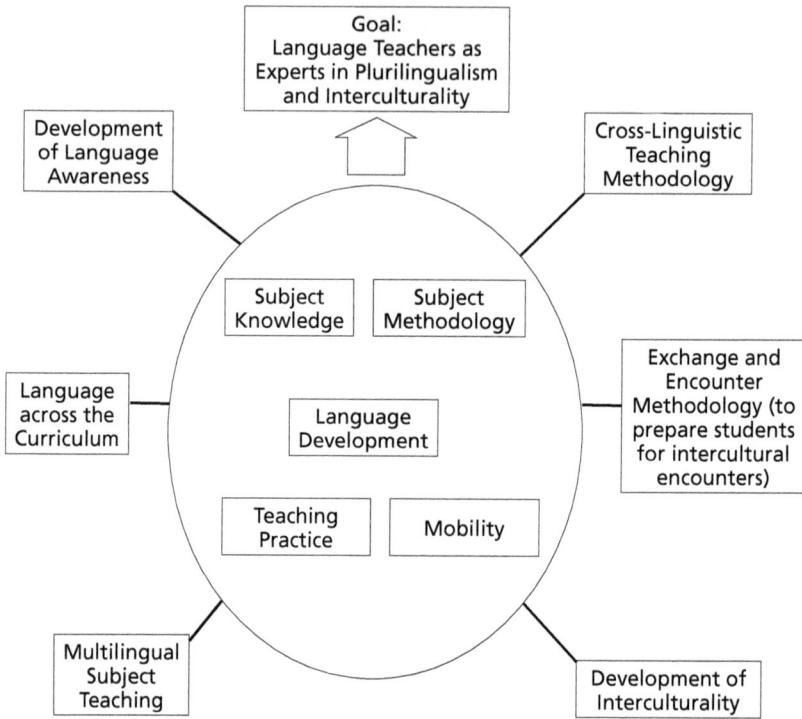

Figure 4.1 Design principles and syllabus areas (Bleichenbacher et al., 2019: 9)

Commentary

Figure 4.1 illustrates how the St Gallen curriculum is built around three core areas, supplemented by courses on topics that contribute to a pedagogical awareness of language, an understanding of the role of language right across the school curriculum, CLIL, the different methodologies associated with other languages and aspects of intercultural awareness. This is backed up by spells of teaching practice and exposure to different language contexts. The aspirational outcome of this model (see top of Figure 4.1) is a graduate teacher whose knowledge and skill base extends far beyond the limits of lesson planning and day-to-day classroom realities. In this respect, the course may be seen as language education with multilingual and multicultural dimensions rather than simply as basic training for the demands of a national school system. Indeed, from this and other similar models we begin to gain an impression of the added dimensions of competence and knowledge required of today's foreign language teachers as compared with the much more limited way in which their role used to be conceived.

Over the last 25 years, there has been a significant move towards more and more involvement of schools in teacher education, and with it a role for school-based mentors in supporting student teachers as they embark on the challenges of school experience and teaching practice. This kind of school partnership is now well established in countries such as the UK (not just for languages but for subjects right across the curriculum) and Hungary (for English language teachers) and is just beginning to take root in other countries. One of the problems with this kind of model has been the increased workload on mentor teachers in schools, who are often not paid for their role, but instead receive a small reduction in their teaching hours. The model works best when there is good liaison between university and partner school, and where there is a phased introduction to school experience, starting with observation, then short periods of teaching before student teachers are asked to take responsibility for whole lessons and are later assessed. This kind of progression reflects the journey that young trainees make from being language learners to becoming language teachers.

Initial Qualifications

In some of these instances, the route into language teaching as a career is no different from the path taken by would-be teachers of any other subject. However, the demand for English teachers, which as we saw in Chapter 2, grew exponentially towards the end of the last century, has led to the establishment of other, quicker ways into the profession, mainly into private language schools. This development was initiated and led by International House, London, who in 1962 began to offer an intensive four-week introductory certificate course, mainly for native speakers who wished to teach at a school abroad. This idea was taken up in the 1970s by the Royal Society of Arts, who formalised and validated a similar four-week programme with a strong emphasis on practical teaching. In 1988, this qualification was taken over by Cambridge Assessment English (CAE) where to this day it remains as the Certificate in English Language Teaching to Adults (CELTA). This is a purely training-based qualification, with an emphasis on pedagogical knowledge of language and on methods, with absolutely no wider educational content. For many teachers of English, however, this (or an equivalent such as the Trinity College Certificate), is still the only qualification they ever acquire, since the prevalent view in many private sector schools is of language teaching and learning as a narrow-focus business with no claim to a wider educational role. This, in turn, tends to strengthen the common view of a language class as simply a forum for learning to communicate in a foreign language, rather than as a route to wider learning and understanding of a different culture, and even of a different way of looking at the world. Nonetheless, CELTA clearly meets a massive demand worldwide, with over 350 active centres offering the course and around 15,000 candidates each year, of whom only about 5% eventually go on to take the diploma level qualification (DELTA) offered by CAE.

A survey of experienced CELTA trainers conducted for this chapter revealed a shared understanding of the limitations of the qualification in terms of both depth and breadth, and they also emphasised the stressful nature of such an intensive programme which compresses so much into such a short period and requires completely inexperienced trainees to prepare lessons from one day to the next. They recognised, too, that the syllabus allows little scope for flexibility to meet participants' differing needs. However, they all saw CELTA as a valuable first step into teaching English and remain convinced that the certificate offers a guarantee of basic teaching competence to private sector employers and school owners. Indeed, it can be seen as a significant achievement of CELTA and equivalent qualifications that they have once and for all laid to rest the beliefs that any native speaker can teach her own language, or that all any non-native speaker needs in order to teach is a certificate of proficiency in the target language. These beliefs prevailed for a very long time in a number of European countries, notably Greece and Switzerland. However, relatively few graduates from this type of initial training course go on to take higher qualifications at diploma level or beyond which would add depth to their professional learning and credibility to their CVs. This may be because private sector employers are reluctant to fund higher studies, perhaps for fear of losing teachers in whom they have invested to higher paid jobs elsewhere in the sector.

Interestingly, there has also been uptake of CELTA in certain state sector contexts despite its stated focus on adult learners. The education authorities in Perm in Russia, for example, saw it as a means of acquainting their secondary school English teachers with modern approaches and methods, and commissioned a large-scale CELTA programme for several hundred of its serving teachers, many of whom had many years of experience of teaching, mainly using grammar translation methods. This initiative is symptomatic of a growing realisation in former Soviet Union countries that English now needs to be seen as a basic life skill rather than just another school subject.

For all their merits, CELTA and the Trinity College Certificate offer a severely reduced view of what it means to be a language teacher, with an emphasis on technique at the expense of in-depth understanding, on a limited view of methodology rather than a range of available options and on survival in the classroom rather than opening the door to further professional development.

Gatekeeping and Assessment Practices

Integrated into the development of programmes such as those discussed above, in both state and private sectors, has been a sharper focus on the assessment of future teachers. There is a stronger awareness of the need to establish minimum standards of language and of teaching competence among entrants to the teaching profession. This is clearly illustrated in the detail of the Ukrainian case study cited above, in which the descriptors can be seen as professional learning outcomes, to be assessed at or before the end of the programme. This is one of the growing number of instances of a minimum language proficiency standard (here CEFR level B2/C1) being set for entry to the profession. Other countries to have introduced minimum standards for future school teachers of English include Albania, Israel, Serbia and Uzbekistan (all at CEFR level B2), and Macedonia (C2) (Bolitho & West, 2017). Given the high cost of international proficiency examinations, most countries striving towards minimum standards are at the time of writing still in the process of painstakingly attempting to benchmark their own language assessment instruments against CEFR levels.

The assessment of methodological knowledge and of practical teaching presents a different set of challenges, and it is here that qualifications such as CELTA have, of necessity, led the way. To achieve a final grade, trainees have to teach six lessons at two different levels, assessed against clear criteria, and to complete four written assignments, each of 750 – 1000 words, focusing on the following topics:

- analysing and responding to adult learner needs;
- analysing language for teaching purposes;
- teaching language skills;
- reflecting on classroom teaching.
  (Source: http://www.cambridgeenglish.org/teaching-english/teaching-qualifications/celta/about-the-celta-course/accessed 29 December 2017)

For the emphasis on reflection in this scheme and in reformed state sector programmes, it is important to acknowledge the influence of Michael Wallace, whose seminal work *Training Foreign Language Teachers: A Reflective Approach* (1991), drawing on the work of Donald Schön (1983), added a key dimension to the way language teacher educators think about assessment in relation to practice. During the long period since Wallace's book was published, many teacher educators have been working towards innovative ways of assessing reflection in relation to practice (e.g. see Kurtoglu-Hooton, 2013), and also ways of assessing those aspects of procedural and pedagogical knowledge ('knowing how to'), such as those mentioned in the first three bullet points above, that are essential to novice teachers. Here, the emphasis has shifted away from assessing purely declarative knowledge about psychology or language systems towards assessing whether trainees know how to apply that knowledge to the reality of working with learners in the classroom. It has gradually become clear that this kind of knowledge cannot be assessed in essays written under examination conditions, and this realisation has led to the introduction of alternative methods of assessment such as teaching practice diaries and portfolios containing teaching materials, samples of language analysis for classroom purposes, coursebook evaluations, case studies of classes and individual learners and notes on lesson observations. The BEd programme for English teachers in Malaysia also requires trainees to include in their portfolio statements from school-based mentors and the host school principal on the extent to which the trainee fitted into the school community and contributed to wider aspects of school life. In a number of countries (e.g. Hungary), training programmes for school-based mentors have been established and the assessment of teaching practice is seen as a shared undertaking between the partner school and the university. In national projects such as those in Uzbekistan and Ukraine, assessment criteria for these task types are included in the curriculum documentation. However, in some contexts, the criteria are still worked out and applied at institutional level, which of course militates against objectivity and standardisation.

The Cultural Dimension in Language Teacher Education

More than any other school subject, foreign language classes open up a window on a wider world, offering opportunities to engage with other ways of thinking, other traditions and other societies, both in the classroom and, through exchanges and cross-national school partnerships, beyond. This points to a need to develop cultural sensitivity and intercultural awareness in future language teachers. While this is probably too much to ask of an initial training course such as CELTA with its already time-limited and packed curriculum, there is no reason why an undergraduate teacher education course should not include a strong intercultural dimension. This is illustrated in the St Gallen course overview presented earlier in this chapter, but is still sadly neglected in many award-bearing language teacher preparation courses. One obvious reason for this is the way disciplines are carved up in universities. The language systems are well covered by specialists who have established their credentials through research in their specialist areas, and who teach courses on grammar, semantics, lexicology or phonology on undergraduate and postgraduate courses. Interculturality is less well represented in language-related research and hence also in teaching, and it is not normally viewed as part of the philological canon. In many universities across Europe and beyond, it is seen as the province of social science faculties and courses in intercultural studies are most often offered in departments of politics or sociology. The work of Michael Byram and his associates has had an impact, largely within

Europe, on thinking and policy in the relationship between language education and intercultural studies, and he has published and lectured widely in this area. Some of his work builds a valuable bridge between theory and practice (e.g. Byram, 2003; Porto & Byram, 2016), but there is much more to be done and on a much broader scale, before the topic is fully explored and understood, and becomes an accepted and integral part of language teacher education.

Teacher Educator Preparation and Trainer Training

While the gateways to the profession of language teaching have been made more secure in recent years and standards at entry have been tightened up in many contexts, there are no clear entry criteria for would-be teacher educators. Some certificate and diploma schemes such as CELTA do run apprenticeship schemes for new trainers, but universities and colleges of education seem to focus solely on academic qualifications, either at MA or PhD level as minimum requirements for their teacher educators, some of whom have never taught in schools. Given that teaching is essentially a 'doing' profession, dependent on the development of skills rather than just on the acquisition of knowledge, there is a self-evident mismatch here. This has been mitigated to some extent and in some contexts by the move towards school-based training, and a division of labour which sees mentor teachers increasingly involved in the supervision of teaching practice, and university tutors taking responsibility for knowledge-based inputs to back up the practical work. However, this kind of model can militate against innovation and progress, as the messages from the methodology course may be at odds with the experiences which student teachers are exposed to when they observe lessons in schools, where practices may be more pragmatic and conservative in nature. Despite the existence of MA courses with optional modules on teacher training and teacher education, and a range of private sector initiatives, there is still no sign of a truly professional route for language teacher educators to take. Most still 'fall' into the role and presumably learn their trade by trial and error.

Yet the role of teacher educator implies huge responsibility. The multiplying effect of a good or poor teacher educator will ultimately reach down to classroom level. To be effective, teacher educators need to be aware of the difficulties that trainees face as they embark on their trip from language learner to language teacher. This involves an understanding of where trainees are when they start out, and of how to guide them gently towards where they need to be (Wright & Bolitho, 2007). Student teachers need to move from analysing their experience as language learners to understanding how to facilitate learning in others, from their declarative or intuitive knowledge of English towards pedagogical language awareness, from dependency to self-reliance, and ultimately towards finding their voice and establishing their presence as teachers. There is nothing easy about any of this, and a teacher educator needs to be grounded in reality, experienced at the chalk face and able to offer good models of language and professional behaviour in addition to being well-versed theoretically in order to carry out the role effectively. Faculty members in universities in Ukraine, Uzbekistan and Switzerland, all referred to in the case studies in this chapter, are now fully aware of these demands and are beginning to respond accordingly. However, there are very few contexts in which provision is made for the preparation of teacher educators and this is clearly a priority for the years ahead.

Concluding Remarks

It is fair to state that language teacher education is still developing as a discipline area. While higher education institutions in some countries still cling to traditional models, others are moving ahead with reforms that are aimed at reflecting in their provision the progress that has been made in methodology, materials and syllabus design, and the demands that are made on language teachers in the 21st century. The most radical change is probably the growing understanding that teachers are concerned with developing language skills in their learners, rather than just language knowledge, and equipping them to broaden their horizons and to communicate in a fast-changing world. This calls for teachers who are able to keep pace with change and teacher educators who are open-minded and outward-looking rather than locked into their own research interests and discipline areas. It also calls for considerable modifications to existing curricula for language teacher education, as in the case of the innovative Swiss curriculum described in this chapter, to take account of the main methodological paradigm shift towards language as communication, but also of multiculturalism and the need for language learners to see beyond the limits of the classroom into a wide world of opportunity. Such changes are only possible if there is a willingness on the part of the academics who determine the content and direction of teacher education to leave their comfort zones and to break down the traditional boundaries of their discipline area in order to embrace the new dimensions that are so evidently needed. Language teaching needs to be seen primarily as principled practice, rather than as an academic discipline which is informed largely by theory.

There are inevitably consequences for the in-service training of teachers, and on a wider level, their opportunities for continuing professional development, a theme which will be explored in detail in the next chapter.

Questions for discussion and reflection

(1) What are the strengths and shortcomings of the main language teacher education programmes in your context?
(2) In language teaching, should practice be based on theory or should theory be derived from practice?
(3) In your context, which traditions of language teaching are valid and should be maintained, and which need to be challenged and changed in teacher education programmes?

5 Language Teachers' Professional Development

The previous chapter discussed in some detail various types of initial teacher education for language teachers from the point of view of policy orientation, content and methodology, and developments that are taking place in some countries to modernise teacher education, including the ways in which language-related issues are covered. But what of the much larger number of language teachers who are already working in education systems and private institutions around the world? What measures are taken by them and their employers to continue their professional development once they have accumulated teaching experience and gained insights that put their initial education and training into perspective, and how effective are they? These questions, which could apply equally to teachers of any kind at whatever stage of their careers, are the focus of this chapter. They are, in our view, critical for the language teaching profession and for education in general, since professional development can have a direct impact on teacher competences and thus on student learning.

In this chapter, we will first consider what professional development for language teachers commonly includes by considering the results of a small-scale survey among teachers and their managers. This will be followed by a discussion of the respective roles of teachers and management in the provision of professional development opportunities, and some proposed principles and quality standards that we believe should inform provision. Although the focus will be on language teachers as these are the teachers we know best, we believe that much of the discussion is relevant to the professional development of teachers of any subject.

What Does Teachers' Professional Development Include?

Over recent decades, a number of different terms have come into use in English (and no doubt in other languages) in the discussion of professional development. 'Professional development' itself and 'continuing professional development', or CPD, have become two of the most current. We will use these terms to include any events or experiences that are designed to contribute to teachers' professional learning.

In many state and private institutions employing teachers, their CPD includes a programme of events, usually organised or funded by the institution, together with observation and other kinds of support such as mentoring and external courses, that are designed to enable teachers to gain new awareness, knowledge and/or skills that will enhance their professional competence. These kinds of CPD organised by the employer or external providers are commonly labelled 'in-service training' or INSET in the UK, or in-service teacher education in North America and elsewhere (we will use the term INSET for convenience). However, teachers should arguably view their CPD as richer and broader than what is provided for them in this way since it concerns their ongoing all-round professional learning.

In a 2005 article on the topic of 'the language teacher's teacher development', Steve Mann summarised some key features of teacher development identified in a review of the then recent literature:

Language teacher development

- is a bottom–up process and as such can be contrasted with top–down staff development programmes;
- values the insider view rather than the outsider view;
- is independent of the organisation but often functioning more successfully with its support and recognition;
- is a continuing process of becoming and can never be finished;
- is a process of articulating an inner world of conscious choices made in response to the outer world of the teaching context;
- is wider than professional development and includes personal, moral and value dimensions;
- can be encouraged and integrated in both training and education programmes. (Mann, 2005: 105)

The key point highlighted here is that teacher professional development is viewed as the responsibility of and under the control of individual teachers, independent of the employer or the institution, and is linked with personal development. It can include any of the activities, experiences and opportunities for reflection and professional learning that occur in the working life of a teacher. These may or may not be organised or suggested by other people, such as managers, mentors or colleagues. For example, opportunities to teach at a new level or to work with a group with specific needs are likely to be offered by those managing the courses and these managers may also organise formative lesson observation. But individual teachers also often have the opportunity, for example, to request new teaching experiences, to observe more experienced colleagues or to prepare and try out tailor-made resources. Similarly, exchanges of experience and ideas about teaching or about how to teach aspects of the target language or the subject (in the case of CLIL teachers) may occur spontaneously among colleagues in a teaching team, or some individuals may take the initiative to carry out some small-scale classroom research to find out more about the usefulness of certain ways of working or about new resources. For many teachers, then, their professional development includes their own initiatives in exploring the subject they are teaching (in this case a language), methods of teaching, learning psychology, the use of language and communication in teaching and learning, etc., through reading, browsing the internet, learning from and collaboration with colleagues, taking a language course and so on. These activities may be undertaken completely independently of the institution where they work.

Decision-Making about Professional Development

An issue that is often overlooked in an institution is whether the aims of CPD and INSET should be decided by managers or by teachers themselves, or whether they should be agreed between the two parties. For example, an employer or a government authority may wish to introduce a new curriculum, new technology or new modes of assessment and is likely to organise specialised training to support the innovation. It may, however, be the case that some teachers are not in favour of the innovation because they feel it does not improve student learning and creates more work for teachers. Nevertheless, they are likely to go along with it and the related training. On the other hand, teachers themselves may propose an innovation that they consider to be important for their work, such as the selection or development of new learning resources, or the analysis and discussion of how certain points in the target language should be handled. To support this, they may request from their managers specific kinds of CPD events, such as workshops with textbook authors, guidance about the development of in-house materials, discussion groups, etc. CPD offered by institutions in the form of INSET is clearly likely to work better when agreed between the manager and the teachers concerned. In contrast with 'pre-service training', a term still often used of intensive initial teacher education for language teachers, INSET often takes the form of a short course, or a series of workshops, or occasionally just a single workshop or seminar, provided for a group of teachers at a specific time face-to-face or more flexibly online. Language teachers may not themselves be first language users of the target language and the same may apply to teachers of other subjects in regard to the language of schooling. CPD focusing on language improvement and awareness as well as the methodology of language teaching is relevant to language teachers in this situation and school managers need to take this need into account when planning

INSET. In the European context, CPD for language teachers may also include EU-funded short courses abroad in the country where the target language is spoken. These may focus on specific language teaching issues such as CLIL or the use of information and communication technology (ICT), but they often also involve a language improvement element. An added benefit is that teachers can interact and share experience and expertise with counterparts from other countries and education systems, and can refresh their communicative competence in the target language in the environment where the course takes place.

The Role of the Institution

As can be seen from the above discussion, the key factor in an institution is the kind of balance that is struck and the degree of harmony and synergy that exists between the objectives and initiatives that come from management as well as from outside the organisation, and those that come from individual teachers and the teaching team as a group. Institutions need to be ever more conscious of the need to keep up with changes in approaches to teaching and learning, and this in turn should heighten awareness of the need for a varied CPD programme to ensure that their teachers do not fall behind. This trend is particularly evident in the private sector, where language schools exist in a competitive environment. It is logical that employers of teachers have their own priorities when organising INSET, which might, for instance, relate to institutional innovations, such as the introduction of blended learning, or to meeting external or self-imposed quality standards and curricular directives or guidelines from education authorities. For the management team, it is important to feel that teachers individually and as a group understand and support these institutional priorities, and this support depends in large part on the nature of interactions and the quality of professional exchanges between managers and teachers. But teachers also have their own individual priorities, for example, relating to the need to become more expert or more competent in a given area of language or methodology, and they also have their own – perhaps individual – interests, which may concern the value of a specific teaching technique, ways of introducing and practising given aspects or points of language, the potential of music or drama as an aid to language learning and so on. For these teachers, the key issue is how interested the management team are in their individual needs and priorities, and to what extent practical support and recognition is forthcoming.

The implication is that there is a clear need for institutions not just to formulate and put in place a well thought-through INSET programme, but also to see this INSET as part of a CPD policy that stresses both individual and institutional needs and perspectives, and specifies the rights and obligations of both parties. In addition, someone within the institution needs to be responsible for implementing this CPD policy and ensuring that effective CPD opportunities are made available to all teachers.

Our own experience of working with teachers over many years leads us to endorse the perspective on teacher development described above by Mann (2005). This is because of the potential breadth and scope of what CPD can encompass for individual teachers as well as for groups of colleagues, and because it potentially empowers teachers to have a clear role and say in deciding what professional learning activities and experiences, including what INSET and CPD opportunities, are organised from above, and in seeking support for their own individual teacher development priorities. As in other employment situations, the power relationship between managers and employees and the degree of mutual respect and collective responsibility can vary considerably, and teacher–management relationships and management styles can have important consequences for the success or otherwise of INSET. Establishing and applying clear principles for teacher development and CPD, and communicating openly with teachers about these, can lead to professional learning opportunities that are productive and enriching for both parties, and, most importantly, for students too.

One could take this characterisation of teacher development further: whether consciously and intentionally or not, teachers develop all the time professionally and as people from lesson to lesson and from one professional experience or encounter to the next. The issue for them and their employers is to try to ensure that the development and professional learning that takes place is positive, constructive and beneficial for all concerned. Given the pressures that many teachers are under and the challenges they face in classrooms, this is not necessarily easy to achieve, but it is important to strive for.

Case study: Views of CPD and INSET for language teachers in the independent sector

In the sections that follow, we will consider snapshots gleaned from research and personal experience into the CPD and other teacher development opportunities available to language teachers in private sector institutions whose prime focus is language education. We begin with a small-scale case study of the perspectives both of individual teachers working in such institutions and of their managers.

> Eaquals is an international not-for-profit association of language education providers, most of them independent. It is dedicated to the enhancement of quality and effectiveness in the field and has its own accreditation scheme, which specifies certain standards including in the area of CPD policy and provision. An informal survey by written questionnaire was carried out among teachers at five Eaquals member

institutions in the private and independent sectors in late 2017. The 11 teachers who responded had teaching experience that ranged from three months to 40 years. Three of them were teaching language students on intensive courses in the UK, while the other eight were working on extensive courses in Italy, Bulgaria and the Czech Republic. Various questions were asked, including those indicated in Table 5.1, which also contains a cross-section of the responses received.

Commentary

As can be seen from the responses in Table 5.1 below, what teachers view as important to their professional development varies considerably, as one would expect, and not only as a function of their level of experience. It is felt by two of them that 'obligatory' CPD sessions should be optional (teacher A) or are inappropriate if based on 'what works for me' (teacher D). Two others (C and E) highlighted drama, music, cooking, etc. as topics that they personally would like to pursue as potentially useful in their teaching but are more likely to be accessible outside the institution. By contrast, teacher A and teacher D express a wish for research-based CPD. None of the informants highlighted aspects of language, communication or culture, although teacher C mentions pronunciation teaching as an important topic. Although the responses were disparate, the focus was

Table 5.1 Responses from some teachers to questions about their own vision for their CPD

Question: In an ideal world, what forms would your professional development take, and why? What activities would you ideally like to engage in and what experiences would you like to have?

A. Teacher in Italy (13 years' experience)	In an ideal world, I think there should be more choice. I would like to be able to choose whether to attend the obligatory monthly meetings based on their relevance to my teaching practice. I would additionally like another opportunity to build my professional qualifications. Finally, I would like to have the time (paid) to carry out research projects and feed that back into the school.
B. Teacher in the UK (20 years' experience)	I would like to have more training in specific areas, for example pronunciation teaching.
C. Teacher in Bulgaria (14 years' experience)	If I had more free time, I would definitely join a drama club and/or writing class, as well as learn to play a musical instrument and improve my drawing skills. Learning more about beats and rhythm along with techniques used by actors, such as teamwork, self-control, voice control, stage performance, presentation skills etc. would have enormous impact on my work and would give me the necessary skills and inspiration to take my teaching to the next level.
D. Teacher in the UK (11 years' experience)	I need current, evidence-based, peer-reviewed research to be referenced in CPD meetings, so that I can incorporate new ideas into my teaching. Conversely (and I only mention this to be clear), I do not need CPD sessions which are based on 'what works for me in the classroom is …'.
E. Teacher in Italy (40 years' experience)	I'd like to set up reading, watching videos, or songs-for-pleasure groups at elementary and intermediate level, and conversation classes on gossip or topics of general interest; or to do things like shopping, touring the town, or cooking in English, with both adults and young learners.

on topics that in one way or another would aid them to enhance their teaching as well as pursue their individual interests.

It is revealing to compare these responses with teachers' views of the INSET provided by their employers. These views are recorded in Table 5.2 below.

Commentary

Again, there is a very mixed set of responses, which also throw some light on the types of CPD opportunity provided. Teacher A refers to external 'trainers' who are regularly used to provide INSET. This is not unusual when schools provide two or more days of obligatory INSET at the start of the school year, or 'INSET days' at other times. But teacher A's remarks underline the difficulties of such an arrangement. External trainers by definition know relatively little about the specific needs of groups of teachers or individuals in an institution but, on the other hand, are likely to bring in new insights and information, which may be relevant. Teacher B focuses on a different aspect of CPD: peer observation

Table 5.2 Some teachers' opinions of the CPD opportunities provided by employers

Question: Regarding the CPD activities organised by your employer that you have participated in over the last year, how useful have these been for your own professional development? What impact do you believe these CPD opportunities have had on your teaching and your students' learning?

A. Teacher in Italy (13 years' experience)	*Usefulness*: The quality of external trainers has varied since I started, though I would say they have improved a great deal over the years and we have enjoyed some excellent training during the last 2/3 years. The monthly meetings have been mixed.	
	Impact: Focused input from external trainers has certainly been very useful. Internal training sessions are at times not so well structured or can be irrelevant to my teaching, but they can also be a useful reminder of where to pay attention and do offer some input on teaching practice at times.	
B. Teacher in the UK (20 years' experience)	*Usefulness*: I particularly enjoyed peer observation because I could see other teachers in action and could use their good ideas in my classroom too.	
	Impact: It's good to learn new ways to teach students. I think it has made a positive impact on the students.	
C. Teacher in Bulgaria (14 years' experience)	*Usefulness*: Being actively involved in a CPD group aiming at enhancing young learners' motivation meant a great deal of research, long hours of learning new songs, poems, chants, clapping games and tongue twisters. It also required finding and adapting party games to suit the needs of an EFL teacher, and designing new-generation homework assignments and projects.	
	Impact: In brief, the CPD opportunities this year have helped me gain more confidence as a professional. Regarding my students, teacher training sessions have really made a difference. Students enjoy taking part in fun and engaging activities.	
D. Teacher in the UK (11 years' experience)	*Usefulness*: I presented some [CPD sessions] and I attended some. The ones I attended contributed only somewhat.	
	Impact: There was some backwash for the students certainly. It heightened awareness in some areas.	

and learning from one another. This works well if teachers have time to observe one another and the consent to do so, but if not taken further, for example, through follow-up meetings, reflective reports, etc., may be hard to maintain. The enthusiasm of teacher C shows how CPD focused on collaborative projects with a specific objective can contribute positively to a varied programme of CPD opportunities, while the muted response of teacher D at least shows the motivating effect of being asked to lead a CPD session and engage in the preparation necessary. What is evident from these few examples is the sheer variety of options that are available to institutions for actively consulting teachers on and involving them in the provision of CPD opportunities.

> The remarks in Table 5.2 might lead one to believe that the employers in question are not providing sufficient satisfactory CPD opportunities for their teachers. However, this was not the impression gained from the responses to a parallel survey carried out with academic managers of the five institutions concerned. All of them were providing regular INSET of different kinds for teaching staff. Decisions were usually made by the academic management team in consultation with teachers and based on observation records and appraisal meetings. Attending these programmed events was obligatory at least for permanent staff, and temporary and self-employed staff were also encouraged to participate. The academic managers were asked what additional support was offered to teachers. The range of such support is exemplified by the responses below from three of the schools surveyed:
>
> *School in Bulgaria*: Funding for external events, courses leading to qualifications, etc; information about external webinars and conferences in which they can participate and invitations to apply to attend funded courses in the UK.
>
> *School B in the Czech Republic*: Individual development plans, peer observations, discounts on certificated teacher training courses, help with running workshops and preparing conference contributions.
>
> *School in Italy*: Support observations and counselling on request or as deemed necessary; sponsored participation in certificated distance training (offered to one teacher per year); sponsored attendance at external events whenever possible; sponsored training as oral examiners for examinations.

Commentary

It was clear from all the responses that significant efforts were being made to respond to the inevitably diverse needs and expectations of teachers as well as the needs identified by the institutions themselves. The responses indicated not only that efforts were made by the centres concerned to provide regular CPD opportunities to teachers as a team but also support to individuals, Depending on the country, observation of different kinds, including peer observation, often goes on informally, although, depending on the country, in the public sector there may be no legal framework or fewer opportunities for observation of lessons by school managers or mentors and thus fewer possibilities to take into account the insights gained from observations in planning CPD opportunities. In general, it is undoubtedly challenging to provide regular CPD opportunities to all, since teachers are busy preparing lessons or teaching most of the day and the time available for participating in such events is limited. Moreover, identifying and meeting the needs of individuals with different priorities and different levels of training and experience is a major challenge. Added to this, a growing trend for teachers to be employed on a part-time and/or temporary basis, at least in the independent sector, means that some of those who might benefit most from these opportunities are not able or willing to take them up.

Voluntary teachers' clubs, like those in India, or reading groups, where teachers read and discuss the same (or a pool) of articles on topics and research in the area of language teaching and learning or of applied linguistics, are a useful alternative to traditional INSET sessions, especially where these lead to practical classroom research in areas to do with methodology and techniques or specific kinds of resources (e.g. internet-based applications). Other types of collaborative event that involve individual contributions are sessions where resources that individual teachers have tried out and have found effective (e.g. new internet-based resources such as video clips, handbooks for teachers or self-made topical resources) can be demonstrated, shared and discussed, and also opportunities to participate in internal projects to develop new course syllabuses or resources. Like classroom research and peer observation, such 'sharing' events promote the sense of the teaching team, indeed the whole team, as a 'community of practice' (Lave & Wenger, 1991) in which people learn from one another and work together on improving their collective practice.

Observation of Teaching as Part of Professional Development

As mentioned earlier, a measure commonly taken by employers to support teachers, and sometimes to check the quality of their work, is lesson observation in its various forms. This is a practice about which whole chapters and whole books have been written (e.g. see Gower *et al.*, 1995; Maingay, 1988; and chapters in Bailey, 2006; Rossner, 2017b). Kathleen Bailey provides a neat visual representation of the various types of less observation that can be used and the extent to which teachers have any control of these, which is reproduced in Figure 5.1.

At one end of the see-saw, 'surprise' observations may be used by supervisors or inspectors from external bodies to check on the quality

Language Teachers' Professional Development 77

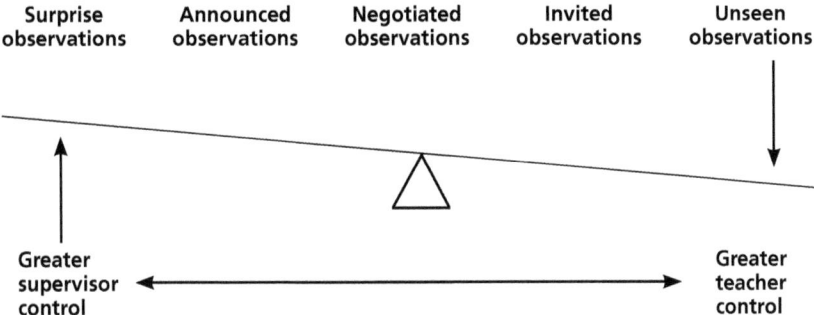

Figure 5.1 Supervisor and teacher control over classroom observation
Source: Bailey (2006: 85)

of what is happening in classrooms by visiting a series of classrooms for brief periods. At the other end of the see-saw, teachers can simply record their own thoughts and reflections on a lesson in a diary or record parts of the lesson on video, for their own purposes and decide whether or not to discuss their 'observation' with a supervisor or colleague. The great advantages of observation are its immediacy, the focus on real teaching and the range of different aspects of the lesson that can be focused on. While supervised observation is likely to focus on standards and general quality issues (motivation, variety, pace, effectiveness of activities in promoting learning, etc.), teachers themselves and their peers may be more likely to focus on techniques, creativity, interaction among students and between students and teachers, resources, the ways in which aspects of language are taught, as well as the teacher's and learners' use of the target language.

Linked to the issue of lesson observation is the practical support that is offered, especially when new and less experienced teachers have been recruited, by more experienced colleagues taking the role of mentors, teacher educators or supervisors, and by peers who request or are invited to undertake observation. When used as part of good quality CPD, the value of any observation lies mainly in what happens afterwards: how the 'evidence' and impressions gathered during the observation are discussed between the observer and the person observed, what insights are gained from the discussion by both parties and what follow-up there is, if any. For language teachers as for all teachers, video-recording segments of lessons and analysing key aspects can if handled well be a very productive means of raising awareness within the teaching team about key features of the teaching-learning process. Such key features certainly include the communication and interaction that takes place between the teacher and the learners, the way language is used and new content, including language elements, is handled, classroom and task management, and the impact on learning of the teacher's interventions, handling of tasks and resources, and the feedback provided. Insights from analysing classroom discourse are, in other words, not simply of interest to researchers but can also provide beneficial opportunities for teacher development. The key is to find motivating and effective ways of facilitating the collection and use of the data from real classrooms.

Reflective Practice and the Use of Competence Frameworks

Linked to observation is the issue of reflective practice (Wallace, 1991) discussed in Chapter 4 and self-assessment. Several resources exist in the form of frameworks that can provide a starting point for self-assessment, such as the *Cambridge English Teaching Framework* (Cambridge Assessment, 2014), the *European Profiling Grid* and *e-Grid* (North *et al.*, 2013), the *Eaquals Framework* (Eaquals, 2013), and the British Council's (2015) *CPD Framework for Teachers* and various specialised instruments for teachers of CLIL and teachers of other subjects through foreign languages. Several of these are discussed in Rossner (2017a). They generally have sections that focus on classroom-related competences such as planning teaching, classroom teaching methods, managing interaction with and between learners, assessment of learning, etc. Many also have sections focusing on competence in the target language, language awareness and intercultural competences. Some have indicators relating to the use of ICT and to professionalism, which includes attitudes to and participation in CPD. A few offer indicators or descriptors organised over successive phases of a teacher's development, from novice to very experienced. This enables teachers and those supporting them more easily to consider and plan ongoing and long-term development. A project called 'A guide to teacher competences for languages in education' within the European Centre for Modern Languages' 2016–2019 programme reviewed 40 such frameworks, not all of them restricted to teachers of language. Brief outlines of many of them can be found on the project website (ECML, 2018) under the 'catalogue of instruments' https://www.ecml.at/ECML-Programme/Programme2016-2019/owardsaCommonEuropeanFrameworkofReferenceforLanguageTeachers/Resources/tabid/3023/language/en-GB/Default.aspx#.

From the point of view of language teachers, the advantage of referring to such frameworks is that they can more quickly comprehend the potential scope of the knowledge and skills relevant to their work and can take a more systematic approach to periodically assessing what knowledge and skills they need and wish to develop further as their careers progress. Regular self-assessment and reflection on the results of this can usefully feed into individual professional development and can inform school managers about current priorities and preferences for team wide CPD as well as individual support. However, it is understandable that some teachers find competence frameworks daunting or even threatening:

will they be expected to endlessly acquire more and more skills and knowledge and gradually tick the corresponding boxes in order to hold on to their jobs? Careful orientation and reassurance are needed to allay such doubts. Some employers, through mentors and academic coordinators, work with teachers to use these frameworks as a means of collaboratively assessing what development opportunities individual teachers need in order to become more versatile and confident, and to progress professionally. However, if it is to be seen in a positive and motivating light rather than as another unwelcome burden, this use of competence frameworks requires sensitivity and a clear mutual understanding of the purpose and benefits of guided self-assessment and reflection.

Criteria for Effective CPD for Language Teachers

It could be argued that the CPD provision exemplified above is still insufficient in some respects. In a 2016 presentation, Simon Borg, whose research work has explored the area of teacher cognition and professional development in some depth, discussed some of the issues that surround and potentially diminish the value of INSET and commented on the resulting lack of impact of most school-based INSET. In his view, this is because it may be seen by the institution and its managers as an 'administrative formality' or does not respond to well-defined needs or because the topics are mainly identified by someone outside the team of teachers. Also, it is often short-term – more a series of separate events than a process – and it is seldom followed up. From a teacher's point of view, on the other hand, in order to be an effective contribution to professional learning, INSET needs to respond to clear needs, which may derive from the teachers themselves, from learners or from the institution. It should also be ongoing rather than a one-off, embedded in the reality of teachers' work, and involve collaboration among teachers and between teachers and management. It should also be subject to review and reflection. Borg concludes that effective in-service training and development needs to be teacher-led, ongoing, collaborative and social, and should involve reflection and inquiry (Borg, 2016). Making provision available that meets all these criteria is a tall order in most educational contexts simply because of the amount of time, expertise and oversight that is needed. It is, however, essential that managers bear such criteria in mind when formulating and implementing their CPD and INSET policies.

Autonomous Teacher Development

CPD opportunities provided by employers are not the only kinds of professional development available to teachers. In the small-scale survey referred to above, teachers were asked about the professional learning they engaged in independently. The questions and some of the responses are summarised in Table 5.3.

Table 5.3 Responses received from some teachers to questions concerning independent steps taken to further their professional learning

- What activities do you engage in as an individual or with colleagues independently of your employer? How frequently do you engage in these activities?
- What other experiences do you believe contribute most to your professional development?
- How important have the independent activities and experiences that you have been involved in over the last year been for your professional and personal development?
- What impact do you believe they have had on your teaching and your students' learning?

A. Teacher in Italy (13 years' experience)	I have a general interest in pedagogy and individual and group psychology, so I am involved in circles that share these interests, informally on a weekly/monthly basis. Systematic experimentation has been most useful. Reflection on strengths and weaknesses and revisiting the basics of teaching and syllabi also help. I integrate much of what I know and continue to learn about psychology, learning, and group dynamics into my teaching practice. The independent activities have been extremely important. I'd be bored to death if I wasn't consistently seeking to do what I do better, and I tend to view teaching as on a never-ending improving curve. They have Improved my teaching a great deal and made classes more stimulating for students and myself.
B. Teacher in the UK (20 years' experience)	I research new material and lesson plans on specialised websites every week. I also share and exchange resources with other teachers.
	Teaching a new level with new materials is most useful. I think teachers should never stop researching new materials and resources – it's very important. It has improved the quality of my teaching and students' learning.
C. Teacher in Bulgaria (14 years' experience)	Discussions with colleagues, sharing ideas, asking for their opinion. It depends on the time we have available, but at least once a week. If we cannot meet in person, we chat on the phone, share ideas, ask for each other's opinion.
	Teaching new levels, designing materials, working on presentations, doing research, and trying out new techniques have been most important for me. Taking a break from my job for a summer job abroad for a couple of months helped be re-evaluate my present job/career and future prospects. It has given me a wider and more accurate snapshot of my abilities and has helped me to redefine my goals.
D. Teacher in the UK (11 years' experience)	Only research for my own publications, weekly. Research is key. Access to new materials on the current research agenda can sometimes be a challenge but this is where I can develop the most. Also, devising effective games for the classroom is very useful.
	[My autonomous CPD] has been crucial. It's something I'm not able to get from/through my job. All of my teaching has been based on my research over the last few years. If I can't back it up through my research, it won't make it into my planning and teaching.
E. Teacher in Italy (40 years' experience)	Finding and sharing 'fun/interesting' input like TV series, talk shows, songs, learning tools etc. on the net in the classroom on a regular basis to encourage students to continue learning for pleasure independently. The awareness of teaching and helping students with learning difficulties has been most important for me, and these activities and experiences have been useful and have had a positive impact on my teaching.

Commentary

These responses show that, on the face of it, these individuals were engaging in explorations and initiatives that were quite different from but often complementary to those that were offered by their organisations, and that these provided a valuable additional dimension to their CPD. The preferred activities span a range from fairly formal research 'for publications', informal study and research circles, conversations and collaboration with colleagues, and making the most of new teaching experiences. It is not apparent from the responses to what extent the information and insights gained from these activities were shared with employers and colleagues, but they do make clear that the teachers concerned felt these activities contributed significantly to their development and had a positive impact on their teaching. We certainly believe that it is incumbent upon employers to discuss such individual interests and initiatives with their teachers, and where possible, to encourage and recognise them. With this in mind, Eaquals has recently developed a scheme to recognise the all-round professional development support given by its member institutions and to enable them to formally recognise such individual initiatives:

> The aim of the Scheme is to enable Eaquals accredited institutions to issue a formal report detailing an individual employee's CPD achievements and activities over a given time period, and with official Eaquals recognition for the local scheme. (Eaquals website, members' area)

Concluding Remarks

The key challenge remains: how can institutions and their teachers, whether in the public or independent sectors, achieve the kind of climate and balance in their provision of CPD opportunities for teachers that both empowers teachers to develop professionally as individuals and also responds consistently (and not haphazardly) to institutional needs and initiatives, and national and global developments in policy and practice? Is it possible to achieve an equitable and viable balance between professional learning initiatives and inspirations that arise 'bottom-up' from teachers as individuals or as a team, and measures considered by the institution to be essential, or at least important, which are organised 'top-down'? Can a comfortable and productive synergy and confluence be achieved between these two currents of professional learning?

The discussion and case studies in this chapter point to a number or prerequisites for achieving this kind of balance:

(1) Teachers themselves need to be orientated and coached towards a belief in career-long professional learning during their initial teacher education as well as subsequently.

(2) Individual teachers need to be given opportunities, encouragement and time to seek guidance and information from employers, associations, colleagues and online, when they feel they need it.
(3) Mentoring and enlightened supervision should be available for all teachers, and this should involve two-way conversation and discussion.
(4) Teachers who do not speak the target language as their first language need to be fully aware of their strengths and weaknesses in the language, especially in the spoken language, and of the need to maintain and, where necessary, improve their competence; moreover, they should be given encouragement and offered opportunities to do this by their employers.
(5) Equally, teachers who are first language users of the target language need to continually work on developing their language awareness, and on finding out more about the issues that confront learners of the language. In situations where they work alongside one another, teachers who are first language users of the target language and those who are second language users have a lot to learn from and to offer one another. The teachers who themselves have learnt the target language are likely to have a very keen awareness of the challenges confronting learners and can sensitise their 'first language' colleagues to these, while teachers who are first language users may be able to help their colleagues to improve their knowledge and use of the finer features of the target language such as varieties of the language, idiomatic use and intonation.
(6) Teachers should be able and be encouraged to initiate individual and group classroom research and experimentation.
(7) A collegial climate needs to be created in which cooperation, professional exchange, development and innovation are the norm, and in which individual initiatives are fully acknowledged, shared and respected.

In summary, as Bolitho and Padwad note, 'A structured approach to CPD and a positive institutional policy will create the conditions needed for teachers to plan and prioritise their development' (Bolitho & Padwad, 2018: 61). Within an institution there needs to be a vision and a policy for CPD that is made known to all staff and can be used as a basis for decision-making on CPD initiatives. In this way, a positive attitude or disposition towards CPD can be created across the institution.

Some employers may view such a scenario as idealistic or expensive in terms of additional finance and human resources. We would agree that it is not a simple matter to reach and maintain a position where pressure on reluctant teachers with differing interests and lengths of experience to participate in professional development is replaced by a desire among them to do so and to contribute actively and collaboratively to the process. However, much depends on other factors such as the communication style and openness that exists within the institution, and the benefits in terms of improved learning outcomes that can be achieved for the ultimate beneficiaries for which the institution exists: the students and the communities which they are part of.

In the next chapter, we examine how language both as a focus of teaching and as a means of engaging in teaching and learning can be productively dealt with in teacher education for all categories of teachers.

Questions for reflection and discussion

(1) Think back to CPD events and opportunities in your own experience. Which of them did you find most fruitful in terms of professional learning? Which were least useful? In both cases, why?
(2) How relevant and important are the points made by Mann (p. 69 above) and the criteria suggested by Borg (p. 79 above) for CPD in your educational context?
(3) From the point of view of managers, what aspect of INSET and CPD provision is most challenging in your context? How do managers deal with these challenges?

6 Language in Pre-Service and In-Service Teacher Education for Teachers of all Subjects

Having discussed in some detail the ways in which language features in teacher education courses and professional development for language teachers in Chapters 4 and 5, in this chapter we make a case for paying far greater attention to language and communication in initial teacher education and continuing professional development for all teachers from pre-primary to higher secondary levels.

Towards the end of Chapter 1, we included a quote from the findings of the Bullock Report (1975), which was to be widely regarded as a basis for policy making on the role of language in education in the UK. We repeat one of its recommendations here:

> a substantial course on language in education ... should be part of every primary and secondary school teacher's initial training, whatever the teacher's subject or the age of the children with whom he or she will be working. (Bullock Report, 1975: 514–515)

The recommendation is expressed in fairly unequivocal terms, and it raises a number of questions about the role and place of language in teacher education in any context. We will address these in this chapter, but before doing so we need to return to one of the topics discussed in Chapter 1 and consider in some detail the place of language in subjects across school curricula, drawing on evidence from both international and UK documents and research.

Literacy and Oracy

A traditional concern has existed in education systems across the world that students should, over the period of their schooling, acquire a good command of the main language of schooling (usually the first language of a majority of students). Many educationalists in the decades since the Bullock Report (1975) have sought to define the objectives of this work more clearly. They have emphasised the importance both of 'literacy', defined as the 'ability to identify, understand, interpret, create, communicate and compute, using printed and written materials associated with varying contexts' (UNESCO, 2004: 13), and of 'oracy', a term coined in 1965 by Andrew Wilkinson and a team at Birmingham University 'to refer to listening and speaking in the same way as literacy refers to reading and writing' (Wilkinson, 1968: 744). It implies an ability to interact, explain and narrate well using spoken language. Literacy and oracy in at least one language are seen as crucial life skills, not only for success in education but in life as well, notably in employment situations, relationships and the exercise of democratic citizenship. As the continuation of the UNESCO definition of literacy (which includes aspects of oracy) states: 'Literacy involves a continuum of learning in enabling individuals to achieve their goals, to develop their knowledge and potential, and to participate fully in their community and wider society' (UNESCO, 2004: 13).

The trend towards equipping children and young adults with oracy and literacy skills and greater language awareness has become a salient feature of policy documents and curricula since the Bullock Report (1975). The National Oracy Project in England (1989–1993), which took the form of a network of research projects in schools across the country, had the following objectives:

- To enhance the role of speech in the learning process [for pupils aged] 5–16 by encouraging active learning
- To develop the teaching of oral communication skills
- To develop methods of assessment of and through speech, including assessment for public examinations at [age] 16+
- To improve pupils' performance across the curriculum
- To enhance teachers' skills and practice [in this area]
- To promote recognition of the value of oral work in schools and increase its use as a means of improving learning. (Johnson, 1994: 34)

Through its scope and results, the National Project went a long way towards throwing the spotlight on oracy as a critical element of education across the curriculum as well as in the teaching of English. This resulted in gradual rather than radical changes in the national curriculum. However, some years later, the Cambridge Primary Review included among its many recommendations for primary education in England a proposed revised curriculum in which 'language, oracy and literacy' constituted one of its eight domains (Alexander, 2010: 266–269).

While these recommendations were not fully accepted, the current national curriculum for England states:

> Teachers should develop pupils' spoken language, reading, writing and vocabulary as *integral aspects of the teaching of every subject*. English is both a subject in its own right and the medium for teaching; for pupils, understanding the language provides access to the whole curriculum. Fluency in the English language is an *essential foundation for success in all subjects*. (UK Department for Education, 2014: 11; authors' emphasis)

However, this does not yet take account of the broader definition of oracy and literacy recommended by the Cambridge Primary Review, which stated 'in England literacy is too narrowly conceived and … spoken language has yet to secure the place in primary education that its centrality to learning, culture and life requires, or that it enjoys in the curriculum [sic] of many other countries' (Alexander, 2010: 268).

The Place of Language and Communication in Curricula for Teacher Education

Given the essential role of language in 'learning, culture and life' discussed above, important questions need to be asked about how the necessary awareness, knowledge and skills are developed during teacher education courses for novice and experienced teachers. We will consider these questions one by one.

Question 1: Do courses on 'language in education' or language across the curriculum exist in modern teacher education programmes?

In looking for evidence of such courses in teacher education curricula in a wide variety of contexts, we were initially constrained by the limits of national policies and practices in this area. In many countries, guidelines and standards for pre-service teacher education are decided nationally, but objectives and detailed curriculum content are determined by the providers – institutions charged with the provision of teacher education programmes. In view of this, it was not surprising to find very wide divergence in the samples we looked at. Some provider institutions in Canada, South Africa, Finland and Switzerland, for example, include modules on language for teachers of all subjects, as the following extracts show.

The University of Northern British Columbia, Canada (UNBC)

Within its BEd programme, UNBC provides a compulsory course in language and literacy across the Curriculum with the following statement about content:

> In this course, Senior Years students study the role of language as a medium of teaching and learning, and develop approaches to

integrating spoken and written language across subject areas to enhance learning. The course includes a substantive focus on English as a Second Language/English as a Second Dialect. Other topics include the nature of language, classroom discourse, narrative, and journals, the construction of meaning, writing and cognition, and diverse oral and literate traditions. The course includes a focus on strategies for integrating language within specific subject areas.

Source: https://ssb.unbc.ca/ssb/dev_web.course_finder.calendar?subject=EDUC

The University of Pretoria in South Africa

The University of Pretoria in South Africa describes a one-year module in Literacies in Education for all B Ed students as follows:

Literacies in Education 300 (JLZ 300)

This module aims to equip students with the necessary communicative and classroom literacies to succeed as a professional in the domain of teaching. Students will show evidence of understanding and being able to implement the theories and strategies underpinning spoken and written communication required within an education context. The development of a critical awareness of language as a nonneutral (biased) conveyor of meaning will also be fostered. An overview of the linguistic diversity encountered in most South African classrooms provides the prospective teacher with strategies for dealing more effectively with multilingualism in a culturally diverse pedagogical context. Students will also enrich their personal language profile by acquiring a functional knowledge of appropriate words and phrases in an African language with the view to facilitating classroom management.

Source: https://www.up.ac.za/yearbooks/2019/pdf/module/JLZ%20300; accessed 19 July 2019

Referring to the national teacher education curriculum in Finland, Kansanen describes the compulsory module in language and communication studies as follows:

> Language and communication studies are basically divided into courses in the mother tongue and in foreign languages. Mother tongue courses include verbal communication, Finnish speech and culture, classroom communication, and didactics of speech education. Written communication courses concern the acquisition of the skills needed to produce academic reports.
>
> The goal of the foreign language studies is to impart to students the capacity to read foreign literature. Many textbooks are in English as are most of the scientific articles in the international journals that are needed for doing research, especially in undertaking the study

> project. Students may also choose to read and study German. Most students, today, however, prefer English. The study of French and Spanish is also possible.
>
> A special topic is the study of the second national language, Swedish. For Swedish-speaking students, this language is obviously Finnish. The second national language is a compulsory subject in the comprehensive school curriculum. In real life, the second national language is actually a foreign language, for nearly all students, despite the fact that it has a formal status in Finland. (Kansanen, 2003: 98)

These samples of course descriptions in different countries and linguistic contexts demonstrate an awareness of the central mediating role of language in schooling and as a necessary component of initial teacher education. However, many institutions in the UK still seem to pay little or no attention to language in their curricula. It is ignored in the official *Teachers' Standards* issued by the UK Department for Education (2011), and hardly touched on in *A Framework of Core Content for Initial Teacher Training* for the UK (Munday et al., 2016). This apparent neglect seems to fly in the face of testimony from so many sources, both historical and modern. For example: 'There is a strong case for revisiting the Bullock Report's advocacy of "language across the curriculum" in order to underline the argument that educationally productive talk is the responsibility of all teachers, not just those who teach English' (Alexander, 2012: 12). Also, 'The readiest way of working on understanding is often through talk, because the flexibility of speech makes it easy for us to try out new ways of arranging what we know, and easy also to change them if they seem inadequate' (Barnes, 2008: 5).

Even allowing for the shift in many contexts towards competence-based models in teacher education and for the crowded nature of the content of many teacher education courses, the lack of an explicit language dimension seems to us to be unjustifiable. It may be attributable to a variety of factors, among them the lack of research studies in language across the curriculum or the tendency to focus on aspects of pedagogy and subject studies, which are comfortably housed in faculty areas whereas language education cuts across faculty boundaries. Whatever the reason, voices such as those of Alexander and Barnes do merit the urgent attention of curriculum designers if we are not to produce a generation of language-handicapped teachers.

Question 2: What might be the objectives and content of a 'course on language in education' in an initial teacher education programme?

The Council of Europe's *Reference Framework of Competences for Democratic Culture*, developed as a reference document for educators in its 47 member states, includes linguistic, communicative and plurilingual skills and knowledge and critical understanding of language and communication as key elements of these competences (Council of Europe, 2018a). The outline of what is included among these skills, knowledge and critical understanding is reproduced in Table 6.1.

Table 6.1 Descriptors of skills and knowledge related to language and communication

Linguistic, communicative and plurilingual skills	Knowledge and critical understanding of language and communication
Linguistic, communicative and plurilingual skills are those skills that are required to communicate effectively and appropriately with other people. They include the following abilities and skills, among others: 1. The ability to communicate clearly in a range of situations – this includes expressing one's beliefs, opinions, interests and needs, explaining and clarifying ideas, advocating, promoting, arguing, reasoning, discussing, debating, persuading and negotiating. 2. The ability to meet the communicative demands of intercultural situations by using more than one language or language variety or by using a shared language or lingua franca to understand another language. 3. The ability to express oneself confidently and without aggression, even in situations where one is disadvantaged through a disparity of power, and to express a fundamental disagreement with another person in a manner that is nevertheless respectful of that person's dignity and rights. 4. The ability to recognise the different forms of expression and the different communicative conventions (both verbal and non-verbal) in the communications employed by other social groups and their cultures. 5. The ability to adjust and modify one's communicative behaviour so that one uses the communicative conventions (both verbal and non-verbal) that are appropriate to one's interlocutor(s) and to the prevailing cultural setting. The ability to adjust and modify one's communicative behaviour so that one uses the communicative conventions (both verbal and non-verbal) that are appropriate to one's interlocutor(s) and to the prevailing cultural setting. 6. The ability to ask questions of clarification in an appropriate and sensitive manner in cases where the meanings being expressed by another person are unclear or where inconsistencies between the verbal and non-verbal messages produced by another person are detected. 7. The ability to manage breakdowns in communication, for example by requesting repetitions or reformulations from others, or providing restatements, revisions or simplifications of one's own misunderstood communications. 8. The ability to act as a linguistic mediator in intercultural exchanges, including skills in translating, interpreting and explaining, and to act as an intercultural mediator by assisting others to understand and appreciate the characteristics of someone or something that is perceived to have a different cultural affiliation from their own. (Council of Europe, 2018a: 50–51)	Knowledge and critical understanding of language and communication have many different aspects, and include: 1. Knowledge of the socially appropriate verbal and non-verbal communicative conventions which operate in the language(s) which one uses. 2. Understanding that people of other cultural affiliations may follow different verbal and non-verbal communicative conventions from oneself, which are meaningful from their perspective, even when they are using the same language as oneself. 3. Understanding that people who have different cultural affiliations can perceive the meanings of communications in different ways. 4. Understanding that there are multiple ways of speaking in any given language and a variety of ways of using the same language. 5. Understanding how the use of language is a cultural practice that operates as a carrier of information, meanings and identities which circulate in the culture in which that language is embedded. 6. Understanding of the fact that languages may express culturally shared ideas in a unique way or express unique ideas which may be difficult to access through another language. 7. Understanding the social impact and effects on others of different communication styles, including understanding how different communication styles may clash or result in a breakdown of communication. 8. Understanding how one's own assumptions, preconceptions, perceptions, beliefs and judgments are related to the specific language(s) which one speaks. (Council of Europe, 2018a: 53)

Source: Council of Europe (2018a)

The skills, knowledge and critical awareness listed in Table 6.1 should be seen as prerequisites for effective teaching that enables students to acquire the competences referred to in order to participate in a democratic culture, but, at a different level, should, in our view, also be essential elements of any initial teacher education programme. If they are not addressed in teacher education, how will teachers be able to help their students to develop the literacy and oracy they need to succeed at school where they are required to express themselves in speech and writing, and later to achieve their potential in life and to participate in democratic cultures?

Distilling elements of the lists in Table 6.1, it seems to us that there are several desirable objectives for a course on language in education for future or practising teachers. These should include the following:

- To raise future teachers' awareness of, and skills in, the many uses to which language can be put in teaching their subject, including questioning skills, the links between talk, thinking and learning, 'scaffolding' concepts and information to provide students with gradual incremental cognitive support, and the ability to explain and clarify key subject-based concepts.
- To enable future teachers to analyse and work with the typical discourse patterns of their own subject area, as manifested in textbooks, articles and other written sources as well as in spoken exchanges in professional contexts.
- To sensitise future teachers to the ways in which children use language to make sense of their learning and of the world around them, and to ways in which language can facilitate or impede children's learning.
- To promote and manage dialogic teaching and learning, which involves opening up the classroom to discussion and interaction between teacher and learners, but also, importantly, among learners themselves.
- To train future teachers in ways of promoting oracy and literacy in their learners.

The following extract from the two-year BEd curriculum mandated for providers by the National Council for Teacher Education in India goes some way towards meeting these objectives:

> (1) Understanding the language background of students, as first or second language users of the language used in teaching the subject. The aim will be to create sensitivity to the language diversity that exists in the classrooms ...
> (2) To understand the nature of classroom discourse and develop strategies for using oral language in the classroom in a manner that promotes learning in the subject area ... oral language in the

classroom; discussion as a tool for learning; the nature of questioning in the classroom – types of questions and teacher control.
(3) To understand the nature of reading comprehension in the content areas (informational reading). Writing in specific content areas with familiarity of different registers should also receive attention. Reading in the content areas – social sciences, science, mathematics; nature of expository texts vs. narrative texts ... text structures; examining content area textbooks; reading strategies for children – note-making, summarizing; making reading-writing connections; process writing; analysing children's writings to understand their conceptions; writing with a sense of purpose – writing to learn and understand.

Source: http://ncte-india.org/Curriculum%20Framework/B.Ed%20Curriculum.pdf

Standards for teacher education in Ghana include the following statement and set of expected outcomes for student teachers under the heading:

Literacy Studies: Ghanaian Languages and English

Language is the key to success in education and life. Getting this right is the most critical issue for our children's future and for education in Ghana [...]

- Communicate fluently and effectively to engage learners in Ghanaian language and English.
- Use the L1 to teach other subjects ...
- Assist transition from L1 as medium of instruction to the use of L2 from Primary 4 onwards.
- Identify children with literacy problems in both Ghanaian language and English and provide remediation.
- Use L1 as a springboard for improving L2 learning and communication, especially at the lower primary level: oral, reading and writing skills. (Source: Ministry of Education Ghana 2017: 23–24)

It might be considered that, because both Ghana and India are countries with complex multilingual contexts, it is appropriate that such modules should be an integral part of teacher education, while in other less linguistically diverse national contexts the language and communication issues are included within other modules related to theories and practices of education and classroom pedagogy. We would not agree with this view for reasons explained below.

The diagram in Figure 6.1 was developed for another linguistically and culturally complex environment, Hong Kong in the 1990s, but it is one way of representing the close relationship between language and 'content' in the teaching of any subject.

For us, Figure 6.1 neatly illustrates the first of three arguments for including language and communication modules in teacher education for teachers of all subjects anywhere: if language is so crucial to learning, it is evident that all teachers should focus on how language and communication function in the world beyond the school gates as well as in the narrower context of the educational organisation. Young adults entering the teaching profession, like those beginning careers in other professions, may be highly literate and very competent communicators, but depending on the way language was dealt with in their own education, they may well never have consciously thought about how language works in interaction and discourse, let alone in teaching and learning. They need at the very least to become aware of the linguistic and communicative options that are available to teachers, and those which are likely to be most effective for different educational purposes. Figure 6.1 also demonstrates the relationship between concepts in any

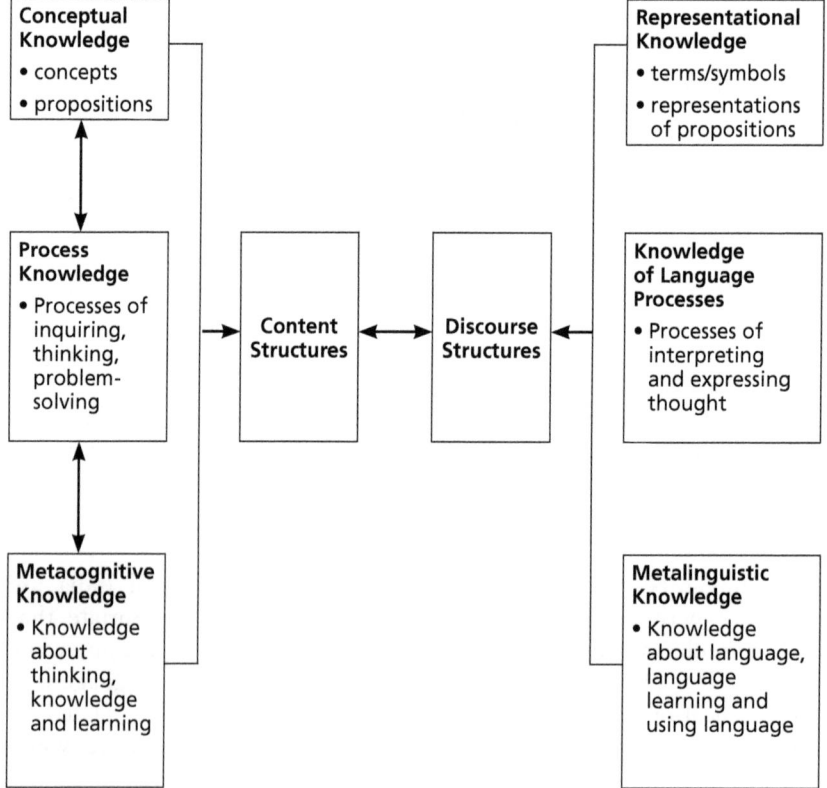

Figure 6.1 The relationship between content and language
Source: Adapted from Clark et al. (1994: 19)

school subject or discipline area on the one hand, and the language that is used to explain these concepts on the other. It also draws attention to the role of language in different thinking processes and to ways in which metacognitive awareness and language awareness complement each other.

Also, as illustrated earlier in the chapter, whatever subject is being taught, a priority task for teachers is to help students to develop their 'transversal' oracy and literacy skills, which will be important for later life as well as for success in the subject in question. This will be much more of a challenge for novice teachers if their initial training has not provided opportunities for them to focus on how language functions in oral and written discourse and in interactions in the classroom around the subjects they will be teaching. The third argument is that, whatever the national context, diversity, including linguistic and cultural diversity, is an increasingly salient and challenging feature of education at all levels. As explained below, it is likely that, in most countries in Europe and elsewhere, teachers of all subjects will need to acquire the expertise to cope with groups where several first languages other than the language of schooling are spoken and where students, including young children, come from diverse cultural and educational backgrounds. A separate dimension of any focus on language and communication should concern handling these situations in a manner that ensures that the diverse linguistic and cultural backgrounds of students are not only acknowledged and respected but are built on in learning.

One means of handling language issues in teacher education and professional development is through observation schemes, including peer and self-observation (through audio and video recordings). There is evidence that some providers of teacher education do this for certain elements of their courses. For example, the University College London Institute of Education developed a postgraduate certificate of education (PGCE) module on 'Removing barriers to learning' for children with special educational needs which is accompanied by a variety of handouts. One of these is the 'inclusive teaching observation checklist', part of which focuses on the issue of the language and communication strategies used by teachers for pupils with special needs, as shown in the extracts in Table 6.2. The observation checklist, also covers various other areas such as motivation, managing peer relations and formative assessment in its six pages. There are many ways of formulating questions and criteria in such observation checklists, whether they have a broad focus, for example the general effectiveness of teaching through subheadings such as these, or a narrow one that homes in on certain aspects of teaching, such as, for example, teacher-student and student-student interaction. Further checklists of the kind illustrated below exploring in greater depth the use of language and communication strategies with and among all pupils at primary and secondary level would be very useful resources in all initial teacher education courses. It is very difficult to determine whether oracy

Table 6.2 Selected questions from the 'Inclusive teaching observation checklist' PGCE handout

Communication between adults and pupils	Yes/no	Evidence
• Are questions pitched to challenge pupils at all levels? • Has the teacher planned some open-ended questions for pupils with communication impairments? • If necessary, do pupils with communication impairments receive support, for example, pre-tutoring, to help them answer open-ended questions?		
• Does the teacher check that pupils understand instructions – for example by asking pupils to explain them in their own words?		
• Is new or difficult vocabulary clarified, written up, displayed and returned to?		
• Does the teacher give time or support before responses are required – for example, personal thinking time, partner talk, persisting with progressively greater 'scaffolding' until the pupil can answer correctly?		

Source: UCL Institute of Education (2012: 37–38)

and literacy issues and teachers' use of and attention to language are consistent features of observation and discussion during teaching practice in initial teacher education but, in our view, they certainly should be. In the UK, several non-governmental organisations are working on this. The Communication Trust, for example, has developed a *Speech, Language and Communication Framework* (Communication Trust, 2017) detailing the competences needed by people including teachers working with children, including those with special language and communication needs. The descriptors of competence cover four successive levels of expertise and areas ranging from speech and language development to 'the communication environment'. In another initiative, Voice 21, a London-based organisation campaigning for greater attention to be paid to the development of oracy skills in British schools, has published a report on the issue of oracy development in schools (Millard & Menzies, 2016). It includes insights gleaned from a survey of more than 900 teachers. Among these insights are that:

> The greatest barrier standing in the way of quality and consistent oracy in all lessons is a lack of time, but other constraints include:
>
> • Teachers' lack of confidence and expertise, exacerbated by a paucity of training
> • Teachers' perception that oracy is only occasionally relevant when teaching, or relevant only in certain subjects such as English
> • A lack of active support from school leadership' (Millard & Menzies, 2016: 5)

Voice 21 and the University of Cambridge Faculty of Education have developed *The Oracy Skills Framework* (Voice 21 and the University of

Cambridge, 2018). This provides a simple checklist that enables teachers to work on and assess the various aspects of oral communication that children need to develop in their schooling. This covers physical, linguistic, cognitive, social and emotional dimensions of oracy.

Question 3: Would the objectives of a language in education course be the same now as they were back in 1975, or might they have changed over time?

The objectives we listed above might equally have been priorities back in 1975 at the time of the Bullock Report, but the world has changed in many ways since then, and for 21st century purposes, we would add at least two more:

- to raise future teachers' awareness of the links between language and culture, with particular reference to the multilingual and multicultural dimensions found in many modern classes; and
- to raise teachers' critical language awareness, thereby enabling them to assess the value and relevance of ideas found in internet sources and information in news media, and to support the development of this skill in their future learners.

The above extracts from curriculum documents from India and South Africa show evidence of multilingual and multi-ethnic dimensions and it would be useful, in this age of mass migration in the face of conflicts in different parts of the world, for these aspects to be addressed in European and North American teacher education curricula. In Austria, for example, some teachers report that they have found it difficult to deal with the sudden diversity which refugees have brought into their classrooms. Morawski and Budke (2017) report that some classrooms in Germany include up to 30% of students of non-German origin. In the German state of Nordrhein-Westfalen, a module called 'German for students with migration backgrounds' has been an obligatory part of all teacher education since 2009. Its aim is to raise teachers' awareness of the challenges that arise in culturally and linguistically heterogeneous classrooms.

Question 4: What place do language issues and language awareness have in CPD and in-service teacher training (INSET) for subject teachers?

As is clear from the discussion in Chapter 5, INSET is a crucial if very heterogeneous type of teacher education. In any education system, many times more teachers are working in schools and other institutions than are undergoing initial training. Moreover, these practising teachers may have had little opportunity for training since they first qualified, are often very experienced or may be under pressure and suffering from low motivation or 'burn out'. INSET and CPD can give a much needed boost to professional engagement as well as providing opportunities to acquire new knowledge and skills and to exchange expertise with colleagues, which can itself be very motivating.

In 2004, research was carried out by two educational foundations in England, the Esmée Fairbairn Foundation and the Villiers Park Educational Trust, to explore the nature and quality of CPD opportunities experienced by teachers across the secondary curriculum in England and Wales (Leaton Gray, 2005). Fifty-eight teachers responded to the questionnaires and follow-up work was carried out with focus groups of teachers. Among other questions, teachers were asked to describe any types of CPD that they had been involved in during their careers. As one might expect, it was found that professional development in schools took many forms including:

- whole-school training days;
- the induction, mentoring and assessment of individual teachers;
- peer observation;
- collaborative planning and evaluation; and
- self-evaluation.

Looking beyond their individual schools, teachers built or joined networks, for example, by:

- visiting other schools;
- attending conferences;
- undertaking joint training exercises with other schools;
- joining teacher networks; and
- engaging with specialist subject associations.

Outside the school environment, teachers' activities included:

- attending short courses by commercial and not-for-profit providers;
- studying for higher degrees validated by universities;
- taking part in examining processes (e.g. by becoming examiners);
- participating in online courses; and
- taking part in secondments, sabbaticals and exchanges (adapted from Leaton Gray, 2005: 9).

Another interesting aspect of CPD for teachers, which was illustrated in a 2015 Eurydice Report (European Commission/EACEA/Eurydice, 2015), was the degree to which CPD was felt to be needed in relation to certain common topics. This is illustrated in Figure 6.2.

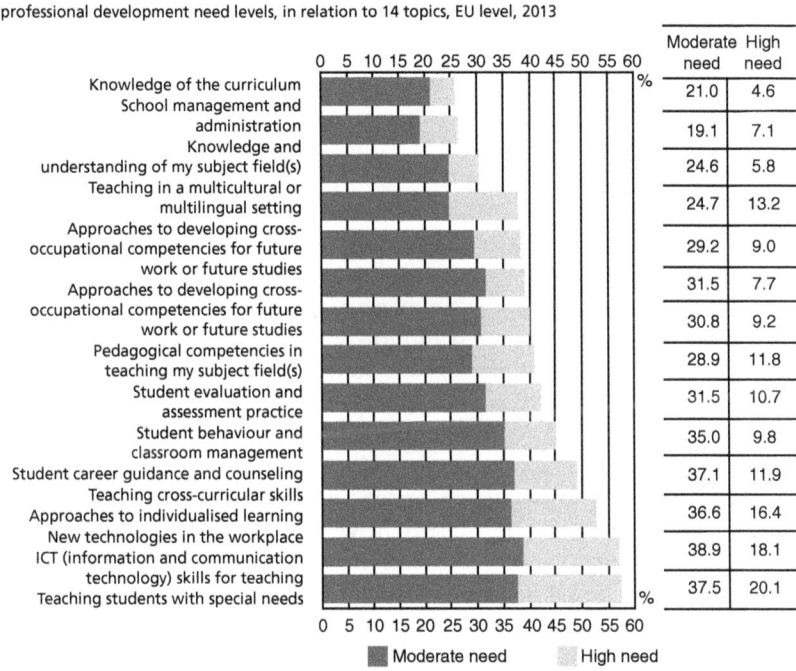

Figure 6.2 Expression of CPD needs in relation to specific topics
Source: European Commission/EACEA/Eurydice (2015: 58)

Of the topics listed, the following can be regarded as closely or quite closely associated with language and communication issues and awareness:

- teaching in a multicultural or multilingual setting;
- approaches to developing cross-occupational competences for future work or studies;
- teaching cross-curricular skills; and
- teaching students with special needs.

Some of these are considered to be quite high priority; however, this EU-wide picture masks considerable differences in levels of felt need between different countries. For example, 'teaching in a multicultural environment or multilingual setting' was more often cited as a priority in Spain, Italy, Cyprus and Portugal, perhaps because of the high exposure of those countries to migration, while it was felt to be less essential in Croatia, Latvia and the Netherlands. It is striking that language across the curriculum, literacy and oracy do not figure among teachers' perceived priorities in this survey.

Nevertheless, there is evidence in some contexts that language issues are taken account of in in-service courses for teachers of all subjects. Informants in Austria and in Germany have told us about courses in 'Sprachsensibler Unterricht' (language-sensitive teaching), in which the central mediating role of language is highlighted with stress on pedagogical language skills such as explaining, questioning, task setting and responding to learners' contributions in a class setting. In one course in the catalogue of the Akademie für Lehrerfortbildung (Academy for Teacher Training and Personnel Development) in Dillingen, Bavaria, the focus is on helping middle schoolteachers to be more aware of the difficulties school pupils have with interpreting task rubrics. In our experience, this is a widespread need in most contexts which applies both to rubrics for tests and examinations and to task instructions given in class, whether orally or in writing. Another course in the same institution ('Leseförderung in allen Fächern') deals with ways of promoting reading skills in all subjects across the curriculum.

In Austria, a project team under the auspices of the Ministry of Education, Science and Research works entirely in the area of language-sensitive teaching and maintains a website with resources and a list of available courses for teachers and teacher educators (see http://www.oesz.at/sprachsensiblerunterricht/main_02.php). The courses listed include some which focus on a specific subject and others that are more general.

In the Moscow Region in the Russian Federation, where serving state schoolteachers are obliged to take 72 hours of in-service courses every five years, the main provider, the Moscow Institute of Open Education, offers courses in 'Metasubject Skills' including the appropriate use of language to scaffold learning. One course on the development of literacy and oracy is described in these terms:

> As a result of training in this program, you will increase the level of professional competence in the field of methods of forming reader literacy (receptive speech actions) and the construction of text (productive speech actions). (see https://www.dpomos.ru/curs/mioo.php?PAGEN_1=19)

However, these are all relatively isolated examples and there is undoubtedly a need for more programmes and resources for practising teachers to enable them to use language effectively in their classrooms.

Question 5: What can subject teachers learn about language from CLIL teachers?

CLIL (content and language integrated learning) was discussed briefly in Chapters 2 and 3. It is a set of approaches that are most often used when teaching a subject such as science, geography or history through a language (most commonly English) that is not the students' first language and is not used across the whole curriculum. The name 'content and language integrated learning' could, however, be applied to all teaching since learning how to talk and write clearly and coherently about a subject should be an integral part of learning subject 'content' or 'knowledge'. While CLIL takes different forms in different European countries, there are examples from research that could well be informative for subject teachers and teacher educators. Some examples are provided below.

As geography specialists, Morawski and Budke make the case for a strong language dimension even for native German students in geography classes: 'Language in geography almost naturally includes complex performances that need to be supported by language awareness' (Morawski & Budke, 2017: 51). Geography teacher education at the University of Cologne includes a practical semester based full time at schools. As part of this 'Praktikum', student teachers undertake an empirical project where they are asked to observe and identify language actions that are specifically relevant in geography classrooms and how pupils are supported in these actions by their teachers. Thus, language awareness has become an essential part of initial teacher education in geography at the University of Cologne as well as certain others, and is also increasingly a feature of continuing professional development for geography teachers.

Morawski and Budke identify teaching in CLIL classes as a potential source of experience that could be transferred to monolingual classes. They also draw on techniques and activity types that are usually found in foreign language classes, for example, strategies such as parallel text work with model texts.

> Pupils receive an example of the required material (e.g. a description or analysis of a pie chart of the economy in the Los Angeles region) from which they can model relevant phrases and structures. Then they transfer these exemplary phrases to a new topic and task (e.g. the description and analysis of a pie chart of the economy in the European Union) using the learned methodical structures and phrases. So the phrases and structures are imitated, copied, and transferred in an example-and-transfer process. This not only improves understanding of geographic phrases and terms [...], but the model texts also define what structural and contextual criteria a description or a discussion contains in geography. (Morawski & Budke, 2017: 58)

Other examples are to be found in a useful article on 'Criteria for producing CLIL learning material' (Mehisto, 2012). An example relating to one of the 10 criteria proposed is reproduced below.

> **Criterion 3: Quality CLIL materials foster learning skills development and learner autonomy**
> Prior to a challenging text, a learning material [sic] could contain a think-pair-share exercise requiring students to brainstorm ways of coping with the language and/or the content in a difficult text. Or, in a similar context, the learning material can guide students through a research exercise to find 10 ways of coping with the language and/or content in difficult texts. Or it could include a pre-reading assignment asking students to skim or scan a text for unfamiliar words and to guess their meaning prior to reading. Or the material could ask students to read a text several times for different purposes such as once for analysing some aspects of language, and a second time to find three key ideas contained therein. (Mehisto, 2012: 9)

While the criteria apply specifically to CLIL materials for use with students taking subject classes in a language that is not their first language, many of the recommendations offered could equally well be applied to materials prepared or created by the teacher for a group of students working in their first language or the main language of schooling. The underlying message is that students need help to progressively develop the literacy and oracy skills required to deal with the information or concepts being taught, and there are standard techniques for helping them to do this, depending on the topic and the focus of the materials. Moreover, these techniques can be creatively adapted, built on and extended by teachers to meet the motivational and linguistic needs of groups that may well be heterogeneous.

It seems that there is a possible point of departure here for the design of modules on language in initial and in-service training courses and that this might be the time to start building on research insights such as these. The same could be said of critical language awareness, which is an accepted area of scholarly research and publication (e.g. see Fairclough, 2013; Ivanič, 1990). This extension of the term language awareness refers to the need to focus on the manner in which discourse is used to exert power of a political, social or socioeconomic nature; for example, between those promoting a product or service and their potential customers, or those with political power and status and the people whose lives will be impacted by their proposed or adopted policies. The necessity of such critical language awareness is evident in a period of increasingly pervasive use (and misuse) of social media, of difficulties distinguishing between real and 'fake' news, that is, what is true and what is not, and real threats to democratic culture in various parts of the world. If it is important that school-age students should become critically aware of the way language is used and of the way they themselves use language, it is essential that initial teacher education gives future teachers opportunities to raise their own critical language awareness and explore pedagogic options for use in their work as teachers.

Another rich source for language and communication elements in teacher education is research into classroom talk and dialogue (e.g. Edwards & Westgate, 1994). While, as these authors point out in their introduction, there are constraints to how much classroom language can be analysed and reflected upon in the time available, it seems to us that there are good reasons why teachers should have the experience of examining student and teacher talk in the context of a partially recorded lesson, preferably including at least one of their own lessons. What the experience, if well guided, can reveal to them spans not only the extent and variety of language used but the power balance between teacher talk and student talk, the usefulness of the questions asked by the teacher, the value of dialogue between pairs and within groups, and ultimately the effectiveness of talk in supporting and leading to learning. In spite of the evident value both of critical language awareness and of research into classroom discourse, we have found only limited evidence of their impact on the design and content of 21st century teacher education programmes.

Concluding Remarks

Having explored issues in language teacher education in Chapters 4 and 5, in this chapter we have sought to make a case for far greater attention to be paid to language and communication in initial teacher education and continuing professional development for all teachers from pre-primary to higher secondary levels, and indeed beyond. It is no coincidence that language centres in universities, for example in the UK, are increasingly providing language and literacy support not only to students coming from abroad but also to students for whom English is their first language. Equally, in adult education, students wishing to gain qualifications are finding that their lack of language knowledge and awareness and the frequently insufficient level of literacy and oracy that they achieved as youngsters in mainstream school are obstacles to achievement that need to be overcome. In our view, it is the duty of teachers of all subjects at all levels, not just of teachers of the language of schooling, to ensure that any school leaver has acquired the necessary language and communication skills to find suitable employment and or to continue their education. To achieve this, initial and in-service teacher education programmes for all teachers need to focus on ensuring that teachers are aware of the importance of language in their teaching and also have the skills needed to develop their students' language competence.

Part 3 moves away from teacher education and professional development to focus on the role and expectations of the various stakeholders in language education, and the ways in which policy is formulated and change is implemented. The stakeholders who are discussed in Chapter 7 of course include teachers, teacher educators and managers of teachers.

Questions for reflection and discussion

In your own context, or one you are familiar with:

(1) How much attention is given to literacy, oracy and language across the curriculum in pre-service teacher education courses?
(2) Which of the skills and competences listed in Table 6.1 stand out as being particularly relevant and important? Please give reasons for your choices.
(3) Imagine you have a chance to design a 20-hour in-service course on language across the curriculum for a target group of teachers of your choice. What would your objectives be and which topics would you include as priorities?

Part 3: Stakeholder Interests

Part 1 considered the role of language in education and the development of language education over recent decades, while Part 2 offered an overview of teacher education for language teachers, and the place of language in teacher education more generally. Part 3 considers the expectations of the various stakeholders in language education, as well as the influence they have on policy development and implementation in the field of language education, and the part they play in determining the role of language and language awareness across the curriculum. 'Stakeholders' covers a wide spectrum of interested parties, from learners themselves and their parents to employers and those admitting students to further or higher education, teachers and other working at 'the sharp end' in educational institutions, ministries of education and their advisors and political masters, as well as suppliers of official examinations, publishers of educational resources and various others.

A key issue we wish to raise in Part 3 is the extent to which these various stakeholders consult with one another and share similar values and goals, and the ways in which it may be possible, where necessary, to improve the status quo. For there is little doubt that policy, including changes in policy, and implementation generally have a considerable impact on stakeholders of all kinds, including on the intended primary beneficiaries of language education, the students, as well as on the development of their transversal skills and their competences for democratic culture (Council of Europe, 2018b), of which language skills and awareness are an integral part.

Part 3: Stakeholder interests

7 The Perspectives of Stakeholders in Language Education

This chapter will examine the perspectives of the various stakeholders in 'the front line' of language education, those who are direct or indirect beneficiaries and those who are providers. Our purpose is to consider how the needs, motivations and views of these various groups are or could be taken into account in the search for improvements in the quality and relevance of language education.

Language Learners

It is logical to start with the most obvious of these, the students or pupils whose lives and future careers language education can make a real and far-reaching difference to. How do they themselves view language learning and what are their motivations and expectations? Various studies have been carried out over the years to look at the main motivational factors and expectations of language learners in various contexts. One of the best-known research projects was the Attitude/Motivation Test Battery (AMTB) led by Robert Gardner. The AMTB was developed in the 1980s to explore attitudes and motivations towards the learning of French and the culture of French speakers in Canada. Gardner's work was in support of a socioeducational model of language learning, illustrated in Figure 7.1.

Here Gardner's contention, based on his much earlier work with Wallace Lambert, (e.g. Gardner & Lambert, 1972) is that:

> the individual's motivation to learn a second language is related to two classes of variables. One is Attitudes toward the Learning Situation. Clearly, the nature of the learning situation will influence a student's level of motivation. An interesting, devoted skilled teacher with a good command of the language, an exciting curriculum, carefully constructed lesson plans, and meaningful evaluation procedures will promote higher

levels of motivation, other things being equal, than a teacher lacking in some of these attributes.

The other variable seen to be important in influencing motivation is Integrativeness [...]. Individuals for whom their own ethnolinguistic heritage is a major part of their sense of identity would be low in integrativeness; those for whom their ethnicity is not a major component, and who are interested in other cultural communities would be high in integrativeness. (Gardner, 2005: 7 – author's emphasis).

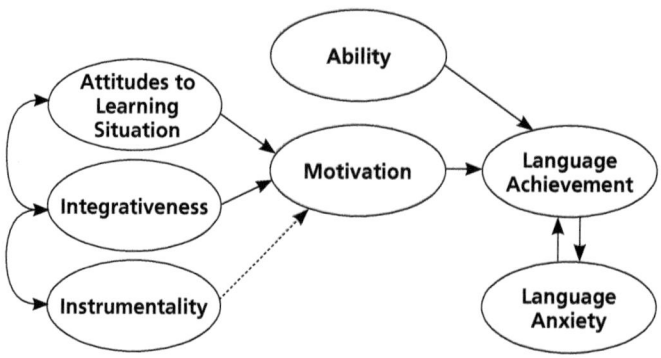

Figure 7.1 The socioeducational model of language learning
Source: Gardner, 2005: 6

It is proposed that these two variable factors, combined with a learner's intelligence help to determine his or her achievement in language learning. As implied by the well-known distinction proposed by Gardner and Lambert (1972), motivation to learn languages can also be positively affected by the desire of learners to be able to use the language for practical 'instrumental' reasons related to work, study or tourism. An international version of the AMTB was developed in the early 2000s to explore whether the correlations between integrativeness, motivation, anxiety and achievement found among English-speaking learners of French in Canada were replicated in other countries: Spain, Croatia, Romania and Poland. The correlations (summarised in Gardner, 2004) were found to be very similar, including across different age groups.

This kind of research underlines the importance of giving attention to these factors. There may be little that can be done to increase learners' readiness to learn languages apart from encouraging at an early age the awareness of language features, such as pronunciation, word similarities and word order. Equally, it may be felt that an individual learner's 'integrativeness' is not easily fostered, although familiarity with and awareness of other cultures and other ways of using language at an early age may well help. Nevertheless, other environmental aspects, such as the ways in which teachers work and communicate in the classroom and the methods and resources they use, may have a strong impact on motivation, on limiting anxiety and ultimately on achievement.

More recent research into learners' motivation and expectations was carried out by a group of Chinese researchers and reported on by Jin *et al.* (2014). Here the focus was on 65 young learners aged 7 years old and 63 aged 9 years old learning English in four Chinese primary schools in Wuhan, and their parents. Unlike the questionnaires devised by Gardner and his colleagues, the method used with the children was the elicitation of metaphors using picture cards. Among the 29 items that featured in the metaphor analysis, the results revealed a strong consensus among the children regarding five of them: the usefulness of English for their future life; the fact that English was felt by those around them to be a 'waste of time'; the importance of 'trying one's best' to learn the language; the perception that learning English is 'interesting'; and the belief that English will be useful if one travels abroad. As might be expected of research among children of this young age, there is a certain amount of conformity evident in the responses, but they do provide evidence that can inform teaching and curriculum design in that context.

An important question arises about what happens to language learning in mainstream education when students move from primary to secondary education. Although we have been unable to find research into learners' views on this transition, the fact that in many national contexts, for example, from our recent experience in Tunisia and Central Asia, it means a break in continuity in both progression and teaching methods that can undermine the attractiveness of language learning. As briefly discussed in Chapter 2, often, secondary teachers of languages, unlike many of their primary level counterparts, see themselves as subject specialists. They also find it challenging to properly assess the language levels achieved in primary school by individual students in their classes. In such cases, rather than setting out to build on what competence has been achieved, they are tempted simply to start again, citing the importance of revision and consolidation, and perhaps adopting the serious-seeming and challenging issue of 'grammar' as a new main focus. Nothing is more likely to dampen any enthusiasm for languages that children have acquired during primary education than being told by implication that what they have learned was not worthwhile. Therefore, it is understandable that adolescents, suddenly confronted with a full and complicated range of subjects, may lose any appreciation they may have had that learning languages is important to them. This is especially noticeable in England, where the curriculum includes study of a foreign or classical (i.e. Latin or Greek) language between the ages of 7 and 14, after which age foreign languages are optional (UK Department for Education, 2014: 252–256). The result has been a noticeable decline in the numbers of students taking school leaving examinations in languages and a consequent shrinking in university language departments. The impact of such a policy on children's communicative and intercultural competences, and their education in general, is yet to be evaluated.

What can be said about language learning in higher education? An example of research into the needs of 284 learners of English at one Indonesian university provides information about the attitudes and expectations of such learners (Poedjiastutie & Oliver, 2017). A questionnaire and focus group discussions were used to elicit information about the learners' views of their language learning needs. Although the course in question is describes as English for specific purposes, a large majority of them (71%) considered speaking the language to be the main priority. The research also focused on their goals in undertaking the course. The top seven goals for these students were:

(1) To participate in overseas training and scholarship programme (nominated by 44.36% of them)
(2) To have better life opportunities – travelling, using more sophisticated technology etc. (42.96%)
(3) To establish business with overseas people. (38.38%)
(4) To be able to work in prestigious international companies/institutions (33.09%)
(5) To improve TOEFL and IELTS scores (32.39%)
(6) To be able to understand English speaking people and cultures (23.94%)
(7) To be able to read and understand English journals and books (21.47%)

(Poedjiastutie & Oliver, 2017: 129)

While these responses reflect the expectations of a limited number of learners in a specific educational context, it is clear that eliciting or accessing such information about learners' goals and priorities could strengthen the focus and relevance of courses and provide invaluable information for teachers. Our view is that too little guidance is given to teachers about building such information gathering and consultation into the initial stages of their courses. This should be given greater priority in teacher education curricula and in-service training.

As evidenced by this example, English, the first foreign language in most countries except those that are English-speaking, is a special case. According to the Eurydice Brief on *Teaching Languages at School in Europe* (European Commission, 2017), by 2014 nearly 84% of all children in primary school were learning at least one language, primarily English, compared with 67% in 2005 (European Commission, 2017: 5), and by 2016 in a majority of EU member states children were beginning a foreign language before the age of 8 years old. Although much depends on the quality of teaching and learning opportunities they experience, many school-age students take a different view of English as compared with other languages they may be required to learn because, even by early secondary level, like the Indonesian students discussed above, they see English as an avenue to the digital world and international connections, as well as to the musical and screen entertainment that they enjoy. In some countries, national policy has for different reasons effectively given English the status of a 'basic skill', allotting more hours in the curriculum and adding options such as CLIL. But other languages may quickly lose out, especially if hours are reduced to allow more time for English and if the teaching methods used remain traditional and provide little opportunity for students to communicate. Less widely used ethnic languages such as Valenciano in Spain or Kashubian in Poland, which may also form part of students' heritage, may be especially vulnerable if hours are reduced. Students may only begin to think about employment and/or further and higher education at a later age and realise how important languages can be (including, where relevant, minority languages). By then it may be too late as, in spite of advertising to the contrary, learning to use another language in the real world of employment or study is not a speedy process.

Parents and their Role

Luckily, many students are actively supported and encouraged – and occasionally pushed – to work on their languages by other stakeholders, especially their parents, who from their own experience and observation are likely to be more aware of the longer-term advantages and opportunities that languages can bring. A key factor in the relentless increase in the prominence of English in school curricula is pressure from parents, who feel that their children's future opportunities and ability to achieve their potential will be damaged if they are unable to communicate effectively in spoken and written English by the end of their schooling. As the Eurydice Report points out, 'it is a common view among parents and educators across Europe that an early start in foreign language learning brings better results in language proficiency' (European Commission, 2017: 5). Many parents who have the means, also send their young and teenage children to supplementary English courses after school or in the school holidays, and some private primary schools, for example in Spain, outsource their English teaching to private sector language schools rather than trying to train or recruit teachers of their own to teach the language effectively. This does not, however, necessarily mean that English is universally well taught. The professional development of practising language teachers is a considerable challenge due to time and resources, and many teachers find it hard to move on from the teaching methods that they were exposed to as students and practised early in their careers. Moreover, parents may have their own views about foreign language learning and many, owing to their own experiences, have a strong interest in grammar and test results rather than in practical language proficiency.

A further issue for parents is that they may find it difficult to understand how they can help their children to learn a language and prepare for exams given the way that modern textbooks are framed and organised, now with much less emphasis on grammar rules and usually no sign of bilingual lists of vocabulary to be learned by heart.

Employers

Another EU document (European Commission, 2012) highlighted the link between language competences and employability within the EU. This working document states (European Commission, 2012: 19): 'There is a mismatch between the supply of, and the labour market demand for, language competences. ... Poor foreign language competences are a serious handicap for young Europeans entering the labour market today, as well as for companies who want to sell their products and services in the global marketplace.' The European Commission's report on *Languages for Jobs* (2011), another strand in the Education & Training 2020 initiative, echoes this sentiment:

> Seen from an employment perspective, language skills are always a means to an end. Academics as well as students in initial vocational education and training need to make sure that their language skills become part of a qualifications profile that matches the future requirements on the labour market. The demand for foreign languages is steadily rising. Gradually more employers adopt recruitment strategies reflecting the fact that they operate in a multilingual society and/or compete on global markets. (European Commission, 2011: 13)

Interestingly, this report points out that according to their sources, employers in certain sectors are finding English is not on its own sufficient and even for English users, being able to communicate in another language can have important advantages in terms of cultural openness, adaptability and being able to mediate between languages if the need arises. Owing to its geographical location and business priorities, a good case in point is Austria.

> The Austrian *Institut für Bildungsforschung der Wirtschaft* has published several reports and research papers projecting future needs in Austria. It appears that English is far from sufficient as a lingua franca for doing business in Central and Eastern Europe, where German and Russian are still frequently used for international trade. In addition to these main languages which, in Austria, also include Italian, companies operating on regional levels and doing cross-border business certainly welcome language skills in Czech, Slovak, Hungarian or Slovene – depending on which partners they do business with. Any such competence will not

> only have a very positive impact on business relations spanning across linguistic and political borders but on the development of social and intercultural awareness and on mutual relations in general. (European Commission, 2011: 17)

In its annex, the *Languages for Jobs* report makes numerous recommendations for improving the supply of potential employees with the necessary language skills, one of which is: 'Improve the structures for dialogue between education and the world of work. Such a dialogue is a prerequisite to match the supply of language skills to demand from the labour market' (European Commission, 2011: 38).

In summary, many employers in Europe and well beyond now see language skills and intercultural experience and competence as important criteria in recruitment and indeed in making their internal training arrangements. The extent to which such factors are decisive in selecting job candidates depends on the type of business and the markets they are dealing with or trying to develop, but the relevance of languages and cultural awareness to employment is not restricted to large international corporations. Small- and medium-sized enterprises (SMEs) are also concerned, as the *Languages for Jobs* report points out:

> As smaller companies are getting more and more international, they gradually become more aware of language barriers and what it takes to break them. According to a study about the internationalisation of European SMEs published by the European Commission in 2010, when companies start exporting, language and cultural barriers are perceived as important obstacles. (European Commission, 2011: 13–14)

One of the issues for employers is how they bring the evolving desired profiles of their employees to the attention of educators, parents and students themselves. This is a classic example of the need for joined up thinking and consultation among stakeholders in education, in this case language education. In spite of valiant efforts and many recommendations from the EU and other bodies, this kind of coordination is sadly lacking in many countries. In countries such as Austria (cited above) and Germany, where there is a strong tradition of vocational education, consultation between educators and employers is in-built and ongoing. Here, there is a stronger current of washback influence on mainstream education, including on language education, and more plentiful opportunities for students and their parents to grasp the potential value of language skills in the job market and to work on developing these early on rather than after leaving school. Schools in several countries have begun to include work placements in their curricula, and in further and higher education internships are an integral part of certain courses. A good example of this was the 'English for the World of Work' project in Romania (https://www.britishcouncil.ro/en/programmes/education/schools/vocational-education-resources/lesson-plans), where students from vocational colleges shadowed people working in SMEs with the explicit task of observing how and for what purposes English was used during their working day. This had a positive impact on motivation and led to students producing their own materials focusing on special purpose uses of English. Such opportunities, whether international or not, which involve the practical use of foreign languages can provide very beneficial experience of language and other life skills relevant to future employment.

Admission to Higher Education

Many European universities do not operate selection or admissions criteria since admission depends on the results of the school leaving examination. However, in some countries, such as the UK, competences beyond the subject being studied can be important when trying to enter one's preferred university and subject specialism, including in some cases language proficiency and cultural awareness as well as general communication skills. Aside from gaining admission, in the modern era of increasing student mobility many more options are open to students to study abroad, such as a semester at a university in another country, government sponsored scholarships and internships in another country.

It is important that students and their parents are fully aware of the additional opportunities in vocational and higher education that may be available if language learning is given priority. For those who want and can access them, undergraduate and graduate courses are increasingly available in the medium of English as well as in the language of the country. Several prestigious universities on India, Malaysia and Singapore now admit international students on undergraduate and postgraduate courses taught in English, and the same is true of courses in medical faculties in Romania and Ukraine, while other international students may attend courses in Romanian or Ukrainian in order to be able to attend courses taught in those languages. Some Russian universities are also broadening the range of courses taught in English to attract international students including those who have fled conflict zones in the Middle East. Depending on the subject there may be advantages for students in pursuing such a course, but the language demands are considerable. It is much easier to develop the specialised language skills necessary for English-medium higher education or courses delivered in other foreign languages if one has become a good independent or expert user of the language as a result of learning it at school and can go on to develop the specialist language skills required for academic study.

Society as a Beneficiary

Interest in education and its outcomes has grown exponentially in most societies and contexts since the 19th century, which is why education is now a key political focus during elections and an obligatory strand of political policy. But in most countries, 'society' is divided about what the critical benefits and outcomes of education, and in this case language education, should be. Should it focus mainly on achieving full employment, economic growth and national competitive advantage, which means meeting the needs of employers and entrepreneurs? Should it aim to equip all citizens with basic literacy and numeracy as well as civic awareness and skills for the digital age? Or should it also focus on higher aims such as developing a culture of democracy, respect and tolerance, as well as ecological awareness and social responsibility? The most likely answer is that education should try to meet all these aims, as well as enabling every individual to reach their potential. But if education should have all these aims, what should be the balance of priorities, and how should educational curricula and institutions be organised to deliver on these priorities?

To think and act in these terms requires a broader view of language and languages in education than the traditional compartmentalisation of 'foreign language' learning, developing literacy, oracy and critical awareness in the national language (or one of them), which is usually also the language most subjects are taught in, and also developing students' plurilingual and pluricultural competences and awareness to enable them to meet the broader and deeper needs of society in the 21st century. A recent European Commission (2018a) recommendation emphasises this point in one of its recommendations, namely that member states of the EU:

> As part of such comprehensive strategies, support the development of language awareness in schools and training centres by:
>
> (a) actively supporting the mobility of learners, including by making use of opportunities provided by the relevant EU funding programmes;
> (b) enabling teachers to address the use of specific language in his or her respective subject area;
> (c) strengthening the competence in the language of schooling as the basis for further learning and educational achievement in school for all learners, and especially those from migrant or disadvantaged backgrounds;
> (d) valuing linguistic diversity of learners and using it as a learning resource including involving parents and the wider local community in language education;
> (e) offering opportunities to assess and validate language competences that are not part of the curriculum, but have been acquired

by learners elsewhere, including through expanding the range of languages that can be added to learners' school leaving qualifications. (European Commission, 2018a: 13–14)

The recommendation is accompanied by an annex that contains some pedagogical principles and examples of good practice designed to raise language awareness in schools, such as:

> - Developing a positive attitude to linguistic diversity and creating a language friendly environment where learning and using multiple languages is perceived as a richness and a resource.
> - Raising awareness of the importance of language learning, and of the educational, cognitive, social, intercultural, professional and economic benefits of the wider use of languages.
> - Integrating language competence and awareness transversally into the curricula.
> - Enhancing the motivation of learners to study languages by linking language lessons to their own lives and interests, taking informal learning into consideration and encouraging synergies with extracurricular activities.
> - Valuing and supporting the entire linguistic repertoires (i.e. all the language competences) of students in school and drawing on these as pedagogical resources for further learning. Pupils can help each other in learning, explain their language(s) to others and compare languages.
> - Establishing bilingual nurseries and schools in border regions so as to encourage children to learn the language of their neighbours from an early age and decrease language barriers in cross-border regions. (adapted from European Commission, 2018c: 1–2)

It is clear from such recommendations and examples that, given the recent intensification of migration into Europe and the rise of populism and intolerance in some countries, member states of the EU, like many other countries, are concerned not just about the economic wellbeing of their citizens, but also about social cohesion and individual and collective wellbeing. If young people at school age can become aware of how language is used for different purposes by different language users and can also view language and cultural diversity as normal and enriching, they may grow up to feel comfortable in societies which are themselves evolving in a diverse, multilingual and multicultural way. Not only that, but they may begin to see how language and languages, and the way they interrelate, can enrich their own lives and bring certain advantages and opportunities. On the other hand, in an age of information overload, social tensions exacerbated by social media and the blurring of dividing lines between factual information and 'fake news', a vital concern for society should be the role of language and languages in developing competences for democratic culture, which were discussed in Chapter 6.

The Service Providers

Another group of stakeholders are those delivering language education and by extension, those engaged in raising students' critical language awareness and seeking to provide language-sensitive teaching across the curriculum, namely teachers. Supporting them are school heads and heads of department. The perspective of these stakeholders is more complex as they are sandwiched between policy implementation and the realities of the educational environment in which they work. The critical environmental factors include the geographical location of the school, its continually shifting population of pupils or students and the linguistic, cultural and social diversity of this population, as well as issues such as the state of buildings and equipment, and the funding available. In the case of language teachers and other teachers as well as those supporting them, a key factor is how much freedom there is to make decisions oneself as compared to the extent to which teaching and learning are governed by external policy, by curricula and/or by testing and examinations. As will become clear in Chapter 8, there are widely differing approaches to school and teacher empowerment from one national context to another. Considering the two extremes, it is as if in some national contexts, schools, head teachers and their staff are trusted and trained to take responsibility for doing what is right for the school's intake of students, while in others centralised systems and policy govern most of what is done in schools. Where language education is concerned things are no different, with little room for manoeuvre regarding the number of hours that can be dedicated to languages, or even regarding which languages are taught and whether space is provided in other subjects for work on language awareness and transversal language skills. There are, however, counter examples. A case from 2018 is cited below.

> Nearly 100 schools in the Spanish region of Castilla La Mancha are abandoning their bilingual programmes, with the local government's approval. Of the 99 schools that petitioned the government of the autonomous region [to be allowed to abandon their bilingual programmes], only one ... was refused permission to drop the bilingual programme after parents voted unanimously to keep it.
>
> In the last decade, bilingual state schools teaching some subjects in English or French have spread rapidly across the regions of the country where Castilian Spanish is the first language.
>
> Educational outcomes in the richer regions, such as Madrid, have reportedly been good across all academic subjects, although critics of the system complain it discriminates in favour of middle-class families who can afford to send their children to private lessons after school. Academic results have been more disappointing in the rural areas where

> it has proved difficult to find teachers with a high enough language level to teach their subject in English. [However] the regional government has already announced the introduction of bilingual teachers into 35 other schools. (Butler, 2018)

This example illustrates the various tensions that language education comes under in the real world. On the one hand, provincial or national authorities devise a policy, such as the decision to introduce CLIL courses in certain schools in order to increase students' opportunities to learn a language by introducing the teaching of one or two other subjects in English or another language, and are supported by many parents in doing this. On the other hand, individual schools find it difficult to identify or recruit sufficient teachers who are able to teach in this way, and at the same time teachers find that certain students, depending on their background, are unable to cope well, and that the divide between students from different social backgrounds is exacerbated by the policy. In this instance, schools were at least able to petition the provincial government to get the policy changed, but no doubt only after facing considerable logistical and other problems for a lengthy period of time as they tried to implement the now discarded policy.

Generally speaking, school heads and their teachers are in a better position to know what will work well and what is likely to work less well in their schools. They also have the advantage of being in touch with parents, although it may be that the more articulate parents who are able to express their opinions and ensure they are listened to dominate parent–school interactions. Depending on the culture of the school, teachers and head teachers should also have a clear idea about what works well with students and how students view innovations in policy. For example, if consulted in the right way, students in secondary education are likely to be able to express an opinion about the kind of language teaching and language learning resources that work well for them, and about whether or not the implementation of CLIL in their curriculum is helping them to develop their language skills as well as enabling them to make progress in the subject(s) in question.

The Key Role of Consultation with Stakeholders

As will be further discussed in Chapter 8, language education and other policies devised by experts and advisors, for example, on the basis of theory, research and experimentation are not necessarily bad policies, and changes of policy, even if they cause logistical and other problems, may not in themselves be negative. But if such policies and changes of policy are formulated and imposed without due and meaningful consultation with those most affected by them, such as students and parents, and with those on whom successful implementation depends, such as teachers and head teachers, then the chances of success will almost certainly be reduced or the policies may not be implemented. A good example of stakeholder power in language education and encouragement of participation in decision-making can be found in the work of the Ontario Multilingual Education (OME) association in Canada, which is 'a group of parents, educators, researchers, and politicians who are advocating for the legalization of multilingual education programs in Ontario schools' (Masson & Ng, 2017: 7). In 2016, it organised a day-long conference with specialists to develop its position on multilingual education, especially as regards children with migration backgrounds, which is reported on in Masson and Ng's paper. In December 2017, OME organised a petition addressed to the Ontario Legislative Assembly to amend the Ontario Education Act to enable their schools to allow languages of instruction other than French and English, such as Mandarin, Spanish or Arabic, to be used in the province's publicly funded schools citing examples in other provinces. A strength of OME appears to be that it deliberately brings together different stakeholders to add weight to their lobbying activities.

The implication is that those devising policy, whether they are in ministries, officials in local authorities or senior staff in schools, need to establish robust and meaningful ways of consulting stakeholders. Many schools have student councils and parent–teachers associations, the work of which can be amplified to include effective procedures for explaining and illustrating new policies and eliciting and analysing feedback on them that can be compared with feedback from other categories of stakeholder. An indication of the likely effects of not undertaking such consultation is to be found in an article on the implementation of the reform programme proposed in Morocco's Strategic Vision for School Reform 2015–2030, which includes ambitious proposals for the reform of language education. The writer quoted an unnamed Moroccan researcher who highlighted the importance of this type of approach:

> All reform attempts [in Morocco] were inspired by Western models that do not take into consideration the possibility of application, and whether the country is ready to apply such reforms on [the] ground. The country has its own identity and characteristics. The setup of any effective reform plan can only be achieved through a participatory approach that should include academics, educational syndicates [trade unions], researchers and [teacher] trainers. Securing logistics and funding are not enough to ensure good educational quality. (El Amraoui, 2018)

Concluding Remarks

Clearly, this kind of 'participatory approach', which we would argue should include parents, students and employers too, takes time and effort. It is in our view critical that national or regional authorities should consult carefully on proposed educational innovations, including those relating to language education, involving not only curriculum designers and school heads but also teacher educators and teachers' representatives in consultative discussions. Similarly, at institutional level, school heads need to organise such discussions with their staff, especially the heads of department and teachers who will be at the sharp end of the implementation of change, but also with parents and students themselves. While they may be time-consuming and challenging to run well, such consultation exercises can reduce considerably the time, effort and cost involved later when unsuccessful or counterproductive policies are introduced. Moreover, if well managed such consultation exercises are empowering for students, for parents, for teachers and for head teachers, and are likely to promote shared values and enhance the sense of community within a school and beyond. This may be particularly true where language and languages are concerned as illustrated by the Spanish and Canadian examples above. Such consultation activities can also provide opportunities for all stakeholders to become more aware of the crucial role that language and languages play in learning, in developing students' transversal skills and critical awareness, and, more broadly, in the development of a robust democratic culture.

In the next chapter we will consider in more detail where different kinds of language education policy initiatives come from, how they are developed and what factors affect their implementation.

Questions for reflection and discussion

(1) In the context where you are working, what steps are taken by schools and teachers to find out about the motivation, the needs and the goals of language learners of different ages?
(2) In your view, how can teachers best find out more about their learners' priorities and their preferences in language learning? How should they take account of these in their teaching, and integrate them within the curriculum they are following?
(3) In your experience, which other stakeholder groups – parents, employers, politicians – can exert most influence on the ways in which languages are taught and learned in schools and higher education? What means are used to consult them?

8 Policy Making

History is littered with examples of the impact of language policies on language education. The two are inextricably linked and are subject to changes of direction when governments change, sometimes even when those in office are replaced. Decisions on language policy are usually motivated politically rather than by cultural concerns, though economic realities are sometimes also an important factor. In this chapter we look at some examples of the part played by language policies in curriculum development, and ultimately in which languages are taught in a nation's classrooms. The *Language Rich Europe* project (Extra & Yağmur, 2012) focused on these issues in some depth, drawing on data from 19 European countries and regions, and we shall refer to some of its key findings in the pages that follow. First, however, we need to consider two fundamental questions:

(1) Where does educational policy come from?

In most countries educational policies are determined nationally by ministries of education. In some larger countries, such as Germany, Brazil and India, and in some linguistically diverse countries such as Switzerland and Spain, policy making and its implementation is wholly or substantially devolved to regional governments. This has also been the case in the UK since the introduction of different levels of devolution to Scotland, Wales and Northern Ireland at the end of the 20th century.

One of the most important aspects of educational policy in any context is the creation of a curriculum, along with ways of putting it into practice and monitoring its implementation. The strongest argument for the creation of a school curriculum at national level centres on the principle of equality of opportunity and on the widespread increase in social mobility, which means that a child can change from one school to another when the family moves without being disadvantaged. A more political reason for centralised decision making is for the state to keep tight control over what is taught, the textbooks that are approved and used, the standards that are set and the means of assessment used at various stages during schooling, and ultimately over the kinds of citizens that the government wants the education system to develop. As we shall see, all this has a significant impact on language teaching and learning in almost all countries.

(2) Who makes educational policy and who influences it?

Practices vary enormously from country to country. At the heart of the answer to this question is the tug-of-war that exists in many countries between ministers and their advisors on the one hand and education professionals on the other. An example of this is captured in an article in *The Guardian* in November 2012:

> How should a national curriculum be drawn up? With meaningful advice from a wide sweep of experienced teachers and academics, or by a clique of advisers whose policy preferences accord with those of ministers? Charges that a group of people who fall into the latter camp have had profound, and in some respects secret, influence are hanging over the government's planned new primary curriculum, which is due to be finalised by September and to come into force for millions of pupils from 2014. (Mansell, 2012)

This kind of tension is often exacerbated by changes in decision makers in ministries. Data that we collected in a survey of 28 countries and regions worldwide indicated most had undergone two or more changes of minister for education in the five years from 2013 to 2018, and in almost half of the contexts, the ministers were reported to be career politicians with no front-line experience of teaching. In such cases, ministers usually rely on expert advice from experienced education professionals and/or senior academics.

When expert advisors *are* called in, for example, to make recommendations about teaching materials or classroom methodology, as was the case in the development of the new primary curriculum in England, there is always a danger that vested interests might be promoted at the expense of what is educationally appropriate. In the worst cases in some countries, the systems used for textbook adoptions are open to corruption on a grand scale, which is not surprising given the profit to be made by publishers when a series of books is given national approval.

As we suggested in the previous chapter, however, ministries are right to seek advice from teachers and other key stakeholders. If this is not sufficiently attended to, as happened when the first version of the national curriculum was introduced in England, Wales and Northern Ireland in 1988, it is likely that many teachers will respond negatively to the change and the policy driving it. This tendency has persisted down the years, and as recently as 2018, one teacher was moved to complain, again in *The Guardian*:

Off went the national curriculum, dragging the poor teachers with it through endless changes, initiatives, an update in 1995, overhaul in 1997, more changes in 2007, more flexibility introduced in 2008, then a new government in 2010, which ordered teachers to abandon the latest changes and return to the 2000 version, then more alterations in dribs and drabs. (Hanson, 2018)

A basic principle of successful management of change seems to have been ignored time and again: meaningful consultation with all key stakeholders, but especially with those in the front line, in this case teachers, is the only way to ensure that the change is owned by the profession and bought into widely. In the case of a national curriculum for schools in any country, these stakeholders include teachers themselves, other education professionals such as inspectors, employers, parents and of course learners, without whom there would be no need for education systems. With broad consultation, there is a chance that the needs and expectations of a society and its citizens will at least be considered and, in the best cases, wholly or partly met.

We will now turn to some of the different dimensions of language policy and the ways in which they are expressed and implemented within education systems in a range of countries in Europe and beyond.

Policies Affecting the Teaching of the Main National or Regional Language

One might reasonably expect to see the teaching of the language of schooling and the development of literacy in school-age children, as a relatively straightforward and uncontroversial matter, but this is seldom the case when it comes to policy making. Some examples from different contexts will help to confirm this.

In the UK, the USA and other English-speaking countries, arguments have continued for decades about the best approach to the early teaching of reading in primary schools. The current preferred method is based on synthetic phonics (cf Johnston & Watson, 2014), also known as blended phonics. This is a method which starts with phoneme recognition and its association with sounds. Given the notorious lack of direct correspondence between sounds and spelling in English, this has always been challenged by proponents of 'look and say', also known as the 'whole word approach', which is underpinned by gestalt psychology and the recognition of the shape of words and also their meanings. The earlier 'pure' phonics approach was partially discredited for this reason and it led to a refinement in synthetic phonics, whereby learners start with the 'transparent' alphabet, in which there is exact correspondence between sound and spelling, before moving on to the 'opaque' alphabet, where this correspondence is not present, as in words such as 'high', 'school' or 'blood'. Since teaching materials and a reliable syllabus for any reading method are needed, ministries looked to expert opinion for guidance on the best method, and reports such as those by Rose (2006), and the one commissioned by the Australian government (Commonwealth of Australia, 2005) came down in favour of a synthetic phonics based approach. While the academic debate about the efficacy of the method still goes on, with researchers citing the lack of conclusive evidence, ministries have enshrined it in curriculum documents and teachers now have ample resources to draw on in implementing the method, which does particularly seem to benefit slow readers and those with learning difficulties (cf Machin *et al.*, 2016).

This kind of interplay between political decision making, academic inquiry and classroom realities is typical of the way in which much educational policy is formulated and implemented in functioning democracies. It is usually a dynamic and iterative process that is subject to revision when changes take place at ministry level or when new research evidence comes to light.

However, not all policy decisions about literacy are so closely linked to research and pedagogy. In a world in which global citizenship and plurilingualism are increasingly seen as desirable features of policy, there are still conservative forces that favour the re-establishment of national boundaries and the need to prioritise the national language in the face of physical incursions of migrants and linguistic incursions, mainly through the dominance of English as the preferred medium of international communication. In France, the Académie Française, established by Cardinal Richelieu in 1635, is responsible for all matters relating to standards in the French language. For many years, through publication of successive editions of its dictionary, the ninth edition of which is still being completed at the time of writing, it has sought to 'defend the French language' and advise on standards of correctness as well as exemplify misuse. This includes offering advice on avoiding unnecessary borrowings from other languages, especially English, such as 'weekend', 'e-mail' and so on, recommending the use of existing or newly coined French words or expressions instead. In 2008, it famously also lodged an objection to the granting of constitutional protection to regional languages such as Alsatian, Basque, Breton and Catalan (cf Allen, 2008).

This kind of linguistic conservatism is currently replicated to a greater or lesser extent in several other European countries, and it inevitably has an influence on decision making in education, notably on classroom language and teaching materials. There are many relatively recent examples of suppression of regional languages through insistence on the national language as the sole medium of instruction and communication in educational institutions. However, that trend has been reversed to a significant degree in many countries as a direct result of pressure by activists, including parents, educators and other stakeholders seeking to preserve their language and the culture which it represents. As a result of their efforts there have been many instances of policies guaranteeing increased recognition and protection for minority languages, as well as permitting schooling in the language at least up to the end of primary level and making television and radio airtime available. This has led to a revival in the standing of languages such as Welsh in the UK and German and Hungarian in Romania, and in some cases even an increase in the number of speakers.

Policies in Post-Colonial Countries

Language and education policies in many post-colonial countries have undergone change and reform since they gained independence in the latter half of the 20th century. In Mali and Senegal, which are former French colonies, for example, French retains its status as the official language, alongside a large number of national languages spoken by the minorities that exist in their regions. While there have been moves to establish the dominant national language (Wolof in Senegal, Bambara in Mali) as an official language with the same status as French, these moves have not gathered significant momentum and French remains the language of government, commerce and post-primary education. In Morocco, by contrast, Arabic and Amazigh (Berber) are official languages and languages of schooling, while French is still recognised as important, though now less so than English.

A rather different situation exists in Central and South America, where Spanish and Portuguese were imposed by the colonial powers in all the occupied countries, though in most of these countries the versions of these languages used commonly have diverged significantly, lexically and phonologically, from those which are current in Spain and Portugal. This is not really surprising given that independence was gained in most of these countries two centuries ago in struggles led by Spanish and Portuguese emigrants. In none of these countries is there a dominant local language that might have challenged Spanish or Portuguese at the national level. It is interesting to note that German and Dutch have not left behind such a strong linguistic footprint in Namibia and Indonesia, respectively. Namibia, thanks largely to its proximity to South Africa, has adopted English as its official language, and Indonesia has its own national language – Indonesian. In South Africa, by contrast, there are 11 official languages, including English and Afrikaans (derived from Dutch). While English is the first language of less than 10% of citizens, it remains the *de facto* lingua franca of the nation.

In all of these cases, official languages are established as the main medium in educational institutions from secondary level upwards, and in most of them, English is learned as a foreign language. The situation in some former British colonies is rather more complex. India has no national language, but it has retained English alongside Hindi as an official language, and both are widely used in the media, in government and in education. In addition, each of the 29 states of India has a number of regional languages, though one usually dominates and has official status, as in the case of Malayalam in Kerala, Tamil in Tamil Nadu and Marathi in Maharashtra. These languages are generally used as the medium of instruction in schools, but in all cases English, and sometimes Hindi, are compulsory from secondary level upwards, and both languages are used for the purpose of communication across state boundaries and, of course, on a national level.

As was mentioned in Chapter 2, the situation is rather different in Bangladesh and Malaysia. In both countries, independence was accompanied by a drive to throw off the vestiges of colonial rule and to establish a new national identity. English lost its status as a national language and was replaced by Bengali and Malay, respectively. For a while, English was no longer taught as a compulsory subject in schools. This led to what both countries came to describe as a 'lost generation' of educated people who had little or no command of English, and by the time the consequences of this for international communication, trade and academic research were fully realised, the situation was too far gone to repair. With their nation-building phase fully established by the last decade of the 20th century, both countries set about reinstating English as a recognised language in all educational institutions. However, in the intervening years, numbers of qualified English teachers and teachers able to teach through the medium of English had fallen to too low a level to reverse the decline in English quickly, and both countries undertook major reform initiatives, backed by policy statements and helped by the UK, to train teachers and to raise standards of English, which had by then effectively become a foreign rather than a second language. Interestingly, in these two countries as well as in India, a local variety of English has developed and is used as a kind of lingua franca, mainly in spoken communication. Malaysian English has absorbed elements of Chinese and Tamil as well as Malay, while Bangladeshi English, like its Indian counterpart, is characterised by what British people recognise as slightly quaint and dated vocabulary as well as some grammatical deviations, such as the widespread use of the present progressive with verbs of the senses, thinking and feeling.

These instances show the extent to which colonial powers exerted control over language policy in their colonies, and some of the different ways in which policies have changed in the post-colonial period.

Policies on the Teaching of Foreign Languages

The opening up of borders across the European Union and the establishment of Europe-wide institutions such as the Council of Europe and the European Centre for Modern Languages have had varying degrees of influence on language policy making in member states and beyond. The recommended commitment to multilingualism (mother tongue plus two for all EU citizens) was first announced in 2002 at a meeting of EU heads of state in Barcelona and has since been backed up by several resolutions and policy statements. The achievement of this so-called 'Barcelona objective' naturally throws responsibility on to individual states and their school systems, and it is interesting to look at the extent to which it has been taken up and acted on in different contexts (NB: data in this section are drawn from Extra and Yağmur (eds) (2012), and from informants' personal correspondence).

Of school students in Hungary, for example, 57% still only learn one foreign language, chosen from English, German, French, Italian, Russian and Spanish. In England, foreign languages are compulsory only until the age of 14 and even then, only one has to be taken. Exam entry statistics show a marked decline in the uptake of French and German in secondary schools, with only 8000 students opting to take French at A-level and around 2500 taking German in 2018. By contrast, Italian schools offer two foreign languages at lower secondary level, in some cases including a regional or minority language as the second option. However, by upper secondary level, the focus is mainly on English as the dominant foreign language. In *Language Rich Europe* the entry for Germany, where education policy is devolved to the Länder, states:

> one foreign language is compulsory in all secondary schools with the exception of special needs schools. A second foreign language is compulsory only for the purpose of reaching the highest school leaving examination (*Abitur*) but is often also offered from grade six in intermediate schools. (Extra & Yağmur, 2012: 127)

In Portugal, by contrast, secondary school students are obliged to learn two foreign languages, almost always English plus one chosen from French, German, Spanish, Latin and Classical Greek. This situation is similar in several other European countries, for example Estonia, Romania and the Basque Region of Spain, though the choice of second foreign language does vary from country to country.

These data suggest that national language and education policies override European policy initiatives and recommendations in many cases, possibly because language policy in particular has always been a sensitive and controversial issue, closely tied up with national and regional identities and the prevailing political climate. But there is also evidence that many countries are falling short of their own targets in foreign language proficiency levels. In spite of parents' support and the increasing prominence of at least one foreign language (and in several cases two) in the curriculum, the results are disappointing. As stated in the executive summary of the results of the 2012 European Survey of Language Competences, which assessed the competence in foreign languages of nearly 54,000 mainly secondary school students across 14 EU member-states:

> [The] results show an overall low level of competences in both first and second foreign languages tested. The level of independent user (B1+B2) is achieved by only 42% of tested students in the first foreign language and by only 25% in the second foreign language. Moreover, a large number of pupils did not even achieve the level of a basic user: 14% for the first and 20% for the second foreign language. (Surveylang, 2012: 5)

These limited data raise questions about language teaching pedagogy and resources as well as about student motivation. Learning a language is a long-term undertaking and school classrooms with 30 or more learners may not provide the ideal environment for it, but it is concerning that in many countries, such a large number of hours of learning over up to 8 years of mainstream schooling does not enable a majority of students to become independent users of at least one language in addition to their language of schooling. This is a concern that the European Council recommendation on 'a comprehensive approach to language teaching and learning' (European Commission, 2018a) discussed in Chapter 7 seeks to address, dovetailing with the objective expressed in the proposal for another Council Recommendation (European Commission, 2018d):

> to improve the development of key competences for all people throughout life and to promote measures needed to achieve this objective. It encourages Member States to better prepare people for changing labour markets and active citizenship in more diverse, mobile, digital and global societies, and to develop learning at all stages of life. (European Commission, 2018d: 4)

Second among these revised key competences listed in the annex is:

> Multilingual competence: This competence defines the ability to use different languages appropriately and effectively for communication. It broadly shares the main skill dimensions of literacy: it is based on the ability to understand, express and interpret concepts, thoughts, feelings, facts and opinions in both oral and written form (listening, speaking, reading and writing) in an appropriate range of societal and cultural contexts according to one's wants or needs. (European Commission, 2018b: 8)

This extract highlights a recommended change of emphasis in foreign language teaching, from the language as a school subject like any other to a view of foreign language literacy as similar in nature to literacy (and by extension also oracy) in the mother tongue, with effective communication rather than knowledge of language systems or basic comprehension as goals. The extent to which this recommendation is put into practice in classrooms in Europe and beyond is hard to evaluate, but there are certainly still contexts in which neither school curricula nor teacher education curricula and practices have developed sufficiently to implement it. In second language teaching, by contrast, effective communication is of necessity prioritised and policies in this area are discussed in the next section.

Policies on the Status and Teaching of Migrants and Migrant Languages

The highly political nature of language policy in many countries is nowhere more strongly in evidence than in the language provision for migrants. At the time of writing, this is an issue which particularly affects those European countries that have accepted migrants and refugees from Africa and the Middle East, but it has at times also been relevant in North America, Australia and New Zealand.

Most countries that have received migrants and asylum seekers have prioritised the learning of the national language as a way of starting the process of integration or assimilation into the host society. In anglophone countries, such as the UK and Australia, this gave rise to the now widely established subdiscipline known originally in British English as English as a second language (ESL), and more recently as English as an additional language (EAL). The assumption was, and still is, that learners, especially adults, would need a different curriculum and different learning materials from those commonly associated with foreign language teaching, and that these would be based on objectives related to initial survival needs, the process of acculturation and the need to understand and cope with civic institutions and authorities in their new environment. This whole process led to the establishment of innovative materials and methods which turned out to have wider relevance in the field of English teaching. Martin (1999) offers a historical overview of the development and impact of the first 50 years of the Adult Migrant English Program (AMEP) in Australia. In an extensive introductory chapter on policy, she reminds us that the original drive towards the assimilation of migrants into Australian society was superseded in the 1970s by a move towards the recognition of multiculturalism as one of objectives of AMEP. She further notes:

> The AMEP plays an important role in the Government's multicultural strategy. Through its range of programs, it introduces the new arrivals to Australian ways of life within the multicultural context of the classroom where students learn about each others' experiences before and after arrival in Australia. AMEP staff recognise, through first-hand contact, the contribution that migrants have made, and will continue to make to Australia. (Martin, 1999: 38)

Here it is worth recalling that the migrant programme in Australia was a deliberate and planned initiative aimed at boosting the population with an influx of skilled and semi-skilled workers in all sectors of the economy.

The particular case of post-war Germany is of interest by way of comparison. As the Federal Republic began to rebuild its economy in the years after World War II, it welcomed many thousands of migrants and 'Gastarbeiter', especially from Turkey, to contribute to the developing 'economic miracle' in the country's economy (Deutsche Welle, 2011). Learning basic German was an urgent priority for these new arrivals and this gave rise to the subdiscipline of 'Deutsch als Fremdsprache' (German as a foreign language), with qualifications and materials offered by the Goethe Institut and courses widely offered in 'Volkshochschulen' (adult evening institutes). Here again, the hope was that the new arrivals would integrate into German society, a hope that has been only partially fulfilled. Despite acquiring German nationality, many of them, even the children and grandchildren of the original migrants, still identify themselves with their original homeland as much as with their adopted home, and in many cases, they feel comfortable living in a district, usually in a big city, where there is a high proportion of fellow migrants. There are similar districts in other European cities, for example in the UK, for migrants and their descendants from Pakistan, India and Bangladesh, and in France for migrants from the Maghreb and sub-Saharan former colonies.

In the UK, the need for joined up thinking on EAL is schools is the subject of a research study by Arnot *et al.* (2014), which looks at the links between language development, social integration and educational achievement. The authors cite official policy:

> the Government's policy for children learning English as an additional language is to promote rapid language acquisition and to include them within mainstream education as soon as possible. (Arnot *et al.*, 2014: 14)

Clearly, if the children of migrants are not to be disadvantaged in the school system, this policy, based within the wider principle of inclusion, is of great importance. However, the authors' recommendations at the end of the study confirm that hard work is needed to put the policy into practice in schools.

These illustrative examples confirm that a policy based around the ideal of assimilation and founded initially on language provision cannot guarantee success. This realisation has contributed, in some European countries, to a policy decision to provide access to classes in the migrants' own languages. The limited extent to which this has been put into practice across Europe is summed up by Extra and Yağmur (2012) in their introduction to *Language Rich Europe*:

Few countries/regions are making immigrant language provision available systematically (three in pre-primary and five in primary), and in secondary eight countries/regions out of (...) 24 responded positively. These are Austria, Denmark, England, Estonia, France, the Netherlands, Scotland and Switzerland. Full state funding is available for immigrant languages in Austria, Denmark, England, the Netherlands and Scotland. In France and Switzerland funding is provided by the countries of origin of immigrant pupils and in Estonia parents meet the costs. The only countries/regions offering immigrant languages in both primary and secondary education are Austria, Denmark, France and Switzerland. (Extra & Yağmur, 2012: 9)

In England, Arnot *et al.* (2014: 14) restate the policy decision that 'the main responsibility for maintaining mother tongue rests with the ethnic minority community themselves.'

This kind of provision is to some extent conditioned and constrained by available human and printed resources and by the work of volunteer groups in the respective ethnic communities, but to a far greater degree by attitudes in government. It is worth noting that most recent arrivals in European countries are either refugees fleeing war or persecution in countries such as Syria, Eritrea or Yemen, or simply economic migrants like many of those arriving from sub-Saharan Africa. It is striking that most of the countries with governments that have imposed limits or a total embargo on immigration have made no provision for the teaching of migrant languages, though there does not seem to be any direct reference to this in language or education policy documents beyond the stated expectation that migrants are expected to learn the national language.

Policies in Multilingual Contexts

Regions where two or more languages are spoken in addition to the 'official' languages pose particular challenges for policy makers. The case of the Indian state of Odisha is of interest here, though it is impossible to be sure how far the language policy adopted there is replicated in other states or in contexts further afield. In Year 1 of primary school, only the local tribal language is taught and used (there are 24 that are recognised for teaching in schools), and the state language, Odia, is then introduced in Year 2 as a second language, but the tribal language is retained as the medium of instruction throughout the five years of primary education. The state authorities have invested heavily in a policy of multilingual education (MLE) and have appointed over 3300 teachers of tribal languages as well as developing teaching materials in almost all of them (data from Barik, 2017). English is then introduced in Year 3. The relevant government document states the reasons for this policy very clearly:

> The mother tongue of tribal children will be used as the medium of instruction for the first five years of primary education in the MLE

programme in Odisha to realize the long-term benefits of MLE for sustained impact on tribal children's educational achievements, high levels of proficiency in Odia and English and positive transfer to post-primary education with a sense of self-efficacy and identity. (Government of Odisha, 2014)

One can think of governments and ministries in other countries that might benefit from taking note of this positive view of multilingual education!

The case of Switzerland is in some ways very different but nonetheless worthy of our attention for reasons that will become evident. The country has four national languages, three of which – French, German and Italian – are the languages of immediately neighbouring countries, though Swiss German is a dialect which deviates markedly in its spoken form from 'High German'. The fourth language, Rhaeto-Romanic is spoken in the canton of Graubünden, and it provides an interesting case study in its own right:

> The trilingual canton of Graubünden represents a linguistically unique situation. The minority language Rhaeto-Romanic has been losing ground for centuries; the *lingua franca* German increasingly threatens the richness and vitality of Switzerland's fourth language. In the attempt to secure a Rhaeto-Romanic-speaking territory, Graubünden has issued a new cantonal language law with new provisions. Now, a municipality is considered monolingual if 40% of its population speaks Rhaeto-Romanic, and multilingual if 20% do. Furthermore, in Rhaeto-Romanic areas, the local dialect is the exclusive language spoken at nurseries and in the first years of primary school. (Berthele *et al.*, 2012: 215)

India and Switzerland have devolved education and language policies to regional governments, and in both cases the relevant authorities have used their powers to formulate their own language policies, in the kind of detail which a national ministry would have been unlikely to devote attention to. In both cases too, one of the main reasons is clearly to prevent local languages from being smothered by majority languages and eventually dying out.

Concluding Remarks

This chapter has looked at different aspects of language policy and in particular how it plays out in education in different contexts. We have pointed to the political dimensions of policy-level decision making and their possible impact on the teaching of languages in schools. We have looked at the deficits in language education policy making, using the example of curriculum design to highlight the need for all-round stakeholder involvement. We have also explored the difficulty of putting into practice at national level aspirational transnational-level policies, relating to multi- and plurilingualism, such as those formulated by the Council of Europe. In the introduction to *Language Rich Europe*, Hope sums up the study's aspirations neatly:

> Through LRE we aim to promote greater co-operation between policy makers and practitioners in Europe in developing good policies and practices for multilingualism. (Hope, 2012: 6)

There is clearly some way to go before this vision becomes reality even within Europe. Beyond Europe, as the instances in this chapter show, there are attempts at national level, and in India at state level, to reconcile policy and practice, but there is little or no evidence of coordinated transnational recommendations or debate about language policy and its impact on practice.

A postscript to *Language Rich Europe* with 10 policy recommendations was published in 2013. The second recommendation calls for a redefinition of the 'Mother Tongue Plus Two' policy:

> The European Commission's trilingual formula of 'mother tongue plus two' should be updated and further developed. For many citizens 'mother tongue' is no longer the same as the national language. The particular position of English also means that in practice most citizens will learn English plus one, so it is rarely any 'two'. (European Commission, 2013: 4)

This serves as a useful reminder that language policy seldom stands still, and that it needs to be rethought and updated constantly to keep pace with developments in societies at national and transnational levels.

In the next chapter, we will consider some of the commercial and vested interests in language education and the influence they have on the quality and variety of the experience of learners and teachers.

Questions for reflection and discussion

In your context, or a context you are familiar with:

(1) How does the prevailing language policy address (i) literacy in the mother tongue and (ii) the learning of one or more foreign languages?
(2) To what extent are minority languages protected by policy?
(3) How much attention is given, in national language policy, to Council of Europe or EU recommendations such as those quoted in this chapter?

9 Commercial Interests in Language Education

Language education in the 21st century is a competitive and high-earning business with many potential beneficiaries. In the UK, commercial activity related to English language teaching accounts for a significant contribution to the national economy – in 2017 it was the fourth-highest contributor. In this chapter, we will look at the balance and some of the trade-offs between commercial considerations and the influence of insights from research and practice. While the global demand for English has opened up lucrative markets for examination providers, publishers, language schools and teacher training institutions, policies around plurilingualism (discussed in Chapters 7 and 8) and provision for international students and migrants have helped to ensure a demand for other languages too and a market share for these same groups of beneficiaries. In this chapter, we describe the role of these beneficiaries, how they are affected by language policies and the extent of the contribution they make to the learning of languages, and we examine the extent and impact of their influence on the teaching and learning of languages.

Examination Providers

The major exam boards for English have seen a huge increase in demand for their certificates of proficiency, and they have now taken steps to ensure that their exams at each level are calibrated against the level descriptors in the CEFR. This demand is led by students who wish to take up or continue their studies in English medium higher education institutions. The British Council has cooperated with Cambridge Assessment English (CAE) to ensure that the International English Language Testing System (IELTS) offers secure and reliable results which can be trusted by universities dealing with applications from prospective students from other language communities. Incidentally, IELTS now accounts for a very high proportion of the British Council's annual income, which is why it is so energetically promoted in countries around the world. For entry to US universities, a designated threshold score in the Test of English as a Foreign Language (TOEFL) is required. However, these international examinations come at a price, which is often beyond the reach of prospective takers and students in many countries have no choice but to rely on the results of their school-leaving examinations or university entrance tests. The problem here is to do with recognition. Despite claims to the contrary, relatively few countries have pools of professional test designers who are capable of aligning their locally produced examinations with CEFR level descriptors and this still restricts the mobility prospects of students who cannot afford to take international examinations. In Ukraine, for example, a recent study (Bolitho & West, 2017) found that some students with a mark of 11 or 12 (the highest grades) in English in their internal school-leaving examination were unable to keep up a simple conversation in the language.

The 'gatekeeping' function that IELTS and TOEFL provide is seen by government authorities and higher education institutions both as a means of exercising some control over immigration and as a way of ensuring that those admitted to higher education in the UK or the USA have the language skills they will need to cope with the demands of studying and living in a new environment. Where other types of international migration are concerned, such as applications for work permits and residency, citizenship or even family reunion, many governments rely on language examination boards to verify whether the individual applicants have attained the proficiency level required. The Third Council of Europe survey on this issue, reported on in Rossner (2014), indicated that among the 36 Council of Europe member states participating in the survey, all but seven had in place language requirements either for residency or for citizenship, or in 18 cases for both (Rossner, 2014: 25). Public examinations are the most commonly used means for obtaining the certification necessary. Examples of the options for obtaining certification of the English language proficiency of would-be migrants to the UK can be found at https://www.cambridgeenglish.org/why-choose-us/visas-and-immigration/. The site makes it very clear that CAE works closely with the Home Office, but it also points to the acceptability of its language certificates in other anglophone countries. The market is potentially huge, though clearly subject to shifts in immigration policy.

The Goethe Institut in Germany and CIEP (Centre International d'Études Pédagogiques) in France operate in a similar way by providing 'gatekeeping' examinations. The Goethe Institut has a dedicated page offering language courses and examinations to immigrants with a visa and also to refugees: http://www.goethe.de/lrn/prj/wnd/idl/iku/deindex.htm?wt_sc=mwnd_integrationskurs.

CIEP offers a test of knowledge of French (TCF) for those seeking to acquire French citizenship, with details on their website: http://www.ciep.fr/tcf-anf.

Testing and assessment are usually viewed as conservative areas in education, slow to change and to take on new ideas, but in fact, each of these three organisations has been relatively quick to spot the increased demand for their products from migrants and to market them accordingly.

CAE have developed a full suite of language examinations, covering all levels from starter tests for young learners at CEFR level A1, through to more challenging and specialised examinations at B2 and C1 levels. Many learners and teachers of English have come to regard these examinations, and the certificates that are awarded to successful candidates, as a way of benchmarking proficiency levels against international standards and thus providing recognition of their level when it is needed in the educational and employment sectors. As discussed in Chapter 4, CAE have also developed and marketed qualifications for teachers of English, at entry level and also for teachers with prior experience. These qualifications are offered at recognised centres worldwide, and, along with the language exams, have done much to raise CAE's profile internationally. To their credit, CAE have always seen themselves as a research organisation and have ploughed profits into research and development, and, in recent years, also into training and professional development for teachers. It is also worth noting that CAE, through their International Board, are also the leading provider of school examinations in English in subjects across the curriculum from lower primary right through to school leaving age. These examinations are taken up widely, mainly in anglophone countries in Africa and Asia, and are seen as a prerequisite for successful applications to universities in the UK, Canada, Australia, USA and even in Germany. However, it is important to note that all the examinations discussed so far focus on language proficiency, and that none of them is specifically intended to predict whether or not examinees will cope with the demands of study or life in general in the communities and institutions they are seeking to enter. IELTS and TOEFL, for example, are not pass/fail examinations and it has been left to receiving institutions and authorities to determine minimum bandings that would probably enable candidates to survive and even to succeed in the contexts for which they are applying.

This leads us to a consideration of the power of examinations and assessment and the ways in which this power is wielded. In every country, examinations, whether internal or international, remain the strongest potential drivers of either educational reform or sticking to the status quo. Because it takes so long to develop and validate examinations, there is often a marked reluctance to change them once they have been shown to serve their purpose. While this kind of conservative thinking is understandable in a narrow view of language education, it has often become an obstacle to reform. Reform initiatives in language education in contexts such as Bangladesh, Belarus and Indonesia have been slowed down by the unwillingness of examination authorities to bring their assessment tools into line with developments in curricula, methodology or teaching materials (see Bolitho, 2012 for examples of this). A further instance of this on a wider scale came in the wake of the 'communicative revolution' in language teaching and learning in the 1970s, which generated great interest in the teaching profession, especially in Europe, and resulted in paradigm shifts in syllabus design, teaching methodology and materials development. Examination authorities were very slow to react to these changes and for a long time, learners who had been exposed to communicative methods and materials were still being asked to take examinations based on knowledge of language systems and on listening and reading comprehension. This raises the need for joined-up thinking between different stakeholders and agents in language education, but it also points up the role adopted by examination authorities as a moderating influence in the face of change. In this connection, it is worth emphasising that, while national public sector examination providers do not have an immediate commercial interest in any decisions about reform or development, the positions they represent and the decisions they take do affect the commercial interests of publishers and language teaching schools and organisations and may have a strong backwash effect on how languages are taught, potentially inhibiting innovations and skewing curricular priorities in both public and private sectors.

Publishers

Mainstream textbook publishing generates huge profits. State sector coursebook adoptions are probably the most significant in terms of volume, but global English language coursebooks released by British and US publishers and sold into markets around the world are also immensely profitable.

English language textbook publishing in the UK is now dominated by the 'big four': Macmillan, Pearson, Oxford University Press and Cambridge University Press. In Germany, Klett and Cornelsen dominate the market for language materials, and in France, Hachette, Didier and CLE International are in a similar advantageous position, especially in the adolescent and adult markets (CIEP, 2016: 21ff). All these companies have fairly conservative publishing policies when it comes to textbooks. Most of them market their books globally and they are generally popular with teachers and learners many of whom prefer their materials to have been written by native speakers (Bolitho, 2019). These teachers may or may not have been exposed to modern methods and approaches such as task-based learning, lexical approaches or project work, which usually means that the publishers take few risks in the content and underlying methodology of their books, preferring to stick to tried and trusted formulae, with only limited concessions to innovative ideas. Interestingly, the most successful global textbook series for English over the last few decades have been written by practising teachers who have a first-hand intuitive understanding of what is likely to appeal to teachers and learners. It is worth mentioning some of these series in order to be aware of the contribution they have made to the history and development of the genre.

Essential English for Foreign Students (Eckersley, 1938–1942) was an early attempt to teach grammar in context with a fixed vocabulary syllabus. It was written on the basis of the author's teaching experience in the Polytechnic Boys' School in London and it was enormously successful, with special editions produced for other countries and updated editions produced until the 1970s. Eckersley was one of the first to take up textbook writing as a full-time occupation.

One of the most successful coursebook writers of the last century was L.G. Alexander who authored four major series for Longman, starting with *New Concept English* (1964) and culminating in 1977 when his books sold 4.7 million copies worldwide, a record number for any author in a single year. His books are characterised by a simple 'text plus exercises' formula that was appreciated by teachers and learners everywhere, and all bear the mark of a practising teacher's knowhow – he spent a number of years at the chalk-face in a school in Greece in the 1950s and 1960s. Robert O'Neill and colleagues also brought all their classroom experience as well as their talent for creative writing to bear on the authoring of the very successful *Kernel Lessons* series (e.g. O'Neill et al., 1971), with its innovative detective story running through the first book in the series. It was immensely popular with teachers and learners alike.

Successful coursebooks also resulted from collaboration between teachers within an institution. In the 1970s, Ealing Technical College in West London (now part of the University of West London) had a thriving ELT department headed up by Brian Abbs. He worked together with one of the lecturers in the department, Ingrid Freebairn, to produce a textbook based on the newly conceived communicative approach. This book – *Strategies* – was at intermediate level and the authors went on to produce a four-book series on the same working principles from 1975 onwards. Rixon and Smith wrote about the series and the authors' work in a review article in *English Language Teaching Journal*, mentioning three ways in which the series was innovative:

(1) ... a robust and consistent focus on 'real' people and 'real' language for 'real' purposes, manifested through the use of language functions as an organising principle....

(2) ... a clear commitment to the importance of (....) the 'production' stage of a P-P-P lesson....

(3) ... an exuberant and varied graphic style that (....) burst the bounds of the neat linear columns and small illustrations typical of most other course materials of the time. (Rixon & Smith, 2012: 385)

Despite the first of these three assertions, Gray and Block (2013), in a detailed analysis of social class representation in global textbooks since the 1970s, point out that *Strategies* contributed to a general trend which increasingly foregrounded middle classes and their values and aspirations, and neglected depictions of working classes. They conclude by complaining:

> The erasure of the working class from ELT textbooks can be seen both as representative of a failure to educate and as a betrayal of working-class language learners. (Gray & Block, 2013: 68)

Nonetheless, the *Strategies* series was hugely successful and it represented a major turning point in mainstream textbook publishing. Until the 1970s, publishers had largely relied on the expertise and talent of their authors, allowing them to stipulate content and methodology, and concentrating on realising the authors' vision in print. By the early 1970s, however, major publishers such as Longman were increasingly aware of the profits to be made in the field, and had assembled in-house teams of highly skilled and pedagogically aware editors and designers, and from that time onwards, textbooks such as *Strategies* became the products of author-publisher collaboration, with the balance of influence gradually shifting more and more away from authors and towards decision-makers in the publishing houses, for whom commercial viability became the key criterion in commissioning new textbook series. This gradual power shift certainly also led to the kind of 'norming' on middle class values that Gray and Block (2013) objected to. However, it has also led to a situation in which authors are commissioned to write to a brief that publishers produce, including in some cases tight vocabulary control, the avoidance of controversial topics to ensure that books are acceptable in all countries, specifications about the length of reading and listening texts, and so on. Zemach (2018), in her address to the annual conference of the International Association of Teachers of English as a Foreign Language (IATEFL) in Brighton, drew attention to many of these developments and particularly bemoaned the growing trend to pay educational writers a flat fee for their work, rather than percentage-based royalties, claiming that this reduces an author's motivation and ultimately leads to a reduction in the quality of materials.

Our purpose in offering this potted historical overview of the development of English language coursebooks is to highlight the significance of the genre in educational terms and the many responsibilities that authors and publishers bear when they produce and market materials. However, it is in their commercial interest to foster a high degree of dependency among schools, teachers and learners, to encourage brand loyalty and to target repeat business. Novice teachers nearly always rely on coursebooks rather than the syllabus to plan their lessons and the accompanying teachers' guides in some cases almost obviate the need for a teacher to think independently about their classes. The extent to which this leads to a kind of deskilling or deprofessionalisation of teachers is bound to vary from one context to another, but there are undoubtedly many instances of teachers starting a lesson by asking learners to open their books on page xx, only for them to remain open for the entire lesson. Wright (1987) refers usefully to the distinction between teaching 'with and through' a coursebook, meaning either 'coursebook as one resource among many' or 'coursebook as the sole resource' for teachers and learners.

As global markets became more accessible, for example after the opening up of Eastern Europe following the collapse of socialism in 1989, coursebook series were usually supplemented by workbooks, more sophisticated audio and video material, and readers, all produced by extended teams of writers, usually working to tight specifications. While the early textbooks were mainly produced for adult learners at language schools or on state sector evening courses, the market for textbooks for different age and interest groups began to emerge from the seventies onward, and all the 'big four' UK publishers have long had series for young learners, teenagers and adults, and to cater for different professional and academic specialisms.

Despite the huge inroads the major publishers have made into textbook markets in so many countries, they do not have it all their own way. Most countries have a fairly robust and long-established educational publishing industry, some of it through nationalised state companies. In many cases, language textbooks are authored by local academics who have developed a loyal base of teacher-followers. Interestingly, their books are often referred to just by the author's name, resulting in a kind of 'personality cult'. For instance, in former Soviet Union countries, teachers might be heard saying: 'We use Arakin with our first-year students' or 'Vereshagina is great for young learners', in contrast with the Western tradition of referring to books by their titles rather than their authors.

In many countries, textbooks are typically adopted for school use by expert vetting committees charged with reviewing and recommending titles as being suitable for the target age groups and domestic teaching context. This process, often accompanied by heavy lobbying and not immune to the offer of 'sweeteners' in the form of discounts, local licensing arrangements or exclusivity deals, has often proved to be a stumbling block for big international publishers trying to penetrate local markets. The reviewing process typically takes into consideration:

- National traditions of teaching and learning and the degree to which submitted titles are compatible with them.
- Match between the allocated hours in the national curriculum and the number of units or lessons in the submitted textbooks.

- Match between curriculum objectives and content and those in the submitted textbooks.
- Compatibility with national assessment and examination requirements.
- Cost.
- Delivery times for bulk orders.
- Cultural content and the values which are explicit or implicit in the submitted textbooks.

In all these respects, global textbooks (GTs), despite their many attractions, may suffer by comparison with locally produced series. For example, Clare Maas reports on the situation in Germany:

> the most successful materials in Germany tend to stem from local publishers and are targeted quite specifically at the German-speaking market. (Maas, 2018)

In some countries, Uzbekistan and Mongolia for example, local authors have been recruited and trained to write books for all levels of state schooling, partly to maintain local authoring capacity but also because global coursebooks are too expensive to allow widespread adoption in the school system.

Gray (2010) looks in some depth at how English language and culture are represented in global textbooks and quotes Pulverness (2003) in recommending local projects like these as a way of ensuring that content is culturally appropriate and of avoiding the '"one size fits all" principle on which the global coursebook is based' (Gray, 2010: 188).

This realisation has encouraged global publishers to consider 'localised' versions of their major textbook series, often involving a local author in the process to ensure that the main criteria for selection are successfully addressed. This also goes some way towards dealing with the criticism that the widespread adoption and use of GTs results in the deskilling of local authors and is a threat to their livelihood. This issue was recognised by agencies such as the British Council and gave rise to textbook writing projects in Russia, Mongolia, Romania and Belarus. For instance, this could involve the training of teams of local authors, in some cases in partnership with UK publishers and the production of series which have been used nationally: *Pathway to English* in Romania (cf. Popovici & Bolitho, 2003), *New Millennium English* and *Millie* at secondary and primary level respectively in the Russian Federation, *English 1–6* in Mongolia, and *Magic Tour* and *Magic Box* in Belarus. In all of these cases, the ability of local authors to make their work relevant and acceptable to teachers and learners has been decisive, and the degree to which local authoring capacity has been built through the projects is evidenced by the fact that several of the writers involved in these teams have gone on to produce further books, either individually or in teams. Where publishing partnerships were established, as in the case of the Russian project, the local publisher benefited from the UK partner's expertise in production standards, while the UK partner was able to access valuable insights about the possibilities and constraints which apply to publishing in the Russian market. In each of these instances, the books were adopted for use in the public education system, thereby generating significant income for the respective publishing houses.

In an article looking at and researching the impact of GTs, Hadley (2014) observes:

> The scholarly debate surrounding GTs leaves one with the impression that, for many language teachers, GTs have taken on a role similar to a fraught relationship where people find themselves inextricably bound to someone they both hate to love and love to hate. (Hadley, 2014: 207)

Drawing on a longitudinal study in an institute of higher education in Japan, Hadley goes on to conclude that GTs 'can play an important role in helping ... second language learning' albeit with the caveat that 'a considerable investment of time and effort is needed to make them work' (Hadley, 2014: 230).

This is a lesson that has not been lost on publishers. As was pointed out earlier in this chapter, most publishers, whether global or local, now understand that to see a long-term return on their investment, they need to back up their marketing efforts by providing training, both face to face and online, to accompany their materials, and to be prepared to engage first-hand with teachers, parents, authorities and any other stakeholders in language education. This includes investing considerable sums in sending authors around the world as conference and touring speakers to promote, indirectly or directly, the books they have been involved in writing and the methodologies they depend on, as well as in sponsoring events and setting up and staffing imposing exhibition stands at conferences and other professional gatherings. In this connection, it is clear that publishers have become even more conscious of the need many learners have to pass examinations, and all major textbook series now carry a claim in their blurb that they are suitable to prepare learners for a specified CEFR or public examination level. Thus, the commercial interests of publishers and examination providers may be seen as interlinked, if not completely interdependent.

Objections to the use and overuse of textbooks have long featured in teachers' magazines and journals, but they have been crystallised by the 'Dogme' movement (Meddings & Thornbury, 2009) who proposed as an alternative, that teaching should be based solely on the resources that teachers and students bring to the classroom and whatever happens to be in the classroom. This ensures relevance and immediacy of content as well as cultural appropriateness, but it does place a burden on teachers who are not trained or ready to rely on their own resources rather than on the omnipresent textbooks. While publishers might initially have been concerned by the rise of interest in the movement, as a potential threat to their profit margins, they probably need not have been concerned, as most teachers are reluctant to throw away the convenient crutch that their textbook offers.

The Role of the British Council

All this has to be seen critically in the context of allegations of linguistic imperialism (Phillipson, 1992, 2003). The worry remains that the whole process of globalisation, at least in the case of English, is now accompanied by the implication that it is the key to educational and career success in any context, thereby devaluing local languages and local culture. The British Council is charged with promoting the English language, British culture and education, often through support for British publishers and examination providers, and yet there is a need for them not to be seen to be doing this at the expense of a commitment to multilingualism and multiculturalism: a difficult balancing act! Yet there is, inevitably, still more than a whiff of cultural and linguistic imperialism about their mission.

The British Council has developed a strong presence in the areas of English teaching and examinations in countries where it is represented across the world, as this extract from their 2017–2018 annual report illustrates:

> In 2017–18 we taught 400,000 students in our teaching centres, had 79 million visitors to our global websites for learners and teachers of English and on our social media channels we engaged with a further 9.6 million learners and teachers of English. We deliver the International English Language Testing System, IELTS, which provides UK employers and higher education institutions with a secure, reliable test to successfully recruit employees and students. In 2017–18 we delivered a record 3.2 million tests and over 10,000 organisations now recognise the test worldwide. (British Council, 2018: 17)

'Exams generated an income of £486.9 million, equivalent to 41% of total income for the year, while teaching provided an income of £212.9 million, or 18% of total income' (British Council, 2018: 66). These figures give an idea of the extent to which the British Council has had to become commercialised as financial support from the government (grant-in-aid) has declined over time to its 2017–2018 level of around 14.3% of total income. Nonetheless, the Council sees all this commercial activity as totally compatible with its mission and its charitable status, in spite of accusations of unfair competition from some providers of English language courses and would-be providers of exam services.

> Our research demonstrates that the strongest predictor of trust in the UK is a person's ability to speak English. It facilitates international trade, diplomacy, opens doors to international study and enhances career opportunities. Learning English through the British Council also leads to a greater understanding of UK culture. (British Council, 2018: 15)

Interesting from a historical perspective is the impact that the Council has had even in countries where it is not or no longer directly involved in teaching English. Names such as 'Britannic House' or 'Cultura Inglesa' abound in parts of Latin America, for example, and this kind of association with 'Britishness' remains an important selling point.

Language Schools

The history of language schools goes right back to the late 19th century, when Maximilian Berlitz founded his first school in Rhode Island. This was the era of mass immigration in America, and the learning of English was an immediate priority for new arrivals. There are now over 500 Berlitz franchises across the world, and the textbooks and teaching method associated with the schools have also survived, through numerous revisions and updates, to this day. Other schools, both chains such as Eurocentres and Inlingua and smaller, family owned institutions, followed in the wake of Berlitz's early success, and thus arose the enduring tension between educational and business interests which still characterises the language school sector today.

While the Berlitz schools focused initially on teaching adults, language schools have diversified their offering greatly since World War II. Some schools have specialised in teaching teenagers, others younger learners, others still professional people needing English or another language for work purposes. In some countries, language schools compensate for poor standards in state school language teaching by offering courses aimed at helping pupils to pass their examinations. This has been a priority for many schools in Greece such as the so-called 'frontisteria' (crammers), where parents are prepared to pay to ensure that their children achieve good grades, but it is a common phenomenon throughout southern Europe and Turkey. These schools offer smaller classes than in state schools, in some cases individual tuition and strict teaching, and in many cases, they can boast a record of success in preparing their students for examinations such as those offered by CAE.

A newly revived and prosperous Europe in the 1960s and 1970s opened up a lucrative market for holiday language courses, initially in the UK, but later in other countries and also for other languages. Some of these courses were (and still are) offered by established language schools while others were run by organisations specialising in short courses with a recreational element attached. This course model remains attractive to this day, with many providers specialising in courses for teenagers, tapped into gratefully by parents who want to see their children gainfully occupied and well looked after during long school holidays. The contribution of these language organisations to the local economy in locations such as the seaside towns on the south coast of England has been immense. Students need lodgings, often with local families, and many of them spend freely during their stay, bringing welcome income to shops, taxi companies and food and drinks outlets.

Quality Assurance Bodies

The private language school sector in the UK was largely unregulated until 1960, when the Association of Recognised English Language Services (ARELS) was established with four main objectives:

- to encourage member schools to raise their high standards even further;
- to represent their interests to government and official bodies;
- to give students recourse to action if they have a complaint against a member school; and to promote high quality English language teaching in Britain overseas abroad.

This was a first tentative step towards establishing order and standards in the sector, and ARELS soon went from strength to strength, with over 220 members at its peak.

In the state sector, an analogous organisation was formed in the eighties to bring together state sector providers of English language courses in further and higher education, many of which offered fee-paying courses to students from overseas. This was known as the British Association of State Colleges in English Language Teaching (BASCELT). It soon became clear that the two associations had a great deal in common and in 2004 they merged to form an umbrella organisation, English UK, which was founded to bring all English language providers together in the interests of promotion, quality assurance and ongoing professional and institutional development. English UK now has over 400 registered members with strong representation from both state and private sectors and, working together with the British Council, it does a great deal to enhance the reputation of British ELT through its inspection and recognition scheme, Accreditation UK, and its global marketing reach.

Meanwhile, in 1991, the European Association for Quality Language Services (EAQUALS) was founded by a group of 10 representatives of language schools and organisations from several European countries. Like English UK, it has welcomed members from both state and private sectors, and under its rebranding as Evaluation and Accreditation of Quality Language Services owing to its expansion beyond Europe, it now has over 140 accredited members worldwide, operates a self-funded accreditation scheme and has developed a strong professional development dimension, including regular conferences and other events. EAQUALS member schools teach 25 different languages and are committed to multilingualism. The advantages of belonging to an international quality assurance association like EAQUALS are numerous according to the feedback received from members:

- it brings international quality standards within reach of providers of language education everywhere, even if they are geographically isolated, and provides them with an internationally recognised quality kitemark to support their marketing;
- it creates a community of practice in which professionals from quite different contexts providing courses in different languages can learn from one another and collaborate on development projects, such as the *Eaquals Framework for Language Teacher Training and Development* (EAQUALS, 2013);
- it links providers of language education with associate members such as national language organisations (e.g. Goethe Institut, Instituto Camões), examination providers, publishers and national associations;
- it provides access to resources and new ideas through conferences, webinars and meetings and the website; and
- it facilitates 'cascading' by enabling (for example) national associations of providers to learn from one another and move towards greater alignment of their standards and procedures.

Language schools and organisations have come a long way in the period since World War II, and most have clearly recognised the benefits of self-regulation and all-round professionalisation as a means of adding value to their offering. Long before EAQUALS was founded, associations had been established in some other European countries, for example the Associazione Italiana Scuole di Lingue (AISLi). Many European and South American countries now have analogous organisations and they also exist in Australia, Canada and the USA.

Self-regulation, while it does not come cheaply, has done a great deal to establish quality assurance in all aspects of course provision, including teaching, resources, accommodation and welfare, safeguarding for under-age students, and, not least, qualifications and professional development for teachers. Schools and organisations have come to understand the need to sign up to these measures in order to ensure that they can still make the profits they need to prosper or, as a minimum, to stay afloat. In a number of countries, there are still rogue providers who put profit before standards, and one of the challenges in the years ahead will be to bring them under some kind of regulatory control, a step that will probably require legislation. Still open, also, is the question about the role of language schools in relation to state education in schools, and this does give rise to soul-searching among teachers and managers: is a language school there simply to provide a narrow-based compensatory service to its students, in the form of 'pure-protein' language proficiency work or is it incumbent on teachers at these schools to be 'educators' in a broader sense, addressing values, transversal skills, and contemporary issues, for example, as part of their course content? We suspect that the answer is context-related, with some more educationally progressive countries being much more open to a broader-based approach, and more conservative societies just looking for a provision focusing on narrower, proficiency-related learning outcomes.

Teacher Training Providers

The language teaching industry, as outlined in the previous section, needs to be 'serviced' in order to survive and develop. We have already discussed physical resources in the form of textbooks, but there is also a continuous demand for human resources. Training organisations recognise this and, although profit margins in this area of work are much tighter than in direct teaching, there is still a need to be met and a reputation to be gained in the field. Indeed, many larger private language schools run teacher training courses partly in order to meet their own internal need for additional teachers in the high season.

Providers have different areas of focus in language teacher training and professional development. Let us start with initial training and specifically with the Cambridge Certificate in English Language Teaching to Adults (CELTA). Worldwide, there are now more than 350 centres offering the course, usually on a four-week intensive basis, and mainly, though not exclusively, in the private sector. Its precursors include the International House Certificate in Teaching English as a Foreign Language, established by the organisation's founder-director, John Haycraft, as a means of ensuring a flow of new recruits to his franchise schools and others ready to accept the new qualification. As of 2017, there were typically more than 15,000 CELTA candidates per year. By common consent, CELTA is now seen as opening the door to a career in teaching English initially to adults in the private sector. The syllabus for a CELTA course is fairly tightly prescribed and, in many ways, it has remained true to a successful and long-established formula, with input, lesson observation and teaching practice, all usually within the four walls of the training provider. If there is to be an opening for innovation in the whole area of ELT, one might expect it to be through these training programmes, which are meant to be taught by trainers who are up to date and involved in critical thinking about methods and approaches. Instead, as one experienced CELTA trainer commented recently in a personal communication, many CELTA courses have become repetitious and mechanistic, espousing low-risk, traditional teaching methods and approaches to language in the interests of 'delivering' graduates who, at the minimum level, are 'safe to teach'. Language schools everywhere need a constant flow of such novice teachers, and they, too, would rather have teachers who are steeped in accepted orthodoxy rather than potential free thinkers and revolutionaries. However, there is no doubt that this militates against innovation both in the certifying body (here CAE) and in the course providers.

As mentioned in Chapter 4, a striking recent development has been the uptake of CELTA as a compensatory programme for experienced but untrained teachers, allowing them to be exposed to modern methods and materials for the teaching of English.

By contrast with CELTA, Cambridge's diploma level qualification (DELTA) has developed fairly radically in both content and delivery mode since its inception as the Royal Society of Arts Diploma in the Teaching of English as a Foreign Language in the 1970s. DELTA is intended as a modular, in-service qualification that can be taken at distance or on a cumulative, part-time basis over an extended period. As of 2017, typically more than 3000 DELTA modules were completed annually by serving teachers worldwide. It is recognised by many universities as a postgraduate-level qualification which earns credit towards a language teaching-related master's programme in the UK. (statistical data provided by Cambridge Assessment English, personal communication).

Cambridge also offers the Teaching Knowledge Test (TKT), which as the name suggests, is focused on knowledge rather than teaching skills and has no practical component. This test has been taken up in high volume in China, where it is offered in 15 centres, presumably as an element of professional development for local teachers.

Trinity College London also offers internationally recognised qualifications at certificate and diploma level, though with fewer centres and candidates than those opting for Cambridge certificates.

All of these programmes have become increasingly professional over the past few decades, with stringent requirements for course centre approval and for the training and induction of tutors. This has had a positive impact on standards and consequently on the reputation of the qualifications, all of which started from an initial fairly low base, with a great deal of improvisation along the way. While the 'service' nature of the programmes provides a needs-driven incentive to maintain them, they have to be commercially viable and most centres are able to see at least a small return on their investment, despite the need to pay trainers well and to spend regularly on library resources.

There is also a considerable market in most parts of the developed world for short in-service courses for language teachers. A number of UK schools and institutes have specialised in this area over many years, with teacher participants often able to draw on European funding for their study trips. Most of the provision is in the form of open enrolment courses with a specific focus, such as teaching young learners, language and culture, or teaching English for academic purposes. Participants from different countries then meet for the course and hope that their needs will be met. Most courses are carefully described in terms of content and approach, and all provide a forum for exchange of experience and ideas, but there is no cast-iron guarantee of satisfaction such as may be expected on a carefully tailor-made programme, commissioned and taught in-country. Indeed, there has been a growth in demand for this kind of programme, and the same providers will often send their trainers to work for short periods at institutions in other countries, thereby saving the client the expense of travel to and accommodation in the UK. This kind of exercise is less profitable for providers, but it does raise their profile in any country they work in, paving the way for possible future business. Franchise organisations such as International House also offer courses for teachers in their centres in different countries

In the UK, a number of universities offer master's courses in ELT or applied linguistics. These are seen by many language teachers as the ultimate step on a personal career ladder and the longer-established programmes regularly attract full fee-paying students from all over the world. For some universities, this is part of a significant income stream, which they rely on to fund some of their work in research and development. It is all part of the commodification of higher education in the UK, whereby universities have become increasingly commercialised and reliant on effective marketing to generate the income they need to meet their costs.

All of these course types have an established place in British ELT and many providers are now looking at new modes of delivery to supplement traditional face to face courses, either online or by a blended learning approach. Many universities now offer postgraduate modules at distance and the DELTA can also be taken remotely. This suits many practising professionals who cannot afford to take time out from their paid employment in order to study full-time. By contrast, CELTA and other initial certificates have to carry a strong teaching practice component and this clearly presents an obstacle to distance delivery, although some centres do offer the courses on a part-time basis over an extended period.

Across Europe and the rest of the world, the main route into language teaching as a career is through a university degree, in some countries at bachelor level and in many others at masters. However, the

Goethe Institut has a long history of offering training and qualifications on a commercial basis for the teaching of German as a foreign language, for example its 'Deutsch Lehren Lernen' programme, as does the Instituto Cervantes for teachers of Spanish. CIEP also designs in-service programmes for teachers of French, servicing the worldwide network of Instituts Français. While these programmes provide a service for institutions concerned with the recruitment or professional development of their teachers, they all operate at much lower volume levels than the programmes for teachers of English described above.

Concluding Remarks

There is clearly a high level of interdependency between these providers and interest groups, all of whom are driven to a greater or lesser extent by the need to make income in order to survive. However, there has been a widespread recognition that this income depends essentially on quality, and the development of quality assurance systems has gone hand in hand with the prioritisation of commercial considerations. Examination providers and publishers, while reluctant to depart too far from established, successful traditions, have introduced very careful quality safeguards into their research and commissioning procedures. Language schools and organisations, while also committed to quality assurance, have no choice but to buy into what the examination providers and publishers offer, and teacher training providers, perhaps the lowest down in the food chain, have to be aware of priorities in both state and private sectors. This all adds up to a somewhat sterile overall picture. Fifty years ago, when what we see today as the language teaching industry was in its infancy, there was a buzz about it, with scope for innovative practices and new ideas. There was no over-powerful establishment to call the shots. With the 'comfort blanket' of commercial success wrapped around so many players in the field today, however, the incentive to innovate and take risks seems to be less attractive than ever.

Our final chapter looks back over the issues raised in the book and offers our own thoughts on the future priorities for language education in our changing world.

Questions for reflection and discussion

(1) Have exam providers become too dominant in setting the agenda for language teaching and learning in both state and private sectors?
(2) In your context, is there enough dialogue between examination providers, publishers and language teachers? Should there be a forum for this?
(3) Have the major publishers become too risk-averse in their commissioning policies, and is this stifling innovation?

(4) In general, throughout the sector, are commercial considerations beginning to outweigh educational and pedagogical priorities, and are too many decisions taken by people with business rather than pedagogical backgrounds?

These are questions that we believe those working in the field of language education need to consider carefully, and that the stakeholders themselves need to address and respond to, in their own interests as well as the interests of those who rely on their services.

10 Language in Education and in Teacher Education: Towards New Paradigms

Having looked in some detail at a wide range of issues related to language education and language in education, in this final chapter we bring together the main conclusions and recommendations that we wish to put forward. We do this out of a conviction that, for language education to respond effectively to the needs of society as well as to the beneficiaries of education in a rapidly changing world, new paradigms must be found and a more enlightened approach taken to policy making and practice than is currently the case in most education systems we know about. This is because, owing to their critical role in enabling individuals to reach their potential and be full participants in their societies, language and communication are absolutely central to all education.

The Story So Far

The preceding chapters have looked in selective detail at language education and the role of languages in education. Readers will have noticed that we have frequently referred to examples and case studies taken from the European context and have regularly referred to documents and projects developed under the auspices of the Council of Europe and the European Commission, and we do so again in this chapter. These examples and references do not diminish the importance of developments in language education elsewhere in the world and do not simply reflect the fact that we have lived and worked mostly in Europe. Rather, they exemplify the considerable emphasis that European institutions have placed on language education since their foundation, which in the case of the Council of Europe, now with 47 member states, took place in 1949, only four years after the end of World War II. The rationale for the focus on language education in the European Cultural Convention of 1954 was clear: the enhancement of language learning in Europe was seen as an important part of bringing the continent's societies together and of helping to avoid such horrendous conflicts in the future. Over the past 60 years, European institutions and the specialists working under their auspices have concerned themselves more intensively and broadly with language policies and language issues than has been the case in other countries. While developed for European contexts, some of these initiatives (such as the CEFR) have begun to influence policy makers and researchers in other parts of the world, such as Uzbekistan, Malaysia, Japan and Argentina.

We began the book with an overview of how language, thought, learning and education interrelate and are interdependent before illustrating the central role that language and communication play in all teaching, whatever the subject. We ended the first chapter by citing some of the recommendations made in an important UK government report of the 1970s (Bullock Report, 1975), which were not implemented in the UK, but we believe are relevant to education systems worldwide. The remainder of Part 1 offered an overview of developments in language teaching and learning in general since the middle of the 20th century before turning to the 'special case' of English and the debate about its role in the world, including in the world's education systems.

Part 2 of the book moved on to consider teacher education and teachers' continuing professional development (CPD), starting with the initial teacher education and CPD for teachers of languages, where we were able to draw on data gathered from these fields of activity. We also discussed the place and space that is given to language, language awareness and 'pedagogic' communication in initial and in-service education for primary teachers and teachers of all subjects in secondary education. Here we found it surprisingly difficult to obtain clear information, but came to the conclusion that there is little evidence of consistent or sufficient attention being paid internationally to language and communication issues either in initial teacher education or in CPD.

In Part 3 of the book we turned to the issue of policy, in particular the ways in which stakeholders are typically able to influence policy or are left out of the policy development process. In many countries, policy is developed top-down in consultation with experts who may be working at some distance from the schools and classrooms where policies will be implemented. In most national systems, among the various stakeholders, academics and government advisors, and in line with their vested commercial interests, textbook publishers and examination boards have sought to have decisive influence on policy development and seem to be directly or indirectly involved in policy development to a far greater extent than representatives of school heads, teachers, parents and students, for example.

Where Do We Go From Here?

In this section we put forward our own recommendations concerning the main topics explored in the preceding chapters. Without minimising the context-related and practical challenges faced in implementing such proposals, our aim is to contribute to and move forward the discussion of what needs to be done to ensure that language and languages in education are given the urgent attention and prominence they deserve.

Policy initiatives

Our intention is not to be critical of those around the world who are responsible for policy in education, language education and teacher education – far from it. We understand the challenges they face as the pace of change in the environments around schools and the new generations of children entering them accelerates, sometimes in unpredictable ways. Change is inevitable and essential, but the processes by which changes are decided on and implemented are fraught with challenges. As Michael Fullan (2007) points out:

> [...] *change is a process, not an event*, a lesson learned the hard way by those who put all of their energies into developing an innovation or developing legislation without thinking through what would have to happen beyond that point. (Fullan, 2007: 68, author's emphasis)

As Fullan also points out, it is not as if schools have to deal with only one innovation at a time. 'Thus, when we identify factors affecting successful initiation and implementation, we should think of these factors operating across many innovations and many levels of the system (classroom, school, district, state, nation)' (Fullan, 2007: 68). While often innovation is felt to be essential to meet the changing needs of society, there is no question that it must be initiated, piloted and implemented with great care and after wide consultation. For the effects of misguided or poorly implemented new policies can be damaging to those they are intended to benefit, and long-lasting.

Our first concern, therefore, goes well beyond language education. Especially in cases where new initiatives impact on school curricula, on teaching and assessment, and on teacher education, it is critical that, in national or regional systems where this does not already happen, wide and thorough consultation takes place with all the stakeholders who will be affected by the changes. Moreover, such consultation needs to be ongoing and to take place at various stages: it is necessary when the initiative and the rationale for it are first proposed, when the specific implications of the changes are fully specified, and later when the actual plans for implementation are made.

Clearly, the ways in which consultation and participation are organised will depend on the context of the proposed initiative and the nature of that initiative, but meaningful consultation and a readiness to listen to concerns and alternative ideas need to be part of the overall change process. This may take time and require some additional expenditure, but only in this way can the various stakeholder groups play a meaningful and constructive role in the change process, and it is the only way to guard against the potentially damaging influence of lobbyists and of those with vested political or financial interests. Thus, in the case of languages in education and language education, the teachers concerned, pupils, their parents and other relevant stakeholders need to fully understand the rationale behind and the implications of an innovation, such as the introduction of CLIL classes or the inclusion of language awareness in subject teaching, before implementation.

Language as a key feature of the school curriculum

At secondary level, in most educational systems the development of competence in the 'language of schooling' – generally the language used in the country or region where the school is situated and the first language of a majority of students – is seen as the responsibility of the teachers concerned. Teachers of other subjects pay relatively little attention to the language of schooling except where technical vocabulary and formulations relating to the subject are concerned. However, as has been highlighted in earlier chapters, language and communication skills, literacy and oracy, are fundamental 'transversal' skills needed by all students in many aspects of their schooling and their post-schooling lives. We have referred earlier to the concept of 'linguistic repertoire'. This is a way of considering all the languages and varieties of languages that a person can use in different contexts and for different purposes, however limited their ability may be. Leaving aside for the moment languages other than the language of schooling, students' repertoires in the language of schooling affect their learning. The narrower that repertoire, for example, the more limited it is to one variety or register of the language, say the informal spoken language of home life or the playground, the harder it is for students to learn from resources and in situations where other varieties and genres are used. The language used for explaining topics in the science curriculum is different from the language used to debate contentious ideas or to make an oral presentation about the results of an investigative project. As we pointed out in Chapter 1, the gradual broadening of literacy and oracy to encompass and develop competence in a range of varieties and registers of language is an essential aim of education internationally and should be the responsibility of all teachers, whatever their subject specialism. But the work of teachers on developing language and communication skills and developing a critical awareness of language that can help students to cope with the ways in which language and communication are used in their actual and virtual environment inside and outside education needs to be well-informed, well planned and well-coordinated. This point is reflected in the *Framework of Competences for Democratic Culture* (Council of Europe, 2018a) touched on in Chapter 6:

> Language learning is always part of subject learning, and the learning of subject-specific knowledge cannot happen without linguistic mediation. Language competence is an integral part of subject competence. Without adequate language competences, a learner can neither properly follow the content that is being taught, nor communicate with others about it. (Council of Europe, 2018a: 17)

This means that there must be cross-curricular collaboration and guidance available such as was recommended over 40 years ago in the Bullock Report:

> 'Each school should have an organised policy for language across the curriculum, establishing every teacher's involvement in language and reading development throughout the years of schooling'; and: 'Every school should have a suitably qualified teacher with responsibility for advising and supporting his colleagues in language and the teaching of reading'. (Bullock Report, 1975: 514)

At that time, reading was seen as the main route to developing greater literacy and it is still very important, but the work on oracy that has been done since the 1980s supports the contention that being able to participate in oral communication effectively in different situations is no less important.

More than 40 years after the publication of the Bullock Report, the attention paid by researchers, policy makers and practitioners to the important relationship between language development and the development of thinking skills, especially 'higher order' thinking skills and critical thinking, is in our view still insufficient. We would urge that more concerted attention should be paid across the curriculum to this key relationship and its importance and potential impact. It should involve focused collaboration among department heads and teachers across the curriculum and establishing language and communication as prominent elements in the curricula for *all* subjects as well as in teacher education. As has been highlighted in another Council of Europe publication on the subject:

> It is no longer appropriate for language education to be conceived narrowly and confined to one or two areas of the curriculum. Instead it needs to be seen as central to every school's mission and culture, and it needs to extend to all subjects in the curriculum. Only then will the

inequalities caused by taking language too much for granted be rectified. (Beacco *et al.*, 2015: 129)

Integration and coherence of curricula

Our own experience has spanned many different aspects of language education. It is an area which provides copious examples of the way in which curricula often lack coherence and miss opportunities for cross-fertilisation and cross-referencing. Like certain other subjects, in secondary education in particular, 'foreign languages' have traditionally been seen as belonging in a separate department with its own special needs and characteristics, and with little if any overlap with any other subject. Yet according to the view of language education that we have presented it is no longer right (if it ever was) to see 'foreign languages' as unrelated to the teaching of the language of schooling. With the explosion of global mobility and migration in the 21st century, the number of languages spoken by students in a given school or classroom has increased dramatically, as has the diversity of cultures that the students represent. The social advantages of a plurilingual repertoire, however limited, were discussed in Chapter 7. Such a repertoire potentially also enables students to use their knowledge of one language to support the learning of others, and to utilise more than one language in learning and in life, while expanding their understanding of how languages work. In 2019, the British *Guardian* newspaper published a series of articles decrying the lack of encouragement to learn foreign languages in the UK. In one of them, Sean Harford, national director of the agency responsible for school inspections in England and Wales, made the following case for introducing measures to tackle the issue:

> Languages are an essential part of a broad, balanced curriculum. Not only do they provide an opportunity to communicate more effectively with others […]: they also help pupils to understand what it is to be a global citizen, including the importance of tolerance and understanding. And they explicitly celebrate difference and highlight that which we all have in common. This is crucial knowledge in today's world. (Harford, 2019)

There is also a strong case for somehow dovetailing the learning and use of other languages with the efforts to develop competence in the language of schooling across all subjects, and for the knowledge and learning of other languages to be encouraged by those teaching other subjects, thus fostering plurilingualism across the curriculum. Moreover, in primary and secondary schools, linguistic and cultural awareness can be enhanced in motivating ways by allowing space for the increasing numbers of children with migration backgrounds who have other first language and cultural backgrounds – other repertoires – to talk about and draw on their languages and cultures. As the teacher may well not be familiar with these, such activities can provide ideal opportunities to temporarily move away from the dynamic in which the teacher is in ultimate control of the flow of knowledge and learning.

There is nothing new about this kind of proposal. A similar line of thinking is put forward in the discussion on curricula in the CEFR itself, where two key principles reproduced below are outlined:

> Discussion on curricula should be in line with the overall objective of promoting plurilingualism and linguistic diversity. This means that the teaching and learning of any one language should also be examined in conjunction with the provision for other languages in the education system and the paths which learners might choose to follow in the long term in their efforts to develop a variety of language skills.
>
> ... Considerations and measures relating to curricula should not just be limited to a curriculum for each language taken in isolation, nor even an integrated curriculum for several languages. They should also be approached in terms of their role in a general language education, in which linguistic knowledge (savoir) and skills (savoir-faire), along with the ability to learn (savoir-apprendre), play not only a specific role in a given language but also a transversal or transferable role across languages. (Council of Europe, 2001: 169)

To summarise the implications of the paradigm shifts proposed above, we see huge advantages in bringing together in one interlocking educational effort:

- Teaching and learning the language of schooling, including developing literacy, oracy and critical awareness of the ways it is used in the various school subjects, in society, in the media (including the social media used by students), in creative works, in political discourse, in marketing and so on.
- The role of language(s) across the curriculum in developing these different kinds of literacy, higher order thinking skills and critical awareness.
- Acknowledging the various home/first languages that form part of the language repertoires of all the people in the school and its environment, and of the cultures they represent, and encouraging them to draw on these when relevant.
- Teaching and learning at least one foreign language for active use and raising students' awareness of the practical and cognitive value of plurilingualism.

Internationally, some systems may well be moving towards such a curricular transformation but most that we are familiar with have yet to make a start.

The promotion of pluralistic approaches to language and culture

In Chapters 1 and 6 we drew attention to the important role of language awareness and of language and intercultural competences in the development and deployment of the constellation of competences that enable us to participate effectively and responsibly in democratic culture. Recent decades have seen a seismic increase in mobility and migration across the world, which has contributed to growing social, cultural and linguistic diversity and pluralism in our societies. Many of us consider this increased diversity to be an enrichment of our societies. However, following the devastating wars and upheavals of the 20th century, governments in Europe, mindful of the potential and historic fragility of democracy, have become especially sensitive to the potential for this increased diversity to be an excuse for extremism and intolerance. The *Reference Framework of Competences for Democratic Culture* developed by the Council of Europe (2018a) as a support for policy makers and educators across its 47 member states is one of several pan-European responses to this situation.

Plurilingualism, the ability to draw on one's knowledge and awareness of other languages and varieties of language, however modest that knowledge may be, in everyday interactions, and pluriculturalism, the willingness to take account of and embrace cultural diversity in one's everyday encounters, are important life-skills:

> Effective learning of one or more languages, awareness of the value of diversity and otherness, and recognition of any (even partial) competence are necessary for anyone who, as an active member of the community, has to exercise his or her democratic citizenship in a multilingual and multicultural society. (Beacco *et al*., 2015: 17)

This point gains added significance in some contexts in today's Europe, where pride in one's language and cultural heritage too easily spills over into nationalism, particularly in cases where people may feel that their national identity is being swallowed up by the growth of 'Europeanism'. School language classes, both in the mother tongue and in other languages, are surely an appropriate forum for discussion of the balance that needs to be achieved in this sensitive area.

Work has been done on defining how schools and teachers of all subjects could approach the task of helping students of all ages to develop plurilingual and pluricultural competences (see Candelier *et al*., 2012; Cummins, 1996). But this is no easy task for teachers whose initial training and experience may not have included guidance and practice in this area. Our view is that, for pluralistic approaches to education to become a reality, much more work needs to be done on the practical and curricular implications of such an approach.

In other words, establishing the worthy principles of a plurilingual and pluricultural approach to education and developing an awareness of its importance is not enough, and in many contexts that we are familiar with where diversity is a salient feature too little work has been done even on this. For effective application of these principles, teacher educators and teachers need to have access to or to create concrete and motivating activities and resources that can be used in classrooms, and ongoing support in using them needs to be provided. A concerted and collaborative effort on the part of specialists, teacher educators, school leaders and publishers of educational materials, along the lines raised in the questions at the end of Chapter 9, is needed if such a paradigm shift is to occur.

Teacher education

An implication of the international paradigm shifts recommended above is that further reform is needed in initial and in-service teacher education. As discussed in Part 2 of the book, the limited research we have carried out indicates that most teachers, irrespective of their subject or of the kind of school they work in, are not given the training needed to take on the challenges of understanding and implementing the kind of holistic language education policy outlined above. While in many countries increased mobility means that teachers themselves bring with them competences in other languages and familiarity with other cultures, the approach to language development and language awareness that we are advocating almost certainly was not a feature of their own school education, and, as discussed in Part 2, our limited research indicates that generally teacher education does not systematically include a focus on language and communication and its role in teaching and learning. Apart from the initial education of foreign language teachers we could find few examples where teacher education courses included modules on language, communication, their role in teaching and learning across the curriculum, and the rationale for cross-curricular attention to the development of literacy, oracy and plurilingualism during schooling. This means that teachers are generally left to learn about and learn how to cope with these issues 'on the job'. Even where teachers of foreign or additional languages are concerned, the language focus of initial teacher education courses tends to be on the technical and discourse features of the so-called 'target' language rather than the encompassing broader aspects discussed, for example, in the *Common European Framework of Reference for Languages* and the recently published Companion Volume (Council of Europe, 2018b).

In our view, it is essential to build into the curricula for initial teacher education for all teachers of all subjects around the world a significant strand, or more than one strand, that focuses on the key aspects of language and communication relevant to education. Such a development would be in line with another of the insightful recommendations contained in the Bullock Report mentioned above and in Chapter 1: 'a substantial course on language in education (including reading) should be part of every primary and secondary school teacher's initial training, whatever the teacher's subject or the age of the children with whom he or she will be working' (Bullock Report, 1975: 515). As indicated in further detailed recommendations in that report, the language dimension of the teacher education curriculum should straddle the building of critical awareness, knowledge and knowhow and the application of this knowhow in everyday teaching practice. For example, the ways in which student teachers and practising teachers use and deal with language and communication in their teaching could be a regular focus of observation of teaching and discussion of feedback, and this could be enhanced by group discussion of video-recorded samples of teaching of different subjects.

This recommendation is not relevant only to initial teacher education: it is essential that language issues should also be regularly included in in-service teacher education and support for the continuing professional development of all teachers, especially in systems where curricula are being reformed to encourage a more inclusive and holistic approach to language. The evidence we have been able to gather indicates that, for most teachers, there are few opportunities in their INSET programmes within and outside their institutions to work with other teachers of the same and different subjects on key issues such as oracy, the development of subject-related academic literacy, handling multilingual and multicultural groups, or looking closely at the language and communication strategies they themselves use in the classroom. In many respects, practising teachers are in an advantageous position since they can build on their experience and current practice to carry out collaborative or individual classroom research focusing on language development and subject-related language use that can inform others, including teacher educators and those implementing curricular reform. Literacy and oracy development and language use do not, however, only affect pedagogy: an enlightened approach to them is also needed in assessment, especially the ongoing assessment carried out by teachers.

The simple fact is that it takes language-aware teachers to develop language awareness in their pupils and students, it takes critically thinking teachers to help pupils and students to develop their critical thinking skills, and it takes teachers committed to a pluralistic approach to develop plurilingualism and pluriculturalism in their classrooms. A systematic structured approach to these and other language-related topics is therefore essential in the CPD of all teachers.

Ways Forward

It is not our place to add more detail to these proposed new paradigms. This prerogative belongs to those working on the formulation and implementation of curricular innovation and changes in the given local, regional or national contexts. The need for concerted action and joined-up thinking is evident, but where would the impetus come from and which stakeholders' initiatives would have the best chances of success? In some countries, such as Finland, it may be possible for individual schools to plan, pilot and implement such reforms, but in many national and regional systems, for such changes to be brought about carefully judged and well-researched policy initiatives are needed 'from the top'. It seems to us that those responsible for curriculum development and the design of teacher education programmes are best placed to instigate such initiatives, as these are two of the most powerful drivers of educational reform. By working together to develop new paradigms of this kind and to pilot new approaches with the help of researchers who are themselves committed to innovation and to breaking out of traditional subject boundaries, convincing evidence could be gathered to persuade those ultimately responsible for policy and its implementation of the importance of this kind of paradigm shift. Once such changes are finalised and implemented in a given context, examination providers, publishers and other stakeholders, who contribute to inertia in education and should not be driving policy, would find it in their interests to pay attention and to respond positively in their own areas. Indeed, as the balance of power and influence in language education shifts and develops, it is important that commercial interests should not be allowed to dictate policies, curriculum design and standards. These areas must remain in the hands of ministries and language teaching professionals, guided by but not dominated by academic institutions and research findings, where these are relevant.

Figures 10.1 and 10.2, taken from Bolitho (2012), are simplified representations of the way in which the impact of an innovation can be diluted depending on its origin and the 'direction of flow'. In Figure 10.1, let us imagine that the policy change originates at national ministry level, in the centre circle. As the structure of the innovation project is based on dissemination or cascading from this centre of activity and energy through regional and institutional levels, there is a likelihood that change messages will be diluted and distorted by the time they reach the teachers working in the outer circle.

In Figure 10.2, on the other hand, activity and energy is generated initially at classroom level, with high levels of involvement of both teachers and learners in the centre circle, which reverses the direction of flow in Figure 10.1.

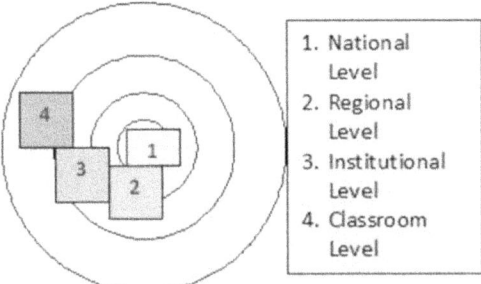

Figure 10.1 Change initiated 'top-down' at national level

1. National Level
2. Regional Level
3. Institutional Level
4. Classroom Level

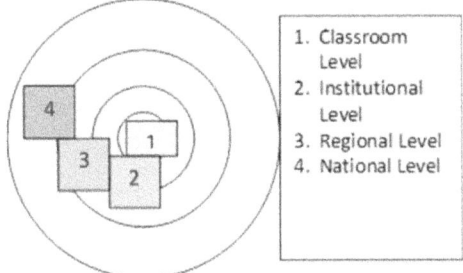

Figure 10.2 Change that starts in the classroom and works 'bottom-up'

1. Classroom Level
2. Institutional Level
3. Regional Level
4. National Level

However, it is equally hard for good practice at classroom level to be disseminated as far as the national level, where the impact might be heeded and lessons learned that can be applied nationally (Bolitho, 2012: 42–43). The key point is that in a sense change needs to be initiated and embraced in each of the concentric circles. This implies a careful process of needs assessment, consultation, trial implementation and further consultation. Only in this way can 'dilution' of change initiatives be avoided.

Figure 10.3 below illustrates a potential relationship between key stakeholders. The different categories of stakeholder are again organised in concentric circles, with teachers, learners and their parents 'at the sharp end' nearest the centre where the new policy will be developed, tried out and implemented, the most prominent stakeholders in the middle circle, and the advisers, researchers, funding agencies and, in the case of Europe, European bodies in the outer circle. But the key condition for these various stakeholders to be effective in delivering policies that reflect the new paradigms, we suggest, is that they must continually communicate with one another and take into account the views and experiences of fellow stakeholders. There needs to be constructive cooperation and communication within each layer of the circle as well as among stakeholders in different layers. In other words, joined up thinking and collaborative action along the lines we have indicated is essential for effective policy initiatives.

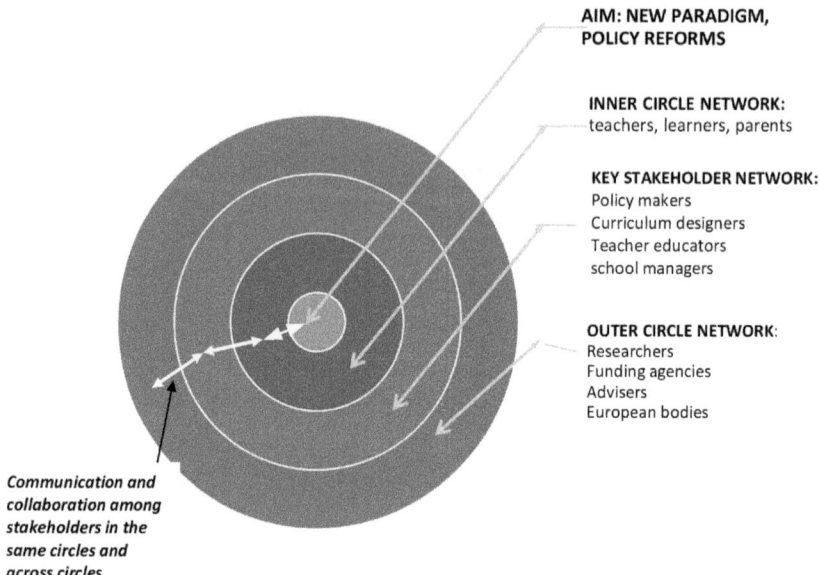

Communication and collaboration among stakeholders in the same circles and across circles

Figure 10.3 Involvement of and collaboration among different groups of stakeholders in a language-related reform process in education – a schematic view

Concluding Remarks

Educational reform in most countries in the world is driven by the twin concerns of employability and international competition, as well as the attention paid to national rankings in the triennial Programme for International Student Assessment (PISA) studies. But accompanying and underlying these preoccupations should be a desire to enable each student to reach his or her true potential in education and in society, and to become active and well-informed citizens. The first volume of *The Reference Framework of Competences for Democratic Culture* cited above summarises these objectives of education well:

> Democratic education should be part of a comprehensive and coherent vision of education, of an education of the whole person. The Council of Europe, in Recommendation CM/Rec (2007), provides a vision of education that includes four major purposes:
> - preparation for the labour market;
> - preparation for life as active citizens in democratic societies;
> - personal development;
> - the development and maintenance of a broad, advanced knowledge base. (Council of Europe, 2018a: 14)

To achieve these goals, it is crucial for each individual to be able to use a well-developed language repertoire across disciplines, and in all aspects of life outside and beyond education, and it is essential that teachers and curricula in schools enable them to do this. In this book, we have looked at some of the possible means of achieving this in any context internationally, in the hope that they will be re-examined and acted upon by educational decision makers.

Questions for reflection and discussion

(1) How relevant are the proposals on curriculum reform in the context where you work? In your view, what steps are needed in your context to ensure a more coherent policy in language education across the curriculum?
(2) How many languages and how many cultures are typically represented in schools in the educational environment in which you work? What steps are taken to cater for and take advantage of this diversity? What challenges, if any, does this kind of diversity present to teachers?
(3) Do you agree that language and language awareness should be more intensively and broadly focused on in the initial teacher education and professional development of all teachers? How could this best be achieved in your context?

References

Abbs, B. and Freebairn, I. (1975–1978) *Strategies* (series). London: Pearson-Longman.
Alderson, C. and Clapham, C. (1995) *Language Test Construction and Evaluation*. Cambridge: Cambridge University Press.
Alexander, L.G. (1964) *New Concept English, Books 1–4* London: Longman.
Alexander, R. (2008) *Towards Dialogic Teaching – Rethinking Classroom Talk* (4th edn). York: Dialogos Ltd.
Alexander, R. (ed.) (2010) *Children, their World, their Education – Final Report and Recommendations of the Cambridge Primary Review*. London: Routledge.
Alexander, R. (2012) *Improving Oracy and Classroom Talk in English Schools: Achievements and Challenges*. See http://www.robinalexander.org.uk/wp-content/uploads/2012/06/DfE-oracy-120220-Alexander-FINAL.pdf (accessed October 2019).
Anderson, L.W. and Krathwohl D.R. (eds) (2000) *A Taxonomy for Learning, Teaching, and Assessing: A Revision of Bloom's Taxonomy of Educational Objectives*. New York: Longman.
Allen, P. (2008) France's L'Académie Française upset by rule to recognise regional tongues. *The Daily Telegraph* 16 August. See https://www.telegraph.co.uk/news/worldnews/europe/france/2569651/Frances-LAcadmie-Franaise-upset-by-rule-to-recognise-regional-tongues.html (accessed 21 August 2018).
Arnot, M., Schneider, C., Evans, M., Liu,Y., Welply, O. and Davies-Tutt, D. (2014) *School Approaches to the Education of EAL Students*. Cambridge: The Bell Foundation.
Bailey, K.M. (2006) *Language Teacher Supervision – A Case-Based Approach*. Cambridge: Cambridge University Press.
Barik, S. (2017) Tribal communities in Odisha are speaking up to save their dialects. *The Hindu*, 4 June 2017. See https://www.thehindu.com/news/national/other-states/tribal-communities-in-odisha-are-speaking-up-to-save-their-dialects/article18713925.ece (accessed 24 August 2018).
Barnes D. (1974) In the foreword to National Institute of Education (1974): p. 1
Barnes, D. (1976) *From Communication to Curriculum*. Harmondsworth: Penguin.
Barnes, D. (2008) Exploratory talk for learning. In N. Mercer and S. Hodgkinson (eds) *Exploring Talk in Schools* (pp. 1–16). London: Sage Publications.
Beacco, J.C. and Byram, M. (2007) *From Linguistic Diversity to Plurilingual Education: Guide for the Development of Language Education Policies in Europe*. Strasbourg: Council of Europe. See http://www.coe.int/t/dg4/linguistic/guide_niveau3_en.asp (accessed October 2017).
Beacco, J.C., Byram, M., Cavalli, M., Coste, D., Egli Cuenat, M., Goullier, F. and Panthier, J. (2015) *Guide for the Development and Implementation of Curricula for Plurilingual and Pluricultural Education*. Strasbourg: Council of Europe.
Berthele, R., Lindt-Bangerter, B. and Obermayer, S. (2012) Switzerland. In G. Extra and K. Yağmur (eds) *Language Rich Europe* (pp. 215–224). Cambridge: Cambridge University Press.

Bleichenbacher, L., Kuster, W., Heinzmann, S., Hilbe, R., Annen, M. (2019) *Entwicklung sprachenübergreifender curricularer Elemente für die Ausbildung von Sprachenlehrpersonen Sek I* (2nd rev edn). St Gallen: Pädagogische Hochschule St.Gallen. See https://www.phsg.ch/sites/default/files/cms/Forschung/Institute/Institut-Fachdidaktik-Sprachen/CV/ESCEAS_Bleichenbacher_et_al_2019.pdf (accessed November 2019).

Bloom, B.S. (ed.) (1956) *Taxonomy of Educational Objectives, the Classification of Educational Goals – Handbook I: Cognitive Domain.* New York: McKay.

Bolitho, R. (2012) Projects and programmes: Contemporary experience in ELT change management. In C. Tribble (ed.) *Managing Change in English Language Teaching* (pp. 33–46). London: The British Council.

Bolitho, R. (2019) Issues and relationships in the use of materials. *Folio* 19 (1), 4–7

Bolitho, R. and Padwad, A. (2018) *Continuing Professional Development.* New Delhi: Cambridge University Press (India).

Bolitho, R. and West, R. (2017) *The Internationalisation of Ukrainian Universities: The English Language Dimension.* Kyiv: British Council.

Borg, S. (2016) Enhancing the impact of in-service training. Presentation at TESOL Arabia, Dubai, 9–12 March 2016. Slides available at: http://simon-borg.co.uk/wp-content/uploads/2013/03/Borg-TESOL-Arabia-Plenary-2016-slides.pdf (accessed May 2016).

British Council (2014, 2015) *English for Academics* (books 1 and 2). Cambridge: Cambridge University Press.

British Council (2015) *CPD Framework for Teachers.* London: The British Council. See https://www.teachingenglish.org.uk/article/british-council-cpd-framework (accessed January 2018).

British Council (2018) *Annual Report and Accounts 2017–2018.* London: The British Council.

British National Corpus (1991–2007) See http://www.natcorp.ox.ac.uk/ (accessed October 2017).

Bullock Report (1975) *A Language for Life. Principal Recommendations.* London: HMSO.

Butler, M. (2018) Spanish schools ditch bilingual programmes. *EL Gazette* July 2018.

Byram, M. (ed.) (2003) *Intercultural Competence.* Strasbourg: Council of Europe.

Cambridge Assessment (2014) *Cambridge English Teaching Framework.* See http://www.cambridgeenglish.org/teaching-english/cambridge-english-teaching-framework/ (accessed January 2018).

Candelier, M., Camilleri-Grima, A., Castellotti, V., de Pietro, F., Lorincz, I., Meissner, F-J., Noguerol, A. and Schröder-Sura, A. (2012) *A Framework of Reference for Pluralistic Approaches to Languages and Cultures (FREPA).* Graz: ECML.

Carter, R. (ed.) (1989) *Language in the National Curriculum (LINC) Project.* London: Department of Education and Science.

Carter, R. and McCarthy, M. (1997) *Exploring Spoken English.* Cambridge: Cambridge University Press.

Carter, R. and. McCarthy, M. (2006) *Cambridge Grammar of English.* Cambridge: Cambridge University Press.

Carter, R. and McCarthy, M. (2011) *English Grammar Today.* Cambridge: Cambridge University Press.

Chaloner, J., Evans, A. and Pragnell, M. (2015) *Supporting the British Economy through Teaching English as a Foreign Language.* London: English UK. See http://www.englishuk.com/uploads/assets/members/publications/statistics/Economic_impact_report_WEB.pdf (accessed November 2019).

CIEP (2016) *Répertoire de Méthodes de Français Langue Etrangère.* Sèvres: CIEP. See http://www.ciep.fr/sites/default/files/atoms/files/repertoire_methodes_fle.pdf (accessed October 2018).

Clark, J.L., Scarino, A. and Brownell, J.A. (1994) *A Framework for Target-oriented Curriculum Renewal in Hong Kong.* Hong Kong: Hong Kong Bank Language Development Fund & Institute of Education. Scanned mimeograph available at https://files.eric.ed.gov/fulltext/ED387417.pdf (accessed May 2018).

Commonwealth of Australia (2005) *Teaching Reading: National Inquiry into the Teaching of Literacy*. https://web.archive.org/web/20110812024503/http://www.dest.gov.au/nitl/documents/report_recommendations.pdf (accessed 21 August 2018).

Communication Trust (2017) *The Speech, Language and Communication Framework*. London: The Communication Trust. See https://www.slcframework.org.uk/how-to-use/ (accessed October 2018).

Cope, B. and Kalantzis, M. (eds) (2015) *A Pedagogy of Multiliteracies*. Basingstoke & New York: Palgrave Macmillan.

Council of Europe (1954) *European Cultural Convention*. Paris. See https://www.coe.int/en/web/culture-and-heritage/european-cultural-convention (accessed 14 August, 2017).

Council of Europe (1992) *The European Charter for Regional or Minority Languages*. Strasbourg: Council of Europe. See https://rm.coe.int/168007bf4b (accessed September 2018).

Council of Europe (2001) *Common European Framework of Reference for Languages: Learning, Teaching, Assessment*. Cambridge: Cambridge University Press. See also http://www.coe.int/en/web/common-european-framework-reference-languages/ (accessed October 2017).

Council of Europe (2014) *Final Report on the 3rd Council of Europe Survey*. Strasbourg: Council of Europe. See https://rm.coe.int/CoERMPublicCommonSearchServices/DisplayDCTMContent?documentId=09000016802fc1ce (accessed October 2019).

Council of Europe (2018a) *Reference Framework of Competences for Democratic Culture* (vols 1–3). Strasbourg: Council of Europe. See https://www.coe.int/en/web/education/competences-for-democratic-culture (accessed September 2018).

Council of Europe (2018b) *CEFR Companion Volume*. Strasbourg: Council of Europe. See https://rm.coe.int/cefr-companion-volume-with-new-descriptors-2018/1680787989 (accessed October 2018).

Cox Report (1989) *English for Ages 5 to 16*. London: Her Majesty's Stationery Office. See http://www.educationengland.org.uk/documents/cox1989/cox89.html#04 (accessed October 2018).

Crystal, D. (1997) *English as a Global Language*. Cambridge: Cambridge University Press.

Cummins, J. (1996) *Negotiating Identities: Education for Empowerment in a Diverse Society*. Los Angeles: California Association for Bilingual Education.

Deutsche Welle (2011) Vom Gastarbeiter zum Nachbarn – 50 Jahre deutsch-türkisches Anwerbeabkommen. Video clip. See https://www.dw.com/de/auftakt-der-serie-vom-gastarbeiter-zum-nachbarn-50-jahre-deutsch-t%C3%BCrkisches-anwerbeabkommen/a-6704913 (accessed October 2019).

Dewey, J. (1910) *How We Think*. Lexington, MA: D.C. Heath.

Doiz, A. and Lasagabaster, D. (2017) Management teams and teaching staff: Do they share the same beliefs about obligatory CLIL programmes and the use of the L1? *Language and Education* 31 (2), 96–109. See https://www.tandfonline.com/eprint/2gHA7aw9DjFnERCAKj9M/full (accessed May 2019).

EAQUALS (2013) *The Eaquals Framework for Language Teacher Training and Development*. London: Eaquals. See https://www.eaquals.org/our-expertise/teacher-development/the-eaquals-framework-for-teacher-training-and-development/ (accessed January 2018).

Eckersley, C.E. (1938–1942) *Essential English for Foreign Students* (Books 1–4). London: Longman.

ECML (2019) A guide to teacher competences for languages in education. See https://www.ecml.at/ECML-Programme/Programme2016-2019/TowardsaCommonEuropeanFrameworkofReferenceforLanguageTeachers/tabid/1850/language/en-GB/Default.aspx (accessed October 2019).

Edelenbos, P., Johnstone, R. and Kubanek, A. (2006) *The Main Pedagogical Principles Underlying the Teaching of Languages to very Young Learners*. Brussels: European

Commission. See https://ec.europa.eu/assets/eac/languages/policy/language-policy/documents/young_en.pdf (accessed November 2019).

Edwards, A.D. and Westgate D.P.G. (1994) *Investigating Classroom Talk* (2nd edn). London: The Falmer Press.

El Amraoui, A. (2018) How an education crisis is hurting Morocco's poor. Al Jazeera website, March 2018. See https://www.aljazeera.com/indepth/features/education-crisis-hurting-morocco-poor-180306225706337.html (accessed August 2018).

European Commission (2011) *Languages for Jobs – Providing Multilingual Communication Skills for the Labour Market*. Brussels: EU Commission. See http://ec.europa.eu/assets/eac/languages/policy/strategic-framework/documents/languages-for-jobs-report_en.pdf (accessed July 2018).

European Commission (2012) Language competences for employability, mobility and growth. Commission Staff Working Document. Brussels: EU Commission. See https://eur-lex.europa.eu/legal-content/EN/TXT/?uri=celex%3A52012SC0372 (accessed July 2018).

European Commission (2013) *Language Rich Europe: Review and Recommendations*. London: The British Council.

European Commission/EACEA/Eurydice (2015) *The Teaching Profession in Europe: Practices, Perceptions, and Policies*. Eurydice Report. Luxembourg: Publications Office of the European Commission. See https://eacea.ec.europa.eu/national-policies/eurydice/content/teaching-profession-europe-practices-perceptions-and-policies_en (accessed July 2019).

European Commission/EACEA/Eurydice (2017) *Eurydice Brief – Key Data on Teaching Languages at School in Europe*. Brussels: EU Commission. See https://eacea.ec.europa.eu/national-policies/eurydice/content/eurydice-briefkey-data-teaching-languages-school-europe_en (accessed July 2018).

European Commission (2018a) Council recommendation on a comprehensive approach to the teaching and learning of languages. Brussels: EU Commission. See https://eur-lex.europa.eu/legal-content/EN/TXT/?qid=1527006129608&uri=COM:2018:272:FIN (accessed July 2018).

European Commission (2018b) Council recommendation on key competences for lifelong learning. Brussels: EU Commission. Seehttps://eur-lex.europa.eu/legal-content/EN/TXT/PDF/?uri=CELEX:32018H0604(01)&from=EN (accessed November 2019).

European Commission (2018c) Annex to the proposal for a Council recommendation on a comprehensive approach to the teaching and learning of languages. Brussels: EU Commission. See https://eur-lex.europa.eu/resource.html?uri=cellar:1cc186a3-5dc7-11e8-ab9c-01aa75ed71a1.0001.02/DOC_2&format=PDF (accessed July 2018).

European Commission (2018d) Proposal for a Council Recommendation on Key Competences for Lifelong Learning. Brussels: European Commission. See https://data.consilium.europa.eu/doc/document/ST-8299-2018-INIT/en/pdf (accessed September 2019).

Fairclough, N. (2003) *Analysing Discourse: Textual Analysis for Social Research*. London: Routledge.

Fairclough, N. (ed.) (2013) *Critical Language Awareness*. London: Routledge.

Fullan, M. (2007) *The New Meaning of Educational Change* (4th edn). London: Routledge.

Gardner, R.C. (2004) International AMTB Research Project. University of Western Ontario. See http://publish.uwo.ca/~gardner/docs/englishamtb.pdf (accessed June 2019).

Gardner, R.C. (2005) Integrative motivation and second language acquisition. A plenary address to the Canadian Association of Applied Linguistics. See http://publish.uwo.ca/~gardner/docs/caaltalk5final.pdf (accessed June 2019).

Gardner, R.C. and Lambert, W.E. (1972) *Attitudes and Motivation in Second Language Learning*. Rowley, MA: Newbury House.

Garside, R., Leech, G. and Sampson, G. (eds) (1987) *The Computational Analysis of English: A Corpus-based Approach*. London: Longman.

Government of Odisha (2014) Department of School and Mass Education: notification dated 1/7/2014. See https://sme.odisha.gov.in/resolution/2014/14118.pdf (accessed October 2019).

Gower, R., Walters, S. and Phillips, D. (1995) *Teaching Practice Handbook*. London: Macmillan.

Graddol, D. (2006) *English Next*. London: The British Council.

Gray, J. (2010) *The Construction of English: Culture, Consumerism and Promotion in the ELT Global Coursebook*. Basingstoke: Palgrave Macmillan.

Gray, J. and Block, D. (2013) All middle class now? Evolving representations of social class in the neoliberal era: The case of ELT textbooks. In N. Harwood (ed.) *English Language Teaching Textbooks: Content, Consumption, Production* (pp. 45–71). Basingstoke: Palgrave Macmillan.

Gulyamova, J. and Isamukhamedova, N. (2012) English reforms in Uzbekistan. *The Teacher Trainer* 26 (1), 7–9

Hadley, G. (2014) Global textbooks in local contexts: An empirical investigation of effectiveness. In N. Harwood (ed.) *English Language Teaching Textbooks: Content, Consumption, Production* (pp. 205–240). Basingstoke: Palgrave Macmillan).

Hanson, M. (2018) Teaching is on the road to hell – the story of the national curriculum proves it. *The Guardian* 12 February. See https://www.theguardian.com/lifeandstyle/2018/feb/12/teaching-is-on-the-road-to-hell-the-story-of-the-national-curriculum-proves-it (accessed July 2018).

Hartley B. and Viney, P. (1978–1980) *Streamline English* (series). Oxford: Oxford University Press.

Harford, S. (2019) Foreign language learning more vital than ever in post-Brexit world. *The Guardian*, 4th July 2019. See https://www.theguardian.com/education/2019/jul/04/foreign-language-learning-more-vital-than-ever-in-post-brexit-world.

Holliday, A. (1994) The house of TESEP and the communicative approach: The special needs of state English language education. *ELT Journal* 48 (1), 3–11

Hope, M. (2012) Introduction. In G. Extra and K. Yağmur (eds) *Language Rich Europe* (pp. 6–7). Cambridge: Cambridge University Press.

Jenkins, J. (2000) *The Phonology of English as an International Language*. Oxford: Oxford University Press.

Jin, L., Jiang, C., Zhang, J., Yuan, Y., Liang, X. and Xie, Q. (2014) Motivations and expectations of English language learning among primary school children and parents in China. London: the British Council. See https://englishagenda.britishcouncil.org/research-publications/research-papers/motivations-and-expectations-english-language-learning-among-primary-school-children-and-parents (accessed June 2019).

Johnson, J. (1994) The National Oracy Project. In S. Brindley (ed.) *Teaching English* (pp. 33–42). London: Routledge.

Johnston, R. and Watson, J. (2014) *Teaching Synthetic Phonics in Primary School*. London: Sage.

Kansanen, P. (2003) Teacher education in Finland: Current models and new developments. In B. Moon, L. Vlăsceanu and C. Barrows (eds) (2003) *Institutional approaches to teacher education within higher education in Europe: Current models and new developments* (pp. 85–108). Bucharest: Unesco – Cepes. See http://citeseerx.ist.psu.edu/viewdoc/download?doi=10.1.1.575.8891&rep=rep1&type=pdf (accessed October 2019).

Kaplan R.B. (1993) The hegemony of English in science and technology. *Journal of Multilingual and Multicultural Development* 14, 151–172.

Kelly, M. and Grenfell, M. (2004) *European Profile for Language Teacher Education: A Frame of Reference*. Southampton: University of Southampton.

Kingman Report (1988) *Report of the Committee of Inquiry into the Teaching of the English Language*. London: Her Majesty's Stationery Office. See http://www.educationengland.org.uk/documents/kingman/ (accessed October 2018).

Krathwohl D.R. (2002) A revision of Bloom's taxonomy: An overview. *Theory into Practice* 41 (4), 212–218.

Kurtoglu-Hooton, N. (2013) Providing the spark for reflection from a digital platform. In J. Edge and S. Mann (eds) *Innovations in Pre-Service Education and Training for English Language Teachers* (pp. 17–32). London: The British Council.

Lave J. and Wenger, E. (1991) *Situated Learning: Legitimate Peripheral Participation*. Cambridge: Cambridge University Press.

Leaton Gray S. (2005) *Enquiry into Continuing Professional Development for Teachers*. London: Esmée Fairbairn Foundation.

Littlewood, W. (1981) *Communicative Language Teaching: An Introduction*. Cambridge: Cambridge University Press.

Maas, C. (2018) Germany 1:0 England – ELT publishing in Deutschland. See https://mawsig.iatefl.org/germany-10-england-elt-publishing-in-deutschland/ (accessed 28 September 2018).

Machin, S., McNally, S. and Viarengo, M. (2016) *Teaching to Teach Literacy: Centre for Economic Performance, Discussion Paper No. 1425*. London: London School of Economics. See http://cep.lse.ac.uk/pubs/download/dp1425.pdf (accessed 21 August 2018).

Maddison, L. (2016) Native English speakers are the world's worst communicators. BBC. See http://www.bbc.com/capital/story/20161028-native-english-speakers-are-the-worlds-worst-communicators (accessed 28th September 2017).

Maingay, P. (1988) Observation for training, development or assessment? In T. Duff (ed.) *Explorations in Teacher Training* (pp. 118–131). London: Longman.

Mann, S. (2005) The language teacher's development. *Language Teaching* 38 (2), 118–131.

Mansell, W. (2012) The new national curriculum made to order? *Guardian* 12 November. See https://www.theguardian.com/education/2012/nov/12/primary-national-curriculum-review (accessed July 2018).

Martin, S. (1999) *New Life, New Language: History of the Adult Migrant English Program 1948–1998*. Sydney: Macquarie University.

Masson, M. and Ng, T. (2017) A report of perspectives on multilingual education in Ontario with Greater Toronto Area community members. OME Community Talk Series No. 1. See http://docs.wixstatic.com/ugd/116537_e5db1e00afec435881f557477248c076.pdf (accessed August 2018).

Meddings, L. and Thornbury, S. (2010) *Teaching Unplugged*. Peaslake: Delta Publishing.

Medgyes, P. and Paran, A. (2017) Point and counterpoint. *ELT Journal* 71 (4), 491–510.

Mehisto, P. (2012) Criteria for producing CLIL learning material. *Encuentro* 21. See https://www.unifg.it/sites/default/files/allegatiparagrafo/21-01-2014/mehisto_criteria_for_producing_clil_learning_material.pdf (accessed October 2019).

Mercer, N. (2000) *Words and Mind – How we Use Language to Think Together*. London: Routledge.

Marzano R.J. and Kendall J.S. (2007) *The New Taxonomy of Educational Objectives*. Thousand Oaks, CA: Corwin Press.

Millard, W. and Menzies, L. (2016) *The State of Speaking in Our Schools*. London: Voice 21. See https://voice21.org/wp-content/uploads/2019/10/Voice-21-State-of-speaking-in-our-schools.pdf df (accessed October 2019).

Ministry of Education Ghana (2017) The National Teacher Education Curriculum Framework. Accra: Ministry of Education, Republic of Ghana. See http://www.t-tel.org/files/docs/Learning%20Hub/Teacher%20education%20policies%20and%20protocols/The%20Essential%20Elements%20of%20Initial%20Teacher%20Education.pdf (accessed October 2019).

Morawski, M. and Budke, A. (2017) Learning with and by language: Bilingual teaching strategies for the monolingual language-aware geography classroom. *The Geography Teacher* 14 (2), 48–67.

Morgan, N. and Saxton, J. (1991) *Teaching, Questioning and Learning*. London: Routledge.
Munday, S. (2016) *A Framework of Core Content for Initial Teacher Training*. See https://assets.publishing.service.gov.uk/government/uploads/system/uploads/attachment_data/file/536890/Framework_Report_11_July_2016_Final.pdf (accessed October 2018).
National Institute of Education (1974) Report of Panel 5: Teaching as a linguistic process in a cultural setting. Conference in Studies on Teaching. Washington DC, December 1974, cited in C.B. Cazden (2001) *Classroom Discourse – The Language of Teaching and Learning* (2nd edn). Portsmouth, NH: Heinemann.
North, B., Mateva, G. and Rossner, R. (2013) *European Profiling Grid*. Sèvres: EPG Project. See http://egrid.epg-project.eu/ (accessed January 2018).
O'Neill, R., Kingsbury, R., Yeadon, T. and Scott, R. (1971) *Kernel Lesson Intermediate*. London: Longman.
Phillipson, R. (1992) *Linguistic Imperialism*. Oxford: Oxford University Press.
Phillipson, R. (2003) *English-Only Europe? Challenging Language Policy*. London: Routledge.
Piccardo, E. and North, B. (2019) *The Action-Oriented Approach: A Dynamic Vison of Language Education*. Bristol: Multilingual Matters.
Poedjiastutie, D. and Oliver, R. (2017) Exploring students' learning needs: Expectation and challenges. *English Language Teaching* 10 (10). DOI: 10.5539/elt.v10n10p124.
Popovici, R. and Bolitho, R. (2003) Personal and professional development through writing: The Romanian textbook project. In B. Tomlinson (ed.) (2003) *Developing Materials for Language Teaching* (pp. 505–519). London: Continuum.
Porto, M. and Byram, M. (2016) *New Perspectives on Intercultural Language Research and Teaching*. London: Routledge.
Pulverness, A. (2003) Materials for cultural awareness. In B. Tomlinson (ed.) *Developing Materials for Language Teaching* (pp. 426–438). London: Continuum.
Rahman, A. and Cotter, T. (2014) English language learning through mobile phones. In S. Garton and K. Graves (eds) *International perspectives on materials in ELT*. London: Palgrave Macmillan.
Raising Bilingual Children. See: http://www.raising-bilingual-children.com/basics/language-stimulation/bilingual-schools/other-european-countries/other-european-countries-ii/ (accessed 28 September 2017).
Rixon, S. and Smith, R. (2012) The work of Brian Abbs and Ingrid Freebairn. *ELT Journal* 66 (3), 383–393.
Rose, J. (2006) *Independent Review of the Teaching of Early Reading*. See http://webarchive.nationalarchives.gov.uk/20130321055757/https://www.education.gov.uk/publications/eOrderingDownload/0201-2006PDF-EN-01.pdf (accessed 21 August 2018).
Rossner, R. (2014) *Quality in the linguistic integration of adult migrants. Report on the third linguistic integration of adult migrants* (LIAM) Conference. Strasbourg: Council of Europe. See https://rm.coe.int/CoERMPublicCommonSearchServices/DisplayDCTMContent?documentId=0900001680305c65 (accessed October 2018).
Rossner, R. (2017a) *Language Teaching Competences*. Oxford: Oxford University Press.
Rossner, R. (2017b) *Language Course Management*. Oxford: Oxford University Press.
Sahlberg, P. (2012) The most wanted: Teaching and teacher education in Finland. In L. Darling-Hammond and A. Lieberman (eds) *Teacher Education around the World* (pp. 1–21). London: Routledge.
Schön, D. (1983) *The Reflective Practitioner. How Professionals Think in Action*. London: Temple Smith.
Seidlhofer, B. (2001) Closing a conceptual gap: The case for a description of English as a lingua franca. *International Journal of Applied Linguistics* 11 (2), 133–158.
Seidlhofer B. (2005) English as a lingua franca. *ELT Journal* 59 (4), 339–341.

Surveylang (2012) *First European Survey on Language Competences – Executive Summary*. Brussels: European Commission. See http://www.surveylang.org/media/ExecutivesummaryoftheESLC_210612.pdf (accessed July 2018).

Swales, J. (1990) *Genre Analysis – English in Academic and Research Settings*. Cambridge: Cambridge University Press.

Swales, J. (2004) *Research Genres: Explorations and Applications*. Cambridge: Cambridge University Press.

Thonhauser I. (2012) Plurilingual and intercultural education: Challenges and definitions. Presentation at a Council of Europe Conference, *Plurilingual and Intercultural Education in Primary Education*. See https://rm.coe.int/09000016805a0a97 (accessed October 2019).

Torikai, K. (2018) Chronic reforms and the crisis in English education. Nippon.com. See https://www.nippon.com/en/currents/d00412/chronic-reforms-and-the-crisis-in-english-education.html.

UCL Institute of Education (2012) Removing barriers to learning: Special educational needs and/or disabilities training toolkit for PGCE courses, handout 1. See http://dera.ioe.ac.uk/13763/1/session2.pdf (accessed October 2018).

UK Department for Education (2011) *Teachers' Standards – Guidance for School Leaders, School Staff and Governing Bodies*. London. See https://assets.publishing.service.gov.uk/government/uploads/system/uploads/attachment_data/file/665520/Teachers__Standards.pdf (accessed June 2018).

UK Department for Education (2014) *The National Curriculum in England – Framework Document*. London: Department for Education. See https://assets.publishing.service.gov.uk/government/uploads/system/uploads/attachment_data/file/381344/Master_final_national_curriculum_28_Nov.pdf (accessed May 2018).

UNESCO (2004) *The Plurality of Literacy and its Implications for Policies and Programmes*. Paris: UNESCO. See http://unesdoc.unesco.org/images/0013/001362/136246e.pdf (accessed May 2018).

UNESCO (2015) *Transversal Skills in TVET: Policy Implications*. Bangkok: UNESCO. See https://unesdoc.unesco.org/ark:/48223/pf0000234738 (accessed October 2019)

van Ek, J.A. (1975) *The Threshold Level*. Strasbourg: Council of Europe.

Voice 21 and the University of Cambridge (2018) *The Oracy Skills Framework*. See https://docs.wixstatic.com/ugd/2c80ff_d780ca405ba943e0a1cf01c4431b1365.pdf; details at https://www.educ.cam.ac.uk/research/projects/oracytoolkit/oracyskillsframework/Glossaryofskills.pdf (accessed October 2018).

Vygotsky, L.S. (1978) *Mind in Society*. Cambridge, MA: Harvard University Press.

Vygotsky, L.S. (1986) *Thought and Language*. Cambridge, MA: The MIT Press.

Wallace, M.J. (1991) *Training Foreign Language Teachers: A Reflective Approach*. Cambridge: Cambridge University Press.

Walqui, A. (2006) Scaffolding instruction for English language learners: A conceptual framework. *The International Journal of Bilingual Education and Bilingualism* 9 (2), 159–180.

Wilkins, D. (1976) *Notional Syllabuses*. Oxford: Oxford University Press.

Wilkinson, A. (1968) Oracy in English teaching. *Elementary English* 45 (6), 743–747.

Wood, D., Bruner, J. and Ross, G. (1976) The role of tutoring in problem solving. *Journal of Child Psychology and Child Psychiatry* 17, 89–100.

Wright, T. (1987) *Roles of Teachers and Learners*. Oxford: Oxford University Press.

Wright, T. and Bolitho, R. (2007) *Trainer Development*. Lulu.com.

Zemach, D. (2018) Sausage and the law: How ELT textbooks are made. Plenary address at the IATEFL Conference 2018. See https://www.youtube.com/watch?v=xI-OLoBxENI (accessed October 2018).

Index

Abbs, Abbs & Freebairn 21, 136, 164, 170
Africa 19, 27, 34, 35, 38, 86, 95, 123, 127, 129, 134
AISLi 144
Albania 63
Alexander L.G., 136
Alexander R., 8, 9, 85, 86, 88, 164
Allen 122, 164
Alliance Française 29
AMEP, Adult Migrant English Program 127
Arabic 20, 117, 123
Arnot *et al*. 128, 129
Attitude/Motivation Test Battery 105
Australia 28, 30, 35, 122, 127, 128, 134, 144, 166
Austria 25, 29, 59, 95, 98, 110, 111, 129

Bailey 76, 77, 164
Bangladesh 19, 20, 31, 124, 128, 134
Barcelona objective 125
Barnes 8, 10, 88, 164
Basque 24, 32, 41, 47, 122, 125
BBC 32, 38, 169
Beacco & Byram 23
Beacco *et al*. 155, 157
Belarus 134, 139
Berlitz 28, 29, 142
bilingual education 24, 41, 42, 48
Bleichenbacher *et al*. 60
Bloom 6, 7, 164, 165, 169
Bolitho 45, 63, 65, 82, 133, 135, 139, 160, 161, 165, 170, 171
Bolitho & Padwad 82
Bolitho & West 45
Bologna 26
Borg 79, 83, 165
Breton 24, 32, 122
British Council 27, 29, 30, 31, 44, 45, 53, 57, 78, 132, 139, 141, 142, 143, 165, 167, 168, 169

Bulgaria 26, 27, 73, 75
Bullock Report 14, 15, 84, 85, 88, 95, 151, 154, 159, 165
Byram 64, 65, 164, 165, 170

CAE, Cambridge Assessment English 61, 132, 133, 134, 142, 146
Cambridge English Teaching Framework 78, 165
Cambridge Primary Review 85, 86, 164
Canada 35, 86, 105, 106, 117, 134, 144
Carter 15, 31, 165
Catalan 47, 122
CEFR 21, 22, 23, 29, 56, 63, 132, 133, 134, 140, 151, 156, 166
CELTA, Certificate in English Language Teaching to Adults 61, 62, 63, 64, 65, 145, 146, 147
Chaloner 30, 165
Chinese 107, 124
Chong 38
Clark *et al*. 92
CLIL content and language integrated learning 41, 43, 44, 45, 47, 48, 60, 70, 71, 78, 98, 99, 100, 109, 116, 153, 166, 169
community of practice 76
consultation 108, 116
Cope & Kalantzis 13
Council of Europe 20, 21, 22, 23, 25, 29, 88, 103, 124, 131, 133, 150, 154, 157, 158, 162, 164, 165, 166, 170, 171
Cox Report 15, 166
CPD, continuing professional development 68, 69, 70, 71, 72, 73, 74, 75, 76, 77, 78, 79, 81, 82, 83, 95, 96, 97, 151, 159, 165
Croatia 97, 106
Crystal 35, 166
Cultural Convention 20, 151, 166

curriculum 1, 2, 10, 12, 14, 15, 17, 18, 22, 24, 26, 27, 40, 44, 46, 47, 52, 53, 54, 55, 57, 59, 60, 61, 64, 66, 70, 85, 86, 88, 90, 95, 96, 97, 98, 99, 102, 103, 105, 107, 109, 113, 115, 116, 118, 119, 120, 121, 122, 125, 127, 130, 134, 138, 139, 153, 154, 155, 156, 158, 159, 160, 163, 168, 169, 171
Cyprus 97
Czech Republic 27, 73, 75

DELTA, Diploma in English Language Teaching to Adults 61, 146, 147
Dewey 5, 166
dialogic teaching 8, 9, 17, 90
Dogme 140
Doiz 41, 166

EAL, English as an additional language 127, 128, 164
EAP, English for academic purposes 43, 44, 45
Eaquals 72, 78, 81, 144
Eckersley 29, 136, 166
ECML 25, 26, 78, 165, 166
Edelenbos 24, 25, 166
Edwards & Westgate 101
ELF, English as a lingua franca 36, 37
EMI, English as a medium of instruction 42, 43, 44, 45, 47, 48
English UK 30, 143, 144, 165
ESP, English for specific purposes 43, 44, 45
Essential English for Foreign Students 29, 136, 166
Estonia 125, 129
European Commission 13, 96, 97, 108, 109, 110, 111, 113, 114, 126, 131, 150, 167, 171
European Language Portfolio 23
European Profile for Language Teacher Education 58, 59, 168
European Profiling Grid 78, 170
European Survey of Language Competences 126
European Union 20, 24, 34, 46, 99, 124
exam boards, examination providers 132
exploratory talk 8, 17, 18
Extra & Yağmur 125, 128

Fairclough 44, 100, 167
Finland 58, 86, 160, 168, 170

frameworks/frameworks of teacher competences 6, 78, 79
France 2, 9, 20, 29, 30, 122, 128, 129, 133, 135, 164
French 2, 7, 19, 20, 27, 29, 31, 37, 41, 46, 105, 106, 117, 122, 123, 125, 130, 133, 148
Fullan 152, 167

Gardner 105, 106, 107, 167
geography 36, 47, 99, 169
German 27, 28, 29, 31, 32, 41, 42, 46, 95, 99, 123, 125, 128, 130, 139, 148
Germany 28, 29, 95, 98, 111, 119, 125, 128, 133, 134, 135, 139, 169
Ghana 91, 169
Goethe-Institut 29, 128, 133, 144, 148
Gower *et al.* 76
Graddol 36, 168
Gray & Block 137
Greece 62, 136, 142

Hadley 140, 168
Hanson 121, 168
Hindi 19, 124
Holliday 36, 168
Hungary 26, 27, 52, 61, 64, 125

ICT 13, 71
IELTS, International English Language Testing System 28, 108, 132, 133, 134, 141
India 9, 17, 19, 38, 42, 76, 90, 91, 95, 112, 119, 123, 124, 128, 130, 131, 165
Indonesia 123, 134
innovation 18
INSET/in-service training 69, 70, 71, 72, 74, 75, 76, 79, 83, 95, 96, 159
Instituto Camões 29, 144
Instituto Cervantes 29, 148
integrativeness 106
IRF/INTIATION-RESPONSE-FEEDBACK 8, 10, 18
Irish 47
Israel 63
Italian 125, 130
Italy 73, 75, 97
Ivanič 100

Japan 40, 140, 151
Jenkins 36, 37, 38, 168
Jin *et al.* 107
Johnston & Watson 121

Kaplan 35, 168
Kashubian 24, 32, 109
Kingman Report 15
Krathwohl 7, 164, 169

labour market 110
language awareness 2, 59, 66, 78, 82, 85, 93, 95, 99, 100, 101, 103, 113, 114, 115, 151, 153, 157, 158, 159, 163
language of schooling 2, 3, 14, 16, 34, 41, 46, 48, 70, 85, 93, 100, 101, 113, 121, 126, 153, 155
language policy 17, 24, 119, 121, 124, 125, 127, 129, 130, 131
Language Rich Europe 119, 125, 128, 131, 164, 167
language schools 28, 29, 61, 71, 109, 132, 138, 142, 143, 144, 145
language-sensitive teaching 98, 115
Lasagabaster 41, 166
Latvia 97
LINC 15, 165
literacy 1, 3, 13, 14, 16, 18, 85, 86, 90, 93, 94, 97, 98, 100, 101, 102, 113, 121, 122, 126, 131, 153, 154, 156, 158, 159
Littlewood 21, 169

Maas 139, 169
Macedonia 63
Machin *et al*. 122
Maingay 76, 169
Malayalam 124
Malaysia 19, 42, 59, 64, 112, 124, 151
management of change 121
Mandarin 117
Mann 69, 72, 83, 169
Mansell 120, 169
Marathi 124
Martin 127, 169
Marzano 7, 10, 169
Masson & Ng 117
Medgyes & Paran 58
mentor 27, 52, 61, 65
Mercer 17, 164, 169
methodology 19, 27, 48, 52, 55, 57, 59, 62, 65, 66, 68, 70, 71, 76, 120, 135, 137
Middle East 27, 34, 127
migrants 24, 27, 28, 34, 48, 122, 127, 128, 129, 132, 133, 134
migration 14, 24, 34, 95, 97, 114, 117, 133, 155, 157
Mongolia 139
Morawski & Budke 95, 99
Morgan 9, 10, 170

Morocco 20, 117, 123, 167
multilingualism 23, 24, 125, 131, 141, 144
multiliteracies 13, 18

Namibia 123
National Oracy Project 85
Netherlands 42, 97, 129

O'Neill 136, 170
observation 57, 61, 69, 74, 75, 76, 77, 78, 93, 94, 96, 109, 145, 159
Odisha 129, 130, 164, 168
oracy 1, 16, 85, 86, 90, 93, 94, 95, 97, 98, 100, 101, 102, 113, 126, 153, 154, 156, 158, 159, 164

phonics 121, 122
Piaget 5
pluralistic approaches 157
plurilingualism 23, 28, 122, 131, 132, 155, 156, 158, 159
Poedjiastutie & Oliver 108
Poland 26, 52, 106, 109
policymaking 24, 84, 119, 121, 125, 130, 150
Portugal 97, 123, 125
Portuguese 19, 20, 123
publishers/textbook publishers 22, 23, 24, 31, 43, 103, 120, 132, 135, 137, 138, 139, 140, 141, 144, 148, 151, 158, 160
Pulverness 139, 170

quality assurance 143, 144, 148

Reference Framework of Competences for Democratic Culture 88, 157, 162
refugees 27, 95, 127, 129, 133
repertoire/language repertoire 9, 16, 41, 48, 153, 155, 162, 165
Rhaeto-Romanic 130
Rixon & Smith 136
Romania 26, 27, 106, 112, 123, 125, 139
Rossner 76, 78, 133, 170
Russia 9, 62, 139
Russian 6, 26, 27, 59, 98, 112, 125, 139, 140

Sahlberg 58, 170
Saxton 9, 10, 170
scaffolding 10, 11, 12, 17, 18, 90, 94
Seidlhofer 36, 37, 170, 171
Serbia 63
Singapore 112
socioeducational model of language learning 105, 106

Sorbian 32
Spain 29, 41, 47, 97, 106, 109, 119, 123, 125
Spanish 19, 31, 37, 46, 117, 118, 123, 125, 148, 165
Speech, Language and Communication Framework 94, 166
St Gallen 59, 64, 165
Strategies 21, 136, 137, 164
Streamline 29, 168
Switzerland 59, 62, 66, 86, 119, 129, 130, 164

Tamil 124
Taxonomy of Educational Objectives 6, 9, 165
teaching practice 60
The Oracy Skills Framework 94, 171
Threshold Level 20, 21, 29, 171
TOEFL/Test of English as a Foreign Language 28, 108, 133, 134
Torikai 40, 171
transversal competences 12, 14
Trinity College Certificate 61, 62
Turkey 28, 128, 142

Ukraine 27, 45, 57, 59, 64, 66, 112, 133
UNESCO 13, 85, 171
University College London Institute of Education 93
USA 7, 11, 28, 35, 121, 133, 134, 144
Uzbekistan 27, 45, 52, 53, 59, 63, 64, 66, 139, 151, 168

Valenciano 109
voice 21, 94, 171
Vygotsky 5, 6, 7, 8, 10, 12, 171

Wallace 63, 78, 105, 171
Walqui 11, 171
Welsh 24, 32, 47, 123
Wilkins 21, 30, 171
Wilkinson 85, 171
Woods *et al.* 12
Wright 65, 138, 171

Zemach 137, 171
zone of proximal development 10

For Product Safety Concerns and Information please contact our EU Authorised Representative:

Easy Access System Europe

Mustamäe tee 50

10621 Tallinn

Estonia

gpsr.requests@easproject.com